Guerillas

'By gaining the people, the kingdom is gained;
by losing the people, the kingdom is lost.'

Confucius

By the same author

JUNGLE GREEN
THE SIEGE

Guerillas

a History and Analysis by

Arthur Campbell

THE JOHN DAY COMPANY   NEW YORK

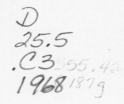
FIRST AMERICAN EDITION 1968

Library of Congress Catalogue
Number: 68-19650

Contents

v

CONTENTS

MAPS

vi

Preface

I have deliberately chosen the form of presentation offered in this book in preference to writing a straight-forward and purely factual history of guerilla warfare. I have attempted to follow the modern development of this form of warfare from its inception in 1808, but I have been concerned more with analysing the problems relevant to guerilla warfare than with relating plain facts.

Guerilla warfare is closer to the people than any other form of warfare so far engaged in by man, because the people are the target for every operation undertaken by the contending forces, whether political, psychological or military, and because the combatants are themselves of the people. For this reason no analysis would be complete without an exposition of the human problems and emotions involved.

The reader will, therefore, find the overall history outlined in a series of chapters which link and give continuity to the narratives, each of which covers in detail an important campaign, either by case history or by personal account. In order to cover all the chosen aspects of the campaign concerned, I have found it necessary to invent a narrator for each personal account and to relate his adventures in my own words, but the reader need have no doubts about the authenticity of these narratives. There is no single incident included which did not in fact occur in the campaign under review and in conditions similar to those described.

The reader may question why I have not included an examination of the present war in Vietnam between the Communist Ho Chi Minh's Vietcong regulars and guerillas, and the South Vietnamese and their American, Asian and Australasian allies. I feel that this war has not yet passed into history and, although the experience of the French and the Vietminh in the Indo-China campaign between 1945 and 1954 point the way to victory over Communism in this area of operations, it is as yet too early to draw conclusions from the present day-to-day happenings in Vietnam. In any case the Americans, who are devoting all the will-power of a great nation, immense physical resources, and the energies of over half a million dedicated men and women to a determined stand in Vietnam against the spread of Communism into South East Asia, have their own operational research teams in the field who are faithfully recording the lessons to be learned from this arduous and protracted struggle.

While writing this book I have been given no help whatsoever by any department of the British government, nor have I asked for any. My government does not necessarily agree with the facts as I have presented them or with the opinions I express. The book is a private venture, and has been completed without access to official documents.

I have been given unstinting help by Joan Abbott, by an excellent librarian, Mr King, and by my patient and helpful family. To them I am deeply grateful.

AFC
1967

Chapter 1

Guerilla Warfare

'War, war is still the cry,
War even to the knife.'
BYRON

During recent years, a variety of phrases and expressions have been introduced to describe the activities of irregular armed forces. We read and hear of, and we study 'insurgency operations', 'partisan warfare', 'para-military operations', 'internal war', 'irregular warfare', 'revolutionary warfare' and 'guerilla warfare'. A diversity of expressions such as these can lead only to confusion because it is impossible to give a precise definition to either one or another. For my purpose in this book I have selected the term 'guerilla warfare' only because it was the original name given to the modern prototype of this form of military activity. The Spaniards, who first evolved this method of fighting on a large scale while resisting the French armies which occupied their country during the years 1807 to 1814, gave to the activities of their irregular bands of warriors the name 'guerrilla' = 'little war'.

Guerilla warfare is a form of warfare, not a type. Today's politico-military theorists have divided warfare into four relevant types, namely:

1 Total war, which is a violent struggle between governments, each aiming at the destruction of the other and using all the means at their disposal to achieve this aim. Since the development of the thermo-nuclear weapon, total war would involve the use of such weapons.
2 General war, which is a struggle between governments each aiming at the destruction of the other, but neither prepared to employ all the means at their disposal to achieve the aim. In its time, World War II was total war; today, barring the use of thermo-nuclear weapons, that war would be a general war.

3 Limited war, which is a struggle between governments in which each has a restricted aim and is prepared to use only limited resources to achieve it. Limited war is fought within a restricted geographical area. The war in Korea was a limited war in so far as it concerned the two chief protagonists, America and Communist China.

4 Revolutionary war, which is a struggle between a governmental party and an anti-governmental party in which the latter aims to overthrow the former, generally employing all available means in its attempt to do so; the governmental party attempts to destroy its opponents by some or by all the means at its command. The campaigns in Indo-China and Malaya were revolutionary wars.

Guerilla fighting is a form of warfare, essentially, though selectively aggressive, which may have a role in any of these four types of warfare. It is as much a form of warfare as, say, the siege, or air bombardment, or naval blockade or, indeed, as the technique evolved by French naval officers in the eighteenth century called the *guerre de course*. At this time, the frigate and the privateer were pitted in irregular fashion against the all-powerful English Navy; the technique was carried over into the nineteenth century by the torpedo boat and cruiser and into the twentieth century by the submarine. Guerilla warfare may be likened in many respects to the *guerre de course*, except only in its elemental environment.

In total war, guerilla warfare may well be resorted to by that side which comes out weaker after the initial exchange of thermonuclear weapons. The weaker side may yet be reluctant to accept the peace terms proposed by the stronger and may hope to gain political concessions by continuing the conflict.

In general war, guerillas play a supporting role to regular forces. We saw many instances of this in World War II, in Russia, in Burma and in many European countries.

In limited war, guerillas also have a supporting role to regular forces. In Korea, four United Nations divisions were contained in the rear areas by Communist Chinese and North Korean guerillas.

In revolutionary war, guerillas play a dominant part during the early phases, when the anti-governmental forces are too weak to deploy regular armies, navies and air forces.

From the foregoing arises a definition of guerilla warfare: it is that form of warfare adopted by the strategically weaker side to give it the capability of taking the tactical offensive at chosen times and in certain places.

It has been argued that guerilla warfare can never be decisive in itself; that to defeat the regular forces of a government, whether of one's own government or another, stronger regular forces must in the final event be deployed against them. We shall, however, see examples of guerillas bringing about political conditions favourable to themselves without the final deployment of regular forces, as in Cyprus and Cuba in 1959 and in Algeria in 1961, but in each case there were other considerations both within and without the area of operations which helped to bring about these favourable conditions.

Guerilla warfare can be decisive only in those cases when the anti-guerilla forces are either not fully bent on defeating the guerilla movement, or are not prepared to employ against them the full resources available. In general, guerilla warfare has been in the past, and is today resorted to by governments and by anti-government parties either when regular forces have foundered or before regular forces are created, or in places where regular forces are unable to function.

The development of revolutionary warfare in the post-World War II years introduces new aspects into guerilla warfare and brings about a need for change in both political and military attitudes towards it. Today, with the thermo-nuclear deterrent containing both political and military leaders, it is the most likely of all forms of warfare, no longer only a resort of the weak, but a form to be deliberately adopted by the strong. Russian leaders, while rejecting total war, approve 'wars of national liberation'. Mao Tse-tung, although not yet publicly rejecting total war, certainly embraces revolutionary war as a means of overthrowing opponent governments.

All revolutionary wars start out with guerilla warfare since the anti-government parties are never at the outset strong enough to deploy regular forces. The guerillas, although only one element, are a strong element in the prolonged struggle to win over the support of a people. Guerilla tactics remain the same today as in the past, but within the setting of revolutionary warfare and employing techniques recently developed, the guerillas' activities

3

now have a far wider influence than before on politico-military strategy. Counter-guerilla forces are now faced with the problem of evolving a doctrine for defeating the guerilla within a broader framework of counter-revolutionary strategy. Such strategy will almost certainly debar a government from employing all the resources at its disposal, particularly those that destroy; such strategy will compel governments to refrain from deploying regular forces in such strength as to weaken their power to deter. A government has achieved little if, while defeating guerillas within a country, it has alienated the sympathy of the people of that country or has let in enemies from over its borders. In revolutionary warfare the political, psychological and administrative offensive is of paramount importance because the aim is to conquer the hearts and minds of a people rather than to destroy their physical means of making war; the military arm should be used offensively but with discrimination and discretion.

Guerilla warfare is as old as warfare itself. History reveals many examples of countries holding out against the conqueror by means of irregular fighting. Many of the campaigns fought by the Israelites against their numerous enemies might be classified as irregular warfare. Gideon, we are told, smote the enemy hip and thigh. The Maccabees engaged in irregular warfare against the Syrian armies. The brilliant Roman general, Fabius Maximus Cunctator, 'the delayer', diverted Hannibal from his main objective, Rome, by unorthodox tactics and by refusing conventional battle in which he would have faced certain defeat. But of the men who led such enterprises in ancient times, although many became legendary figures in their own countries, none made more than a slight impression on military history.

During the Hundred Years War, the Constable of France, Du Guesclin, might have made a considerable impression had the minds of his contemporaries not been closed by the 'rules of war'. At that time, English soldiers occupied many parts of France. Du Guesclin studied the tactical system by which the English conquered on the battlefield, a system based on the prepared defensive position from which their magnificent archers first broke the ranks of the French men-at-arms and from which a final charge completed the rout of the enemy. Du Guesclin refused to attack, but instead, by night raids, ambushes and harassment, compelled the English to surrender most of the lands they occupied.

The American War of Independence threw up a number of brilliant irregular leaders, the best-known of these Major Rogers of Rogers' Rangers, but the land in which they fought was remote from the centres of military thought.

In mediaeval times, and thereafter, the irregular was considered an unnecessary evil on the battlefield – an indecent and unchivalrous amateur. For this reason, the military lessons taught by such men as Du Guesclin and Rogers made virtually no impact on the conduct of war until, towards the end of the eighteenth century, Napoleon Bonaparte introduced new methods and a less scrupulous psychological approach.

It was during the war in Spain, between 1807 and 1814, when the Spanish people, in concert with Wellington's British Army, threw off the yoke of Napoleon's military conquest, that modern guerilla warfare was conceived.

Chapter 2

Introduction to Spain

For many years before the French invasion, the royal house of Spain had been torn by domestic quarrels. Political intrigue and secret machinations were the order of the day; unscrupulous self-seekers trod the corridors of the Court, driven by personal interest and ambition, not least among them Don Manuel Godoy.

Godoy instigated a secret treaty with the French, allowing them to pass an army through Spain for the conquest and division of Portugal; Napoleon Bonaparte, Emperor of France, ratified this treaty on the 29th October, 1807.

But even before the treaty was signed, French troops entered Spain. 'The First Army of the Gironde', under the young and ambitious General Junot, marched on Salamanca, and from there to Lisbon. In December, two more French corps, 'The Second Army of the Gironde' and 'The Army of the Côte d'Océan', marched one on Vitoria, the other on Valladolid.

By the 24 July 1808, a French army of eighty thousand men had completed the occupation of Spain and Napoleon had installed his brother, Joseph, on the Spanish throne. Thus, in the space of a few months, a nation of eleven million proud, arrogant and boastful people had been conquered and their country occupied.

Years of misrule and poverty had, however, rendered the Spaniards both physically and morally weak, so that their reaction to occupation varied greatly. In Zaragoza, in Aranjuez and in Galicia, for example, there was insurrection and resistance, inspired by priests who hated the French both from patriotism and for the threat they presented to privilege and temporal power, but the Spaniards overall, though threatening, in brave and vindictive public and private statements, to throw out the invaders, failed to match their words with performance. In the main, they timidly accepted this swift descent of French military might, but

6

the insurrection at Aranjuez, and the verbal reactions of the people were enough to show the French Emperor that the Spaniards would not remain quiescent under insult.

His instructions to his envoy in Madrid, Savary, Duc de Rovigo, read: 'In a war of this sort, it is necessary to act with patience, coolness and open calculation. In civil wars it is the important points only which should be guarded. We must not go to all places'. Even though Savary failed to appreciate the full meaning of these wise words, the French strengthened their grip on Spain until by the end of 1808 the Spaniards, though restless, were unable to shake off the yoke.

Towards the end of 1808, the situation in the Peninsula was confusing. A French army occupied the main towns and certain fortified strong-points along the lines of communication between them. The Spanish regular army was still in being, though scattered, and was supplied by the English Government through a number of agents. The Spanish peasants, and in some places the townspeople also, were in a state of turmoil but were utterly without leadership. An English army was in Portugal; the English Navy ruled the seas around the Peninsula.

It was in this setting that the Spanish guerilla movement was born.

The story of guerilla warfare in Spain is told by a young Spanish gentleman who was torn from his studies in Barcelona at the early age of twenty-three years to take up arms against the French.

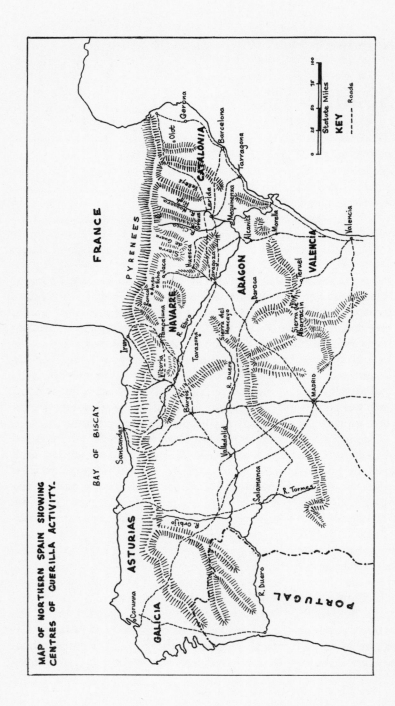

MAP OF NORTHERN SPAIN SHOWING
CENTRES OF GUERILLA ACTIVITY.

Narrative 1

Spain — 1807 to 1813

'... when, as in Spain ..., the war is for the
most part carried on by means of a people's
war ... a truly new power is formed and ...
people's warfare introduces a means of
defence peculiar to itself.'

KARL VON CLAUSEWITZ – *On War*.

It was in October in the year 1807 that the barbarian armies swept
through my beloved country. We who were proud of our peerless
heritage, confident in the authority and independence of Spain,
were led to believe that the Royal Court in Madrid had made
treaty with the Emperor Napoleon to enable his cohorts to journey
through our country for the conquest of Portugal. This they did
under the upstart Junot, but coincidentally, other armies fell upon
Spain itself. Rapine, pillage and all forms of savagery followed in
their wake until, in June of the year 1808, we were compelled by
force of arms to accept a French king upon our throne.

One would rightly have imagined that my people would rise as
one against the brutish invaders, but for years our spirits had sunk
and our bodies bowed under corrupt and incompetent government. In the ante-rooms of the Court of Madrid and in the
provincial *juntas* venal men had introduced themselves into the
branches of government with no other view than to enrich themselves at public expense; ignorant men, thinking themselves
wise, had obtained by intrigue duties which they were not capable
of discharging; perfidious men had taken office who cared not for
the issue of events but would submit to any master.

It should occasion no surprise that while the invaders strutted
and noised their way abroad, clashed their arms and oppressed the
people, young men gathered in places of learning to discuss what
might be done. It was at one such gathering, in the garret which
was my dwelling-place in Barcelona, on a certain spring evening

9

in 1808, that there appeared an emissary from Mina. The man himself, well-known to a number of my friends, was of enormous girth, with short, strong legs and that dark earnest mien worn by the men who inhabit the Pyrenees mountains.

He told us that *partidas* were assembled in the mountains and in the fastnesses of Aragon, Navarre and Catalonia. The bands were composed, in the main, of men from the mountains, men who had for long carried arms for smuggling and who were well-versed in the practice of baffling government troops. But because they were lacking in good leaders he had travelled the long journey from Pampeluna to recruit young men of learning. He told us of bands led by the Catalonians Baget, Pereña and the chief Theobaldo; he talked of bands under Gayan in the Montalvan mountains, and of others in the hills of Moncayo. Mina himself, called 'the student', conducted guerillas from the Pyrenees, while in the High Valleys of Ronçal, Anso and Echo, *partidas* operated under the leadership of one Renovalles. He made claims, claims which were later disclosed to me as being no more than the ranting of a heated mind, that the *partidas*, raised from among the defeated Spanish armies and the peasant people, were in great strength, perhaps twenty thousand men.

This emissary besought us to take up arms in defence of our country, to associate ourselves with the struggle to discard the horrid yoke of French dominion. It was on that same evening that I made the fateful decision to take up the sword with the *guerrilleros*; there followed five years of unparalleled hardship, five years of cruelty, bloodshed, hunger and of unimaginable privation. I set out on the following morning, carrying only the clothes on my person and a few necessities in a small knapsack.

I traversed the length of the Ebro river, to Zaragoza. In that town, a place of importance on the communication-lines between the French armies and their own country, my papers were examined by Spanish guards in French pay. I was constrained only with difficulty from plunging a knife into their guilty hearts, but instead, taking advantage of the confusion of the times, I was able to persuade them that I was to visit my ageing parents in my own village of Huesca.

From Zaragoza I travelled by foot on to the high Sierras called Alcubiere, then in a wide detour along the mountain tops to the north and east, in order to circumnavigate the valley of the Cinca river, infested as it was with French soldiery. From the Sierra de Guara I descended into Huesca where, from among my own people, I found one to guide me to Theobaldo's hideout on the Sierras.

His camp, which sheltered two hundred men, as variegated and as villainous an assemblage as you would meet anywhere in Spain, was situated in caves six hundred metres above the floor of the valley. The men included defeated Spanish soldiers, deserters from the English and French armies, robbers and outlaws and some few poor peasants from my own village and neighbouring Barbastro. There were also, ill-at-ease in the mountains, vagabond townsmen from Lerida. The soldiers had retained their uniforms, though the plumes, cockades, aiguillettes and all finery had been cut away. Like me, the remainder were in civil apparel; many, as though to claim a modicum of uniform, wore a sleeveless leather jacket. The armament they carried was as varied as the men themselves; for myself, I was handed a flintlock pistol which had seen much service and which must have been fashioned as one of the first of its kind, some one hundred and fifty years before. I was never practised in its use and depended more on the two knives which I wore in my belt.

The men, by use of board and blanket, had made some attempt at comfort within the caves but there was little enough; the chill damp cavern was our house, the rock-hard ground our bed. Food there was in abundance, though of a frugal and monotonous nature; it was later disclosed to me that the Governor of Lerida sustained all the *partidas* in Aragon, provisions being delivered to the hideout by peasants or collected by the *guerrilleros* from various appointed places in the plain. Of powder and shot I saw none, except that carried in the powder flasks and in the pockets of those fortunate enough to have obtained some.

I saw but little of Theobaldo; of those others who had assumed the mantle of leadership, some were reckless, some indolent, none with knowledge or skill, and all given to high-flown talk. The activities of the *partidas* were loosely controlled by these men. I presumed that Theobaldo received orders from some ill-defined authority because he spoke sometimes of co-ordination with other bands. But however the many schemes may have come into his head, he discussed them with the others; if all did not agree they were abandoned.

I was first instructed to agitate the natural turbulence of the people of Huesca and to obtain information from them concerning the movements and habits of the French soldiers. I had expected to find no difficulty in this; they were, as I have stated, my own people, but the invading armies had brought to a poor village certain material benefits which the inhabitants had not previously encountered; further, the burden of exactions and provocations had not yet weighed upon the peasants. They seemed reluctant to exchange the quiet, if austere life which they had known for a nebulous resistance to the foreign invader. Yet in the fashion of a volatile people, youths would now and then rush off, unprepared and unrestrained, to attack some French post, only to be slaughtered by disciplined bayonets and only to bring fierce reprisals down upon the heads of their friends and families.

I continued in this work for two months until, in June, I was given leadership of a *partidas* of forty ruffians. After much discussion, we were prevailed upon to destroy a French outpost situated where the road leading from Zaragoza into the High Valleys passes by ferries over the Cinca river. The people said that there were only twelve French soldiers in this place and as is our wont, we accepted this estimate. '*Es verdad; los dicen*' – 'It is true; they say it'.

I led my noisome and motley crew under cover of darkness to a place on the road two kilometres to the north-east of where the French soldiers huddled in their guard-house. As dawn approached so we came nearer to the enemy and when the oncoming light of day illuminated the sky for one hundred metres all around, we rushed upon them. The soldiers, as ever alert, deployed to meet us, more than twenty-five in number. Standing shoulder to shoulder, unflinching and unyielding, they poured into us one volley of musketry. But so sudden was the attack, and so fierce the charge that we were soon among them. There followed a wild and uncontrolled fight, hand-to-hand, their weapon the bayonet, ours the sword and the knife. Finally, our numbers prevailed; the enemy's survivors made off, but not before twenty of my men lay dead or wounded on the road-side. We placed explosive charges against the ferries, but their blast only killed three more of my *guerrilleros*. Then we fled.

Even in the broken ground of the valley we were exposed to view in the daylight which was by now burnished to brilliance by the rising sun. As we rushed for the shelter of the mountains, each one intent only on his own salvation, we were pressed by a French horse patrol which appeared as if from nowhere; we scrambled into the foothills only just in time to evade complete destruction.

We came to Theobaldo's encampment flushed with triumph and passed the remainder of the day in exchanging heroic stories, all of which grew in the telling. Baget, Pereña and Perdoza had come, bringing with them three hundred *guerrilleros*, all vocal with tales of slaughter. Through the Governor of Lerida we were informed that Gayan had pushed his bands out into the plains of Zaragoza; that two regiments of the army had cut the road between that town and Madrid. We heard that the Moncayo bands were active around Tarazona and many more at Pampeluna.

But our triumph was to be short-lived. We knew not at the time, but we were soon to know that General Souchet, *Comandante* of the troops in that district, had determined to drive the *partidas* from Aragon. He first reformed the administration of that rich province so that kindness and good management replaced oppression and corruption, thus increasing our difficulties in bringing the citizens to our aid.

And then one day, while about my duties in Huesca, I perceived a body of French soldiers which I estimated to be more than one thousand strong, marching through the village towards the mountains. Heart in mouth, I secretly followed, having in mind to warn the bands of their coming.

I made fast time into the poor village – a hamlet housing a mere hundred peasants, gleaning a bare existence from the unyielding soil – which lay three kilometres from the encampment, but I preceded by only a moment a forward detachment of the soldiery. I laid low in one of the filthy stone huts while the officer parleyed with the village chief. I heard the latter, in cowardly fashion, his head bowed in shame, submit to the threat of destruction of his entire village and undertake to lead the enemy to where the *partidas* were sheltered.

I crawled away over the fields, barely concealed by the stunted crops, until a fold in the ground, running into a small valley, gave me access to the mountainside. I reported to Theobaldo, who, with the others, determined to stand and fight.

At dawn on the day following, when the French army in all its might – muskets, bayonets and accoutrements glistening in the

13

early sunlight – guided by traitorous wretches approached our positions in martial array and resistance soon melted away We were no match, even on our own ground, for these finely-disciplined men and, when another body appeared to our rear, we fled down the mountainside; down across the road which links Lerida with Huesca, across the Cinca river and up towards the High Valleys. Here we were met by Renovalles, and were determined to stand again between the Cinca and Noguera rivers, but once again we were defeated in pitched battle. I fled into the safety of Lerida.

Now occurred an incident unusual in these times, but later to be repeated in almost every province in Spain. Souchet threatened the valleys of Venasques and Benevarres and this he was compelled to do in order to re-open communications with France, which had been closed by the partidas. Upon learning of his intentions, the inhabitants flew to arms, encouraged and supported by the dispersed partidas. The *migueletes* (armed peasants) defeated a French regiment which had sallied forth from Graus, while from Lerida they menaced the whole circle of French strongholds. Souchet, in space of time, brought the proud and fierce Aragonese to their knees, but only after deploying many thousands of soldiers against them.

It was tragic that after more than one year of the struggle the partides were as yet so unskilled, so reckless, so poorly armed, so ill-supported by their own people, that the French, when they turned against us, could reduce us to such pitiable state. Even the student, Mina, in Navarre, was finally captured in December of this year. He was at once replaced as *caudillo* by 'espoz y Mina', who was to become a legendary figure among the partidas.

I myself partook in yet further tragedy after taking flight from Lerida to my own village. There were assembled many leaders from among those who had been betrayed to the French on the Sierra Guara. They were disillusioned, cold, hungry, bitter to the point of madness. All were bent on the destruction of those who had betrayed them. On a freezing morning in January of 1810 we trudged forth through the snow, heads bent to the storm, sixty armed and vengeful men, to destroy the village. The peasants, unarmed, made no resistance against the unbridled fury, against the knives, the axes and the muskets of their attackers. We hacked to pieces every man and child within the hamlet. First stripping them to the waist, we turned loose the women on to the snow-covered, storm-swept mountainside. Perhaps those who survived, and could cover their shame, would tell others of the price of treachery.

There followed for me a twelve-month of wandering through the provinces of Navarre, Catalonia and Aragon, raiding and ambushing with the various bands and constantly seeking information from, and stirring the emotions of the citizens.

In Aragon, where Souchet had established a beneficial administration, the people were indolent, many, even, sympathetic to the invaders. Convoys passing to and from the French base at Zaragoza were guarded by Spanish soldiers or armed citizens. Beyond the base, the French had fortified all important places on the routes leading out to the provincial boundaries, and even beyond. Lerida and Mequinenza were Souchet's; by fortifying Morella, Teruel and Alcanits, he secured safe passage to the kingdom of Valencia.

In Navarre, Mina, with whom I passed much time, was active at Souchet's rear, in loose concert with the *partidas* of the Moncayo and Albaracin mountains, south of the River Ebro. Mina's supplies now came from the English ships through the great port at Corunna.

In Catalonia, affairs were different. General Augereau, notorious for his perfidious treatment of the garrison of Gerona, and later MacDonald who took over his command, were ignorant of the people and unprepared for the struggle in which they were engaged. Mostly their troops were hired mercenaries – Italians, Poles, Swiss, Germans – and these pressed in great numbers upon a country poor and rugged, barely able to support the inhabitants without the added demands of a foreign army. The lower regions of the Catalonian mountains were swarming with *partidas* connecting Mina in Navarre with the Spanish army located at Olot, both supplied by the English fleet through the port of Tarragona. The Spanish troops, ill-led and defective as they were, none the less menaced the invaders even to Barcelona.

Under Augereau's weak leadership, the foreign mercenaries ran wild over the countryside. The people, already near to starvation, were reduced to the state of beasts by exactions enforced with the utmost ferocity. The Catalonians, possessed of a cruelty natural to a people who must every day fight against nature for their very existence, but hardy too, fled from their villages and, together with the *miqueletes*, daily killed stragglers and small parties of the enemy. Many thousands fell to the enemy's bayonets due to their unskilful ways and mad recklessness. The turbulence in Catalonia, the depredations of the hired mercenaries, the madness of the citizens were utterly wasteful in both material and life.

By December of 1810, the *partidas* throughout the country, in conjunction with units of the Spanish armies, took on some semblance of organisation. Those in Catalonia were called 'The First Army'; in Valencia 'The Second Army'; in Galicia and Asturias 'The Sixth Army'; while the *partidas* of the North, Mina's Longa's, Campillo's and Porlier's, formed the 'Seventh Army'. But we lacked the political leadership, the self-discipline and wise direction needed to make good this organisation. Self-seekers still held sway in the *juntas*.

In the early spring of 1811, while the mountains yet lay under a mantle of deep snow, I transferred to one of Mina's bands. On the 22nd of May we had news that a French column was to pass through the hills above Vitoria. For three days we lay in wait, three thousand strong, among the crags and rocks on the summit of the pass until, in the light of early dawn, we saw the column approach, twelve hundred men in full dress, moving ponderously up the mountain road, bayonets gleaming, heavy accoutrements clanking as they came. At the rear followed numerous baggage wagons carrying treasure to France.

We waited until the long convoy halted at the summit, in our midst. We poured two volleys of musketry into the escorting soldiers, then we dashed down upon them. The very surprise of the assault and the fierce on-rush of our headlong charge favoured our intentions. Many of the enemy fled to the safety of the valley below; the remainder were cut down by thrusting swords, by flashing bayonets and by vicious blows from staves and cudgels. Within twenty minutes the tumult died and the ground was soaked with the blood of six hundred Frenchmen and two hundred Spanish prisoners, who had been mistaken in the mêlée for traitors in enemy pay.

All order gone, we descended like wolves upon the plunder, carrying all that we could load upon our backs, and upon the captured beasts, into the mountains from which we had come. I saw a cackling rabble of riff-raff dragging into a nearby field six Spanish ladies, erstwhile mistresses of French officers. A huge man, his face cut about and running with blood, rushed up to the group crying, *'a muerte! a muerte!'* – 'Kill them!' – at once plunging a dagger into the bosom of the lady nearest. The *canaille*, mad with the lust for killing, stripped off the harlots' finery and tore them limb from limb, scattering the parts over the blood-soaked earth. A breast, roughly severed, fell at my feet; turning it over with the toe of my boot, I pondered how befitting a fate this was for those of Spanish birth who allowed their bodies to be sullied and fouled by the lips and hands of the invaders.

This engagement and its terrible aftermath brought ferocious reprisals down upon the townsmen and villagers of Navarre. The French army sallied out in force and beat the *partidas* back into the high mountains.

Myself, reverting to civilian dress and dispossessing myself of my arms, passed through Catalonia and thence to take part with those bands harassing the French forces now besieging Tarragona. Together, the *partidas* and the Spanish armies outnumbered the French at this place, but our manoeuvres were in vain due to the petty squabbles and the deficiencies of our *comandantes*. The town fell into the hands of the enemy amidst great slaughter.

Even so, at this time, such were the depredations of the *partidas* and the growing strength of the Spanish armies, such was the menace of the English army hovering on the border of Portugal, that the King himself, with many French Marshals and Generals – Ney, Massena, Junot and St Cyr among them – took flight to Paris. Here the Emperor Napoleon met them in conference and set out new measures to prevent oppression of the Spanish people. At the same time, he warned them that armies must be withheld from Spain, withdrawn even, for a further great venture elsewhere. The King and his captains returned to my country in a more sober frame of mind.

Meanwhile Souchet, who in July of this year 1811 was honoured with the title of Marshal, pursued his wise course, his measures for good government now affecting not only Aragon and Valencia, but also Catalonia, where sickness had reduced the French army to a state of ineffectiveness. As the burden imposed by the tyrants lifted from the shoulders of the harassed people, so it became more difficult to incite them to insurrection and hostility, except only in Catalonia, where Lacy and Campo Verde and their accomplices continued their system of murdering French officers in their quarters, of poisoning the wells, of drugging the wines and flour, of firing the powder magazines, all regardless of the safety of innocent citizens.

I continued far into the summer with various *partidas* which harried Souchet's army as it pursued its triumphant march through Valencia where, under the general leadership of the weak and foolish Blake, the *partidas* were helpless spectators of numerous French victories. Disgusted with these operations, I returned, after two weeks of extreme exertion and imminent danger of capture, to Pampeluna, where Mina's group was active.

Let it not be thought that the actions which I describe were either the most or the least effective of those guerillas by which the people of Spain opposed their extortionate invaders.

Throughout the bitter winter of the years 1811–12, the French communications from Salamanca to Irun were continually menaced by the *partidas* of the Montana de Santander, of the Rioja, of Burgos and the Liebana, supported by English squadrons in the Bay of Biscay.

The Galicians harassed Marmont's army on the Orbijo; Mina and Merino continually harried the communications into France, with the utmost ferocity, hanging prisoners, killing the sick, destroying all that strayed in their path, thus bringing down upon themselves and upon the peasants of Navarre the vengeance of the French armies.

The Empecinado, ranging the mountains, pushed his parties up to the very gateways of Madrid. Villa Campa infested Daroca; Gayan raided the surrounds of Zaragoza; Gay and Miralles infested the Garriga.

The *partidas*, by May 1812, together with the Spanish and English armies, held down seventy-six thousand men under Souchet, forty-nine thousand of the 'Army of the Centre', sixty-three thousand under Soult and seventy thousand under Marmont – in all, a force of two hundred and seventy-seven thousand men. Of this number forty thousand were Spanish soldiers in French pay, traitors to their country.

At this time the *guerrilleros* took heart from the Duke of Wellington's great victory over Marmont at Salamanca, which made all the northern province ripe for rebellion and insurrection. In the autumn, following his resounding success, the Duke of Wellington's advance to Burgos, and his retreat therefrom, was

covered and aided by the bands of Ballesteros from the mountains
of Alcarez, by those of Elio, Villa Campa and the Empecinado and
by the *partidas* of Marquinez and Sanchez.

By the end of this year of 1812, the *partidas* were receiving many
thousands of English muskets which allowed them to acquire
cartridges from the English ships, instead of the loose powder
formerly demanded on account of the difference in the bore of the
Spanish muskets. This advantage enabled the bands to improve
their martial skills in the way that regular soldiers train. Our old
weapons we handed over to the citizens so that they could
answer the Frenchman's frequent demands for the surrender of
arms.

In the Northern provinces new and large bands were formed
until several battalions, taking to the field, were able to deny communications to the French through those areas. New leaders disposed of the robber and cut-throat elements and brought in men of
high birth, accustomed to service. Even in Aragon, that province
of plenty, insurrections grew in number and in strength. In
Catalonia, well-formed units replaced the ill-assorted gangs of
miqueletes.

General Cafarelli, posted in the northern states, complained to
the Emperor of this state of affairs. Napoleon replied, not to the
General, but to the King: 'Hold Madrid only as a point of observation; fix your headquarters at Valladolid; concentrate the armies
of the south, of the centre and of Portugal ... to put down the
insurrection in the northern provinces, to free the communications
with France and to re-establish a good base of operations before
the commencement of another campaign, that the French army
may be in a condition to fight the allies if the latter advance towards
France'. It was as well for Spain that King Joseph was less certain
of the methods which should be used against us than was his
brother, the Emperor. Thus, while Joseph pursued notions of
government utterly misplaced among the clash of arms, the *partidas* and the insurgents laid firm hold on his lines of communication
in the north.

Let it not be presumed that the *partidas* operated without
defeat. In the one month, in May, Mina was twice defeated, at first
in the valley of Ronçal, with one thousand men killed and wounded
(I myself escaped this engagement with the utmost difficulty and
with a severe shoulder wound), and again in the mountains. It can,

however, be said with truth that the forty thousand *guerrilleros* now operating in the northern provinces tied down the French army of the North to the rear areas.

Behind cover of these exertions, the Duke of Wellington reorganised his army and, at the end of May in 1813, launched that great march which, in the space of a few months, was to take his well-found troops over the Duero into Spain, over the Tormes, through Salamanca, through Valladolid, Burgos and Vitoria to the gateway into France. In making plans for this ambitious project, the Duke of Wellington exposed his armies to many hazards, since he was in no way superior to the French armies opposed to him, and, as the advance proceeded, despite his moving his bases of supply from the ports of Portugal to Santander, he operated along extending lines of communication. But more than any other thing, the vigorous excitement and sustenance of the northern insurgents and *partidas* occupied the enemy and scattered his forces, thus rendering the success of the project nearly certain.

By November in the year 1813, the impetus of the English advance had carried them into France itself. I was then with Mina's battalions, and side by side with the English armies, we debouched into the territory of the Basques. Here the soldiers of Spain, as we had now become, encouraged by a loosening control and urged on by friends at home, turned to pillage and to every form of wanton destruction. The Basque people fled from their villages and took up arms, and we ourselves discovered how it was to be opposed by *guerrilleros*.

The Duke of Wellington, understanding the reasons for the wrath of the Basques, at once returned Mina's troops to their own country, despite his virulent and excitable objections. Myself, I remained with Morello's division to discover that the Basques, once the Duke of Wellington had removed this threat and shown his resolve to destroy their bands, disregarded all appeals to patriotism and returned to their villages, setting the pecuniary advantages derived from the friendship of the British troops and the misery of the avenging warfare against the evils of further Spanish plunder.

Within this concise account of five years of the cruellest of wars, one which by its very nature must be fought without quarter (*guerra a muerte*), I have mentioned only a few of those actions in which we, the *guerrilleros,* engaged, and only a small number of the many measures which we adopted to shake off the yoke of foreign domination.

From this tale the reader should learn, however, that the *guerrillero* must be able to endure unimaginable hardship. Throughout the long summers, the climatic conditions in Spain are admirably suited to living the outdoor life, but in winter, in the mountains which were at once our refuge and stronghold, the intense cold will of itself kill the weak, the faint-hearted or the unprepared. The extent of the hardships and the dangers which the *guerrillero* has to endure is directly related to the extent to which the people of his country support him with supplies, with information, with shelter and with sympathy; so also the extent to which he either succeeds or fails in his endeavours.

Unless carefully controlled by established authority, the effect of guerillas on the common people may be such as to reduce them to a condition little better than that enjoyed by wild beasts. In the northern provinces, wherein lay the limits of my own experiences, there was no authority except only that imposed by the *comandante* of the *guerrilleros*. The peasants, the villagers and the townspeople were persecuted in turn by the Spanish armies in retreat, by the French in pursuit and in occupation, and by the *partidas*, all in search of men, beasts and sustenance. Brother's hand was turned against brother; son's against mother, father's against son, each one attributing his demands to the exigencies of the time. Further, the *partidas* too often forced ignorant citizens to arms and turned them loose, to their own destruction, against the skill and discipline of professional soldiers.

The *partidas*, particularly when supplied by the English fleets or through English agents, and when supported by their own people, were able to engage enormous numbers of enemy soldiers and to inflict upon them not only hampering delays and material losses, but also the final blow which saps above all the strength of an army of occupation, namely death. The French army lost to the *partidas* one hundred men each day during their occupation of my country.

The *partidas*, when engaged in battle in direct concert with regular armies, were able to make contribution to a successful outcome out of all proportion to their numbers, but despite my many exertions and the deep loathing which I harboured for the barbarians who infested my country, I would say that the *partidas* alone, supported only in part as they were by my people and subjected to the disadvantage of indifferent leadership, opposed as we were by such men as Souchet and Cafarelli and the experienced soldiers whom they led, would never have driven out the French barbarians without the assistance of the Duke of Wellington and the English, Spanish and Portuguese armies which he so ably led.

Chapter 3

Russia, 1812, and introduction to the Boer War

On June 24th 1812, the French army crossed the Niemen river into Russia, a well-found multitude of six hundred and seventeen thousand men, six companies of engineers, one siege train, several thousands of provision wagons, countless droves of cattle, one thousand three hundred and seventy-two pieces of cannon and innumerable artillery and hospital wagons – the largest, most experienced and best-equipped military force that the world had ever seen. They were led by Napoleon, Emperor of France, who ranks as one of the greatest military leaders of all time; his talented marshals, generals and colonels had helped to carry him to victory on a number of the great battlefields of Europe.

This army hurried across immeasurable steppes and plains to a hollow victory on the bloody battlefield of Borodino, seventy miles from the gates of Moscow. Despite a loss of one-third of his force, Napoleon continued on his way, entering the holy city on September the 14th.

After many restless and wasted days, during which he failed to bring the Russian Government to terms, Napoleon decided to withdraw his army and there began, as winter laid its first cold fingers on the land, the most disastrous retreat in the history of military affairs.

In mid-December, the remnants of the Grand Army crossed back over the Niemen – one thousand foot soldiers and nine cannon, with twenty thousand starved and frozen beings, clothed in rags, their heads bowed, eyes dulled in ashen cadaverous faces, beards stiffened with ice – all victims, together with their lost compatriots, of space, of Russian cunning, of the Russian winter and of the Cossack cavalry.

This magnificent army had been destroyed by guerilla tactics adapted and allied to the immensity of space and the ravages of climate. The Russian army, though ever present throughout the retreat, acted only in support of the Cossacks, bringing the French to battle only now and then, as at the disastrous crossing of the Beresina river. But the achievements of the guerillas in the campaigns both in Russia and in Spain were at that time obscured by the contributions made to victory, in the one country by the cruel weather and in the other by the Duke of Wellington's army.

Between 1814 and World War I, guerilla campaigns were waged in many parts of the world. In South America, Paez, later to become President of the Venezuelan Republic, in 1816 and again in 1822, made useful contributions to the struggle of the South American people for independence, at the head of a force recruited from the wild Llaneros, whose home was the vast Venezuelan grasslands. Mexican irregulars seriously hampered Scott's movements in the Mexico City campaign. The Civil War in America produced a number of guerilla leaders, not least among them the redoubtable John Singleton Mosby, who imposed insuperable difficulties of supply upon Grant throughout the Wilderness – Cold Harbour action, and the audacious Jesse McNeill, whose capture of his enemy, General Benjamin Kelley, ranks in boldness with any subsequent guerilla escapade. The Russians were engaged against guerillas among the Turkoman tribes.

Not one of these campaigns had any hope of eventual success and all subsided after initial local tactical victories. All were resorted to rather as a measure of desperation than as part of a proper strategical plan. Kutuzov in Russia, the people of Spain and the Duke of Wellington had shown the way, but those who clearly saw the potential were few in number and committed their convictions to paper rather than to the battlefield.

The British were also gaining experience of guerilla warfare in many out-of-the-way places in their far-flung Empire. We should now take a look at the campaign fought between the British army and the Boer commandos in South Africa at the turn of the nineteenth century.

To Bulawayo

Mafeking

Vryburg

Magliesburg
Witwaters Rand
Krugersdorp
Lichtenburg

Potchefstroom
Klerksdorp

Bothaville

ORANGE RIVER
COLONY

Abraham's
Kraal
Bloemfontein
Dewetsdorp

Hopetown

Strydenburg

Zand
Drift

De Aar

To Cape Town

Aberdeen

Great Karoo

Port Elizabeth

Harts R.

Harts R.

Vaal R.

Sand R.

Modder R.

Orange R.

Orange River

Caledon R.

Limpopo R.

To Pietersburg

Pretoria

Prinsloo

Johannesburg

Vereeniging

Heilbron

Tafel Kop

Tweefontein

Ficksburg

Springhaan
Nek

Odendaal

Delagoa Rly.

Komati Poort

Nooitgedacht

TRANSVAAL

Ermelo

Vaal R.

Langeburg

BASUTOLAND

Orange River

NATAL

ZULU LAND

Durban

INDIAN OCEAN

CAPE COLONY

20 0   100 Miles

SOUTH AFRICA

THE PRINCIPAL BATTLE AREAS OF THE GUERILLA
CAMPAIGN

Political boundaries —·—·—   Railways ++++

Narrative 2

South Africa — 1900 to 1902

'Take a community of Dutchmen of the type of those who defended themselves for fifty years against all the power of Spain at a time when Spain was the greatest power in the world. Intermix with them a strain of those inflexible French Huguenots who gave up their home and fortune and left their country forever at the time of the revocation of the Edict of Nantes. The product must obviously be one of the most rugged, virile, unconquerable races ever seen upon earth. Take these formidable people and train them for seven generations in constant warfare against savage men and ferocious beasts, in circumstances under which no weakling could survive; place them so that they acquire exceptional skill with weapons and in horsemanship, give them a country which is eminently suited to the tactics of the huntsman, the marksman and the rider. Then, finally, put a fine temper upon their military qualities by a dour fatalistic Old Testament religion and an ardent and consuming patriotism. Combine all these qualities and all these impulses in one individual and you have the modern Boer.'

FROM *The Great Boer War* BY ARTHUR CONAN DOYLE

A Dutch community was first established in South Africa, at the Cape of Good Hope, in 1652. During the ensuing one hundred and fifty years the colonists extended their sway inland, showing at all times a characteristic independence from Europe. They were not, however, to escape the after-effects of the titanic struggle between England and France which occupied the twenty-five years following the French Revolution. In 1814, in the final pay-out, Cape Colony was added to the British Empire, at the price of conquest and at a cost of six million pounds.

The Dutch were farmers, and their vast estates were tilled by slave labour recruited from among the native people. In 1834, in a single day and without due warning, the British gave the slaves their freedom. The Dutch farmers, facing ruin, looked towards the enormous tracts of territory to the north of the Colony. Packing their possessions, women-folk and children into huge ox-drawn wagons with teams inspanned, with herds and flocks accompanying, the Boers marched forth across the rolling veld. Among those who set out on this great trek to the north was a ten-year-old boy, Paul Stephanus Kruger. The Boers first crossed five hundred miles of wild country in the direction of Natal, only to find the British flag flying over the small township of Durban. They turned west, and still further north, to found the two republics named Orange River Colony and the Transvaal.

In these new territories fifteen thousand souls spread over a countryside as large as Germany where they led a turbulent existence, warring with the Kaffirs, with other native tribes and even among themselves.

In 1848 the British, no longer able to tolerate a disturbed situation on their borders, annexed a large part of the Orange River Colony, but at the same time, at the Sand River Convention, formally acknowledged the independence of the Transvaal. Only a year later, the British withdrew from the Orange River Colony and a second republic received recognition.

For twenty-five years following the Sand River Convention, the two republics continued to lead a strenuous and violent existence. Threats by Kaffirs and Zulus grew into the menace of large-scale invasion; in 1877, making as their excuse the need to forestall such invasion, the British annexed both the Transvaal and the Orange River Colony.

The Boers were in no mood to accept such annexation, nor were British promises of peace and return to independence immediately realised. In 1880, after a short bout of warfare which gave rise to only a few skirmishes, the British Government, at the Convention of Pretoria, made a new deal with the Boer·republics; by this agreement they became self-governing but subject to an ill-defined suzerainty emanating from the Queen and Her Government in London. Paul Kruger became President of the two republics.

Meanwhile, Cape Colony flourished. By 1872 the white population had risen to two hundred thousand, Dutch slightly predominating over British. In this year the Colony became self-governing; the Dutch, in the majority, at once introduced their own laws and methods of government.

The two republics might well have prospered in peace also but for Paul Kruger's ill-judged attempts to expand beyond his borders and but for the discovery of gold in the good earth of the Witwaters Rand.

Gold brought to the Transvaal thousands of clever, energetic and ruthless men from all parts of Europe and America. These men, their numbers ever-increasing, brought wealth to the Transvaal, but Paul Kruger, labelling them 'Uitlanders', denied them the franchise, taxed them to the hilt and demanded their complete subservience to the Boer.

In 1896 the Uitlanders, by now out-numbering the Boers in the Transvaal, planned a rising against the Government in Pretoria, The Governor of Cape Colony launched from Mafeking the ill-conceived and ill-fated Jameson Raid, ostensibly in their support. The Boers quickly rounded up the ludicrously small force of five hundred raiders and Paul Kruger wasted no time in making worldwide political capital out of the incident, thus receiving moral backing for still further harsh treatment of the Uitlanders.

In 1899 these unfortunate people, the majority of them Englishmen, still denied a voice in the government of the country in which they lived and to which they had brought prosperity, driven to the last extremity, appealed to the Queen for help. Negotiations followed, but in vain; at 5 p.m. on Wednesday the 11th October, 1899, the war opened.

There followed one year of fighting between regular forces of the British Army on the one side and those of the Boers on the other. This stage of the war ended with the occupation by Lord Roberts of Pretoria, the capital of the Transvaal. Lord Roberts had arrived in South Africa early in December, 1899, to find a series of disconnected operations in which the British were invariably worsted; he speedily converted them into a series of connected operations which were almost uniformly successful. Upon his arrival in Pretoria, there remained only one outstanding need, to mop up the Boers' last regular force which had retreated into the east Transvaal. He despatched General Buller to eliminate this force and to take possession of its source and means of supply, the Delagoa railway.

By the end of September, 1900, General Buller had completed his task and it was hoped that this final dispersal of the main Boer army, the capture of its guns and the expulsion of many of the burghers and their foreign mercenaries, would have marked the end of the struggle; but there was to follow eighteen months of guerilla warfare which was as senseless as it was brave.

The arena for this arduous conflict lay in the territories of the two republics and Cape Colony, a tract of land stretching one thousand miles from south to north, and five hundred miles, on average, from east to west. This vast arena was made up of boundless rolling *velds*, huge ranges of forested mountains, enormous areas of broken ground, wide prairies of bush and grassland, the whole intersected by three great rivers, the Orange, the Vaal and the Limpopo, and a thousand tributaries.

Habitation was sparse. Homesteads lay scattered over the extensive plains and in the fertile valleys. Five thousand acres was the average size for a farm, and the Boer's proud boast was that even in the clear air and brilliant light which prevailed over the land for most of the year, a farmer could not see the smoke rising from the chimneys of his neighbour. Here and there were small hamlets, each no more than a cluster of houses. Towns were established only at centres of communication, at Cape Town and Port Elizabeth in the Cape Colony, at Bloemfontein in the Orange River Colony and at Pretoria in the Transvaal.

Communications were based on two main railways, each stretching for one thousand miles from end to end, the first from Cape Town through Mafeking to Bulawayo, the second from Port Elizabeth through Bloemfontein and Pretoria to Pietersburg. Two main branch lines connected Johannesburg with Natal, and Pretoria with Komati Poort, this latter called the Delagoa railway.

The few rutted roads, in dry weather deep in dust, in the wet reduced to quagmires of mud, were barely fit for the ox-cart or the horse-drawn limber. After rain in the mountains the many fords became raging torrents, impassable by man or beast.

The inhabitants in the main were farmers – in the Transvaal and Orange River Colony Dutch almost to a man; in the Cape Colony mixed Dutch and British. Black and brown-skinned natives served on the farms or eked out a bare living in remote *kraals*.

The end of regular warfare found a considerable number of well-mounted and well-armed Boers spread over the land, acting with such aggressive energy that they gave the impression of a powerful force. Making their way into the settled districts, they inflamed the passions of those reverting to peaceful ways and so recruited to their number. Many of these new recruits had

29

previously been released on parole from captivity, together with their horses, and now added their honour to the many sacrifices demanded of them.

Opposed to them was the British army, with contingents from Australia, Canada and New Zealand. In total an enormous force, they had yet to guard two thousand miles of railroad, to escort every convoy, to garrison every centre of communication; thus, they had only small numbers available for mobile operations. But these men, although regular in outlook and in training, after one year of warfare were themselves as skilled in the ways of the hunter as were the brave men whom they encountered on the field of battle. The *'rooineks'*, whose lack of cunning and veld-craft had been a subject of derision, were men of the past.

As a study of this campaign, one can do no better than follow in detail the adventures of Christian De Wet who, set even against such figures as Delarey, Botha and J. C. Smuts, was probably the most famous of the Boer guerilla leaders and certainly the most indefatigable. His strong stocky figure, dressed always in tail coat, tinted spectacles and a stubby top-hat, his tireless energy and reckless courage dominated the Orange River Colony for many months and drew upon his burghers the attention of thousands of his opponents.

The spring of the year 1900 found De Wet lying low in the northern sector of the Orange River Colony after a hectic flight from Prinsloo. Though lying low he had not been idle and by October he was ready for action once more with a commando of two thousand men. Wasting not a moment he rode forth at once to intercept a column under General Barton which was covering the railway between Krugersdorp and Klerksdorp. At this time the long stretches of railroad were protected from enemy action by patrolling up and down the line with complete field forces of infantry, cavalry and guns.

It was upon such a force that De Wet's burghers descended on the 20th of October; an alert British scout, observing the dust-cloud hanging over his body of horsemen, gave brief notice of his coming. The Boers sprang from their ponies and went into action in their usual effective fashion, approaching along the narrow *spruits,* gullies and *nullahs* the line of *sangars* hastily thrown up by the soldiers. Using for cover every fold in the ground, every rock, every boulder, and covered by the fire of several guns, the Boers in their fashion surrounded the British and for five days and nights drew closer the cordon of attack. By the 25th Boer snipers overlooked the Britons' only water supply, so that men of the Scots and Welsh Fusiliers were forced to close upon them. After crossing one mile of ground, in widely extended order and under sustained and accurate fire, the infantrymen gained their objective, thus placing their enemy in an untenable position. The Boers, now themselves under a deadly hail of fire, rushed out from their cover and streamed across the veld to where their horses had been hidden – 'a black, running mob, carrying coats, blankets, boots and rifles'.[1] De Wet, quick to see the threat of defeat, made away without delay, for some inexplicable reason unpursued by his opponents.

But he was not allowed to escape with impunity. Forty-eight hours later two forces of mounted infantry and cavalry, led by officers of great skill and energy, General Charles Knox and Colonel De Lisle, ran into a cloud of horsemen fleeing along the north bank of the Vaal river, seeking for a place to cross. The British rode headlong after them, bringing guns into action at furious speed, firing from the hip as they rode. But darkness and a violent storm gave De Wet his opportunity to escape.

After crossing the river he placed seventy miles, as he thought, between himself and his pursuers, and halted at Bothaville to rest and re-fit, but Knox, De Lisle and one other, Le Gallais, were hard on his heels.

Here, on November the 6th, forty mounted infantry suddenly came upon the Boers' sleeping camp. Without delay, though greatly outnumbered, the small party opened fire, while sending for reinforcements. The camp immediately sprang to life; those guerillas who could reach their horses galloped away across the veld; those who could not occupied a kraal and farmhouse from which to hold off the attack. Guns were brought to bear, accurate and intense sharp-shooting criss-crossed the open ground. Both sides spread out in ever-widening flanking movements, the one attempting to surround the other. For an hour the pressure on the original British force was extreme, but eventually it was the Boers who were out-flanked and De Lisle with his Australians, after a twelve-mile gallop across the plain, arrived in time to deliver the *coup de grâce*. De Wet had lost one hundred and forty men, six guns, a pom-pom and a thousand head of cattle.

[1] From an eye-witness account.

Concurrent with these exertions, a small but efficient Boer force skirted a wide area in the southern regions of the Orange River Colony, falling upon one small garrison after another, stirring up the farmers who were settling down under the wise and conciliatory rule of General Prettyman.

De Wet is next to be seen at Dewetsdorp. The place fell to his commando on November the 25th after a week of creditable defence, but only two days later De Wet was on the move again, once more threatened by General Charles Knox. Knox ran him down at Vaalbank but De Wet again broke away, trekking south for eighteen hours without a halt.

During his journeys across the Orange River Colony, De Wet's plans were aided by the extraordinary leniency of the British in leaving horses on the farms and in returning their mounts to prisoners on parole, a parole no sooner given than broken; there seemed a lack of appreciation that the horse was as much a weapon as the rifle. De Wet was thus enabled to retain his mobility despite his losses on the field of battle.

De Wet planned to invade Cape Colony. In torrents of rain which turned every *spruit* into a river and every road into a quagmire, the Boer leader hurried south. Information came that he was crossing the Caledon and mobile columns were directed, through lashing rain and bitter cold, upon that river, but De Wet had passed. The British followed, the guns dragged over beneath the swirling waters, horses and men wading and swimming.

De Wet's course was not difficult to follow; broken wagons, exhausted animals, discarded litter, the debris of a large mounted force showed his pursuers the way. It led to the Orange river at Odendaal but a British force was already there to oppose his crossing. He doubled back north, back over the Caledon, back to Dewetsdorp, then on to the Springhann Nek. Here, without hesitation, De Wet led his whole force, now two thousand five hundred strong, at full gallop through the pass, through a hail of rifle and gun-fire directed upon his horsemen from either flank. He then disappeared into the Ficksburg mountains.

While British troops hounded De Wet through the Orange River Colony, others were engaged in the Transvaal which had been divided into separate military zones. Within these zones, from Lichtenburg to Komati Poort, a distance of four hundred miles, there was sporadic fighting everywhere, as the commandos attacked scattered posts, tore up the railroad, wrecked the trains and harassed the countryside.

Within their allotted areas British commanders launched their troops on a series of aggressive operations against the elusive foe; Lord Methuen to the east of Mafeking; Hart at Potchefstroom, where he surprised a commando which had occupied this railway town after a march by which his infantry covered thirty-six miles, and his cavalry fifty-four, within the space of fifteen hours. General Paget operated against the commandos of Erasmus and Viljoen to the north and north-east of Pretoria; on the eastern borders, Pole-Carew, Buller and Hamilton engaged in minor skirmishes and in two major engagements. General Clements made vain attempts to remove Delarey's forces from the rugged lines of the Magaliesburg mountains, his efforts being brought to nought during a foray to Nooitgedacht where superior numbers of the enemy concentrated upon his small force.

At the end of the year 1900, honours were about even in the Transvaal, but whereas British losses in men, arms and equipment were easily replaced, this was not so for the Boers; their reserves were infinitely smaller. Against this, the demands of the lines of communication absorbed so many of the two hundred thousand soldiers whom the British kept in the field that they were seldom superior, and often inferior to the numbers of their enemy in the countless local engagements.

The people's dissatisfaction with British rule in the Cape Colony had become unobtrusive as regular warfare turned to guerilla fighting, but later in the year 1900, fanned by propaganda disseminated by a political association known as the Afrikander Bond, and by fictitious stories of British outrages put about by certain newspapers, discontent increased to a dangerous degree. The Boers were quick to grasp the opportunities offered for a fresh invasion, and two main columns were accordingly sent forth across the Orange river, one to operate in the west under Judge Hertzog, the other in the east under Kritzinger.

The columns split into small bands and with the help of information and supplies furnished by the local farmers, wandered for many weeks over the great expanse of the Colony, taking refuge when necessary in the mountain ranges.

To counter this activity, the Commander-in-Chief, Lord Kitchener, proclaimed martial law in those parts of the Colony most affected, raised regiments from among loyalist farmers and organised small mobile columns to seek out and eliminate the invaders.

Inspired by the enterprising Colonel De Lisle, British columns rounded up Hertzog's forces, driving them back, by the 26th February, 1901, on to a new invading force under Christian De Wet. De Lisle's men, during the final forty-eight hours of pursuit, covered no less than seventy-two miles of broken country, but the Boers were quicker yet and made good their escape. Meanwhile Kritzinger had been driven into the wild country north of Aberdeen where his forces disappeared.

At the end of January, with two thousand five hundred freshly-mounted troops, De Wet broke through the wide meshes of the British net and on February 11th, forded the Orange river at Zand Drift, undeterred by a plea for peace sent to him by his brother Piet.

De Wet's invaders headed west through continuous and torrential rain, closely pursued by Plumer. On the 15th of February, after crossing the railroad north of De Aar, De Wet turned upon his persecutors, taking position upon a line of *kopjes* rising out of the great expanse of the plain. There he fought a gallant rear-guard action, but failed to shake off his persistent enemy; instead, he was compelled to abandon his wagons and reserve ammunition and to flee headlong to the north-west.

The two small armies continued the chase over the endless plain, through atrocious weather, rain and hail falling with such violence as to terrify the horses and to test to the uttermost the skill and determination of their riders. Northwards through Strydenburg, past Hopetown to the Orange river, too swollen to cross, back eastward over the railroad again, De Wet continued his way, numerous minor engagements with Plumer's hardy men gradually reducing the strength of his commando. As we have seen, Judge Hertzog joined him in late February, but by this time the Boer leader was as anxious to leave the Cape Colony as previously he had been to invade it.

De Wet was now trapped by the swollen Orange river on his left, by Plumer at his heels and by further columns converging from south and west, but a sudden drop in the flood allowed him to cross the river on the last day of February and escape into his own country.

He had gained nothing; instead he had lost four thousand horses, all his guns, all his convoy and three hundred of his men. Still undeterred, he thrust northward into the Orange River Colony, still menaced by the indefatigable Plumer, until, by crossing the Modder river at Abraham's Kraal, he made good his escape once more, while the British forces fell back on Bloemfontein to rest and re-fit.

Meanwhile events in the Transvaal had taken a different course. There the Boers had adopted a technique of mounting widespread attacks upon a succession of British posts; a few successful but the majority broken up by the accuracy of British defensive fire. The timings of these raids demonstrated good planning and co-ordination by the two leaders operating in that area – Delarey and Smuts.

To add to the difficulties of their enemies, the Boers took to wearing British uniform. Denys Reitz, in his stirring account of a commando's fortunes and misfortunes, claims that these captured uniforms were worn only out of dire necessity when the Boers had nothing else to wear; none the less, the ruse gave them the advantage of surprise on many occasions and Lord Kitchener instructed that captured offenders should be hanged.

The British, forswearing a defensive attitude, initiated a series of wide and long-ranging sweeping movements against the raiders, conducted by separate and highly mobile columns. General French controlled one such sweep through the area surrounding Ermelo; seven columns, each two thousand strong, passing from west to east through this territory. On occupying Ermelo and looking eastwards they saw innumerable herds and countless flocks, long lines of wagons and bodies of horsemen stretching from horizon to horizon; Botha, with a commando several thousand strong, had just passed by.

Aware of his desperate position, Botha turned to attack. First isolating Smith-Dorrien's column, he mounted a formidable assault, but only to be beaten off. Then started a ruthless and prolonged pursuit, every day showing a record of captured men, herds, guns and wagons as the fugitives were rounded up from the north, from the west and from the south. The British forces trampled over fertile farmlands leaving behind a barren desert; they burned the houses, destroyed the crops; they rounded up both cattle and people and transferred them to camps along the railroad. The relentless march of the destroying columns was halted only by torrential rains which turned the countryside into a sea of mud.

While the columns in the Transvaal were taking their toll, while De Wet's forces were being hounded down, Lord Kitchener took further steps towards peace.

On the 20th of December, 1900, he had issued a proclamation offering amnesty to those who surrendered. This had the effect of producing peace movements among the settled burghers, but all their representations to the Boer leaders in the field were turned down. In March, Lord Kitchener offered Botha terms of extraordinary leniency in return for his calling off the fight. Botha replied that nothing short of total independence would satisfy him and the negotiations were broken off; but the peace committees in various districts and townships continued in being.

Peace offers and their refusal had the effect of bringing in thousands more refugees, mostly women and children whose bread-winners were riding the range. They were accommodated in spacious camps, administered entirely by the British authorities. At the same time, the opportunity was taken deliberately to concentrate the scattered population into communities near the railway lines, so that they could be fed and cared for, their activities controlled and no longer dictated by fear of, or sympathy with, the armed commandos.

In the military field, Lord Kitchener instituted new and far-reaching methods to turn to full account the initiative which he had gained. He centralised his bases, withdrawing garrisons from outlying towns while moving their populations. His engineers constructed barriers of barbed wire from strategic point to strategic point, thus canalising the Boers' movements. His soldiers scorched the earth, in order to deprive the guerillas of their livelihood.

He reinforced his cavalry until, by the end of April, 1901, he had under command between fifty and sixty thousand dragoons, hussars and troopers, 'such a force as no British general in his happiest dream had ever thought of commanding and no British war minister in his darkest nightmare had ever imagined himself called upon to supply.'[1]

Finally, he established the famous and marvellous block-house system which contributed more than any other single factor to the downfall of the armed guerillas. The block-houses were small square or hexagonal buildings made of stone, about nine feet high,

[1] Arthur Conan Doyle in *The Great Boer War*.

with corrugated iron above, all sides loop-holed for musketry fire, each small fort holding between six to thirty men. They were dotted along the railways at points not more than two thousand yards apart, and were supplemented by a system of armoured trains. Once established, their frequency was increased, on key stretches, to only six hundred yards, and they were further extended to certain areas away from the railways. All individual accounts by Boers of their exertions and adventures in the guerilla war tell of the dangers and the difficulties they encountered when attempting to tamper with the railways once this system had been evolved, and of the severe restrictions which it imposed upon their cross-country movement. Even at night it proved almost impossible to break across a line of block-houses.

With these effective steps in train, Kitchener launched Plumer on one of those bold, swift strokes which were typical of his military strategy. In seven days Plumer led a force of two thousand rifles from Pretoria to Pietersburg, a key town in the very heart of the Boers' last stronghold. Occupying the place on the 8th of April, Plumer then swept the country all around, wearing down the commandos of Viljoen and Botha.

For the next few months, in both the republics and in the Cape Colony, British forces were engaged in the tiresome and often unrewarding work of hunting down small bands in the wildest country; but attrition was beginning to take its toll upon the Boers' will to resist.

It was not until December, 1901, that Christian De Wet reappeared. It had long been evident that the British tactics of scouring the country for isolated commandos must finally bring the war to a conclusion, and it appeared to De Wet that the Boers' only hope lay in re-assembling a larger body to try conclusions with the British columns.

Serene in his convictions, decisive and aggressive to the last, he brought a force of two thousand men to bear upon a small contingent near Heilbron, his sharp-shooters coming to close quarters, his guns shelling from afar. Leaving the surprised soldiers to lick their wounds, he rode off to the east. Shortly afterwards, with the general aim of checking the building of block-houses, he sprang out of Langeberg mountains upon a covering party of the East Lancashires near Tafel Kop. A rescue column, struggling through weather so atrocious that the veld resembled an inland sea,

37

approached the scene of action in widely extended order. In the centre was the commander, Colonel Damant, his staff, two guns, a maxim and forty men of the Imperial Yeomanry. At a point far removed from their objective, they saw riding towards them a body of men in khaki uniform, keeping British formation, firing volleys towards a distant enemy. Nearer they came and nearer until, throwing off all disguise, the Boers made a dash for the guns. In a moment they had cut out the heart of their adversary and were riding fast away.

Only four days later De Wet surprised another covering force sixty miles further south, at Tweefontein. On this Christmas Eve, the British, encamped on high ground, had relaxed their guard. The Boers stole up to the position in stockinged feet, sprang over the crest and firing upon the pickets rushed into the sleeping camp. Within a few moments one thousand rifles poured a hissing sleet of bullets into the startled soldiers as they rushed from their tents. Resistance was maintained for half-an-hour, but at the end of that time the Boers had the whole camp in their possession. De Wet hurried away, taking two hundred prisoners whom he later turned loose upon the Basuto border.

With this last successful engagement De Wet had shot his bolt, as, indeed, had the whole Boer movement, except only one man, Delarey, in one last stronghold, that wide area of hilly and broken country which lies to the west of Klerksdorp. There lurked Delarey with several thousand tried and trusty stalwarts.

Lord Methuen turned against him in one long trek which took him out to Vryburg, up to Lichtenburg, and back to Klerksdorp as he attempted to bring his elusive foe to battle. Results were negligible and it was Delarey who had the last word, pouncing upon a convoy only ten miles out from Klerksdorp, driving off the escorting soldiers, inflicting one hundred and eighty-seven casualties, capturing two guns, burning the wagons and shooting their teams. Again, on the 7th of March, he came charging down from the hills upon Methuen's own column, the horsemen firing from their saddles as they came, driving off the British cavalry and overwhelming both infantry and guns.

But this was to be the last Boer victory in the war. Lord Kitchener took personal control of the operations against Delarey, with General Ian Hamilton, his Chief of Staff, as supreme commander in the field. There followed a number of intensive drives against the remaining commandos, none of which met with a success commensurate with the numbers of soldiers employed or the exertions to which they were subjected, but all of which had the effect of slowly wearing down the enemy.

The final outcome of this brutal and deadly war of attrition was happily forestalled by overtures for peace. Members of the acting government of the Transvaal at last realised that the military power of the Boers was broken. The only organised force of any size was imprisoned in the fastnesses of southern Transvaal; elsewhere, scattered commandos had been reduced to dejected groups of exhausted men and flagging beasts, clothed in tatters with few weapons and little ammunition.

At the end of March the acting government, giving way to the compulsion of military logic, issued instructions to the men in the field. Christian De Wet, Delarey and other leaders appeared at the British outposts at Klerksdorp, while delegates for peace came forward from all parts of the country. Their appearance led to the assembly at Vereeniging where, by the end of May, it was settled by vote that the British peace terms should be accepted.

At half-past ten on the 31st May, 1902, the delegates arrived at Pretoria to set their names to the treaty of peace.

In the light of our experience in the twentieth century, it may be asked how, in the space of only eighteen months, a regular army of two hundred thousand men, tied as they were to long and vulnerable lines of communication, were able to bring down a highly-organised guerilla movement, composed of the type of men described at the beginning of this chapter, never less than twenty thousand strong and for much of the time at least treble that number, operating in their own country, in terrain ideally suited to guerilla tactics and in which they enjoyed the support of the majority of the people. The answer is to be found in both the politico-strategical field and in the tactics employed by the two opponents.

The Boers were cut off from the outside world. As the guerilla war proceeded and became harsher in its execution, so there were outbursts of indignation in the world press against actions taken by the British, but such outbursts were few – so few as to make little impression upon the British Government and so few as to offer little encouragement to the Boer movement. The British Government's liberal treatment of both the people and the armed enemy, carried out through the offices of Lord Roberts and Lord Kitchener, was devised not only for humanitarian reasons but also to woo away from the Boers the sympathy of foreign governments and of the people of South Africa. This policy succeeded.

As a result, the Boers had no sanctuary upon their borders into which to retreat for rest, re-training and re-equipping. They had no support, either moral or material, from outside; the few supplies which they were able to obtain from across their borders were smuggled in by a handful of money-greedy adventurers.

The Boers were denied the opportunity – by history, by geography and by the politics of the day – of tying the activities of their guerillas to a politico-strategic plan.

The Boer leaders, with the possible exception of Paul Kruger – that obstinate man who directed his nation first from Pretoria, later from The Hague – persuaded either by the logic of circumstance, by humanitarian principles, or by lack of experience, appeared reluctant to commit their people to a prolonged war. Their tactics in the field reflected this policy.

Their commandos were large, often several thousand strong, and were always spoiling for a fight, too often in unfavourable conditions. Their attacks, though skilfully mounted and making expert use of ground and cover and of crack marksmanship, too frequently broke down in the face of British defensive fire. They invited casualties to men and beasts which they could ill afford, and they were too slow to recognise the time for retreat. The bravery, aggressiveness and enthusiasm of such leaders as De Wet, Botha, Delarey, Viljoen and Smuts were not matched by the necessary patience, skill and cunning. But it may well be that they deliberately avoided many of the techniques of the guerilla because of the circumstances prevailing and in the interests of their people. Certainly their chivalry and sense of fair dealing had never before, nor have ever since, been found in an irregular force.

They were opposed by an efficient army brilliantly led. Names which have since become illustrious sprinkled the list of senior officers – Kitchener, Hamilton, Haig, Plumer and Allenby to name but a few. Their brain power, skill and energy were matched in their subordinates. Not only was the mobile warfare carried to the armed commandos with boldness and audacity, but the securing and pacification of territories once cleared was carried through thoroughy and thoughtfully, despite the enormous effort involved.

The block-house system along the lines of communication, linked to the long belts of barbed wire reaching out across the countryside, the clearing of fertile areas of people, shelter, crops and cattle, the well-timed offers of amnesty, the raising of peace committees and local defence units, all in a comparatively short time, denied to the guerillas the essentials of their trade, namely, intelligence, supplies and freedom of manoeuvre.

The soldiers, whether employed on defensive duties in the block-houses, villages and towns, or whether carrying the war to the enemy, displayed resolution, courage and adaptability which enabled them to meet all the demands of their excellent leaders. They learned to endure, to suffer hard marches, harsh weather, hunger and privation. Men trained in the 'line of fire' became individual marksmen, men skilled in the drills of mass formation became expert in the use of ground, men trained as infantry took readily to horseback. The hunter became the hunted, the evader found himself pursued, harried and finally surrounded by troops as mobile as he.

The Boers were beaten by their political environment, by brain power and by a tough and adaptable army of professional and volunteer soldiers. Among these latter was the author's father, one among many who, during the two years and seven months of the campaign, slept only one night under a roof and was never once separated by more than a few yards from his long-suffering horse and his accurate rifle.

Chapter 4

Introduction to the Arab Revolt

The Boer War contributed to the evolution of both guerilla and counter-guerilla warfare. The Boer commandos clearly demonstrated the weaknesses of an unsupported guerilla movement whose main aim was to carry the fight to a well-trained and well-equipped regular army. The British, on the other hand, evolved a number of effective techniques for dealing with the political, military and administrative problems presented by this form of fighting.

If one can except the ancient military philosopher Sun Tzu, and Fabius Maximus who though adopting guerilla tactics commanded a regular army, and certain chieftains and warriors of olden times whose military achievements have never been accurately recorded, the world had yet to produce a man who would deliberately reduce guerilla warfare to a set of rules and adopt it as a form within a proper strategical plan. This need was first met by an Englishman, T. E. Lawrence.

While not a trained soldier, Lawrence was sent to Arabia in 1916 to organise the revolt of the Arab tribes against their Turkish overlords. He found that the Arabs, despite initial success at Mecca, had been beaten in pitched battle at Medina and were on the verge of abandoning the rebellion. Lawrence analysed the causes for failure, concluding that the Arabs possessed neither the knowledge, discipline nor equipment to enable them to defeat a regular army in formal battle. He at once adopted the guerilla form, adapting it to the environment of the desert and offering it as an adjunct to the British government's strategical plans.

The story of the contribution made by Lawrence and the Arab tribes to the campaign against the Turks in Arabia and Palestine between 1916 and 1918 is told by a sergeant of the British army who became involved in the Arab revolt, a man of perception, but one whose previous military training had been devoted to regular warfare in a European setting.

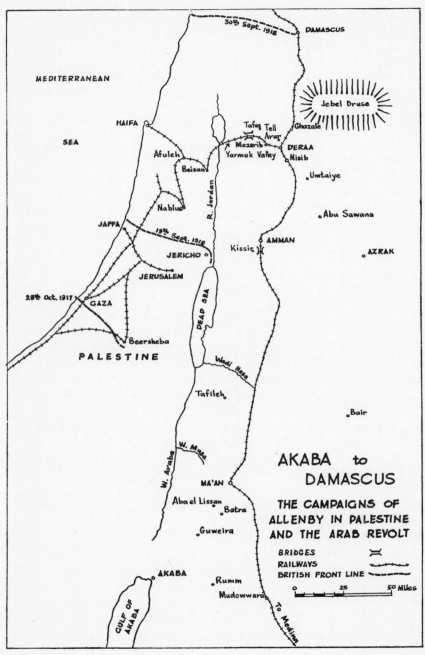

MEDITERRANEAN

SEA

HAIFA

Afuleh

Beisan

Nablus

JAFFA

19ᵗʰ Sept. 1918

JERICHO

JERUSALEM

28ᵗʰ Oct. 1917

GAZA

Beersheba

PALESTINE

R. Jordan

DEAD SEA

Wadi Hesa

Tafileh

W. Musa

W. Araba

MA'AN

Aba el Lissan

Batra

Guweira

AKABA

GULF OF AKABA

Rumm

Mudowwara

To Medina

30ᵗʰ Sept. 1918

DAMASCUS

Jebel Druse

Tafas Tell Arar

Ghazale

Mezerib

Yarmuk Valley

DERAA Nisib

Umtaiye

Abu Sawana

Kissir

AMMAN

AZRAK

Bair

AKABA to DAMASCUS

THE CAMPAIGNS OF ALLENBY IN PALESTINE AND THE ARAB REVOLT

BRIDGES
RAILWAYS
BRITISH FRONT LINE

0   25   50 Miles

44

Narrative 3

The Arab Revolt — 1916 to 1918

'I went up to the Tigris with one hundred Devon Territorials, young, clean, delightful fellows, full of the power of happiness and of making women and children glad. By them one saw vividly how great it was to be their kin, and English. And we were casting them by thousands into the fire to the worst of deaths, not to win the war but that the corn and rice and oil of Mesopotamia might be ours. The only need was to defeat our enemies (Turkey among them), and this was at last done in the wisdom of Allenby with less than 400 killed, by turning to our uses the hands of the oppressed in Turkey'.[1]

Akaba was a strange place, quite different from any other place I had seen. Only two days before I stepped ashore there, one day in July, 1917, I had been teaching the techniques of my favourite weapon, the Stokes mortar, to a number of regular, and to a few not so regular soldiers at the military school in Zeitun, and even as the ship entered that crowded little port I could see that life was going to change for me. At Zeitun I had had regular hours, regular meals, regular sleep, but I could see at once that things were not going to be regular any more.

Akaba was as hot as hell. The heat scorched up from the ground as though from a furnace, stifling movement and thought, opening the pores of the skin so that sweat ran freely, blocking the nostrils with a sickening, foetid smell, parching the throat and glazing the eye-balls until they withdrew for protection deep back into their sockets. I never did like this heat, not during all my two years in the desert, but somehow I learnt to live with it.

There were the flies too, millions of them everywhere. I had to walk around with a kerchief across my mouth so that I could breathe without sucking them in. I passed a fruit stall soon after

[1] T. E. Lawrence, in the Introductory Chapter to *The Seven Pillars of Wisdom.*

45

coming ashore and saw an old Indian vendor waving a stick over
the flies which settled on his wares; the small flies ducked underneath, the big ones jumped over the top only to settle again into
the seething black carpet.

But what amazed me most were the thousands of tents, all of
different shapes, sizes and colours, pitched within and around the
half-ruined buildings of the old mud-built town. They were put
down anywhere and everywhere, all over the place, a queer sight
to me, a regular sergeant in His Majesty's army.

Among the tents were the Arabs, most of them crouching in the
shade of the canvas or beneath the rocks and bushes that were
strewn about, but some striding to and fro in that smooth-flowing
movement which I came to associate with them. Some were
young, clean-shaven, bright eyed, no more than boys; others,
older, were swarthy, bearded, hawk-nosed, their faces lined with
age and hardship. Their colour varied from pale brown to the ebon
of the men from the Hedjaz. Most of them wore loose shirts, many
with cotton drawers underneath, and all wore head shawls which
seemed to be used for almost anything; as sweat rags, as carrier
bags, or as handkerchiefs when the need arose. Many, also, were
armed, with ammunition in bandoliers around their chests. I had
never seen a tougher-looking crowd, and indeed, I came to learn
later that they could ride immense distances on camel-back day after
day, or run through sand and over hills in the heat for hours on end
without apparent pain or fatigue. There was a spirit of lawlessness
about them, yet one of purpose, albeit wild. I felt a real comic in
my khaki shirt and shorts, in my putties and boots and with a
topee on my head; I determined to change into their kit as soon as
I could get permission from whoever was in charge.

This, then, was the Arab revolt about which I had heard so
much back at Zeitun, while never dreaming that I myself would
play a part in it. During the first few days I discovered the history
of this extraordinary uprising, and I soon came to enter into the
spirit of the thing. These Arabs became brothers to me, in a
brotherhood forged in the loneliness of a vast wilderness, in the
rigours of the long rides, in the dangers of short and sharp
engagements with the Turkish enemy.

The revolt had started in 1915 while I was still on a course in
Blighty before coming out to the Middle East. The Arabs were
already discontented with Turkish occupation and I have no

doubt that the flame of their discontent was fanned by the British government who saw, in an armed Arab revolt, a means of drawing Turkish men and material away from the main war fronts on which we fought, and a means of reducing the Turkish threat to our base in Egypt. But it was not until near the end of that year that Emir Feisal, son of the warlike Sherif of Mecca, came out in open revolt, and brought with him a number of the tribes over whom he had loose control.

This Emir Feisal was an unusual man. He was only thirty-one years of age but looked much older, with blood-shot eyes and deep lines set in hollow cheeks. He was gentle and learned in speech but one could feel a great power and strength in his person. He had charm and an easy-going manner, yet when the situation demanded he could be as tough as any of them; I believe that in this combination lay his appeal to the Arabs, and he needed all the appeal and patience a man could muster. The Arabs are not given to discipline like we are, we who accept and know that an order from a superior officer is law and must be obeyed without question. If the Arab does not wish to obey, nor can be persuaded to do so, then, after much argument he will pack up his bags and disappear, or as likely as not take his own course of action. Amidst all the squabbles and tribal jealousies which beset the revolt it was Emir Feisal who held the tribes together, so far as they were ever held, and it was he who called the tune, not by any established principle of monarchy or government such as we understand it in England, but by his own personal qualities.

When the revolt started, after success at Mecca, the Arabs tried to turn the Turks out of Medina, the terminus of the long railway line from Turkey, which crossed the Arab countries and ran right down into the Hedjaz, constituting the lifeline of the Turkish armies which held down their Arab subjects. They attacked this place, but the Turks, under command of Fakri Pasha, a man of bloody reputation, out-gunned and out-manoeuvred them. Here was first proof that Arab ways and equipment did not fit them for attacking regular troops in a defensive position. Ignorant as they were of military tactics and battlefield discipline, equipped as they were with only a few short-range guns to add to their rifle power, they were shelled and shamed into defeat by the Turkish regulars as one tribe after another deserted the battlefield or offered surrender.

47

The Turks then fell upon the suburb of Awali and massacred every living thing within its walls; women were raped and butchered, children hacked to pieces, houses fired and living and dead alike thrown into the flames. The shock of this horrible deed spread throughout the Arab tribes; their rules of war laid down that women should not be harmed, nor children, and that property which could not be carried off should be left undamaged. The Turks had flouted every rule.

Despite this spur the revolt was slow to get under way, perhaps because of the shame of defeat. There was greed for money among the tribes and none would acknowledge leadership from another. Even so, Emir Feisal held together a corps upon which to build.

It was at this stage that Major Lawrence joined the revolt, sent out by the top brass in Cairo as military adviser to the Emir. There will be much argument about this wonderful man in the years to come, and I can only report what I saw with my own eyes and heard with my own ears. He had a way with the Arabs, speaking in their own language and dialects and feeling about things, I thought, much as they did. After only a short time they held him in veneration, so far as they were able to revere anything in human guise; he seemed to them a mystical hero, one who espoused their cause, one who was to lead them to glory and freedom.

As a man, Major Lawrence was a queer mixture, an intellectual, you might say, yet one with his feet on the ground. That he had a vision, I do not doubt, a vision of one Arab land freed from Turkish overlordship, and I believe that he sold this idea to the Arabs, although he always seemed ill-at-ease when discussing this matter with his own kind. He had a far-seeing and clear mind, and from the way in which he worked out the tactics that we should employ against the Turks you would have thought that he had been brought up in the army. However, that was not the case and he always looked upon himself as the amateur he was. As for his body, I have never seen a man so tough and so able to endure. When under stress he seemed to shut his body off from all emotion and feeling so that he rode further than ever did any Arab, with less to eat and to drink, even though subject to many ills – boils, dysentry, fevers – which did not beset the Arabs. He was able to endure hardship and suffering, pain and torture to an extent which few men can ever have known, and this without the least effect on his powers of reason or thought. Whatever anyone may say about his words and deeds among the Arabs, he was first and foremost an Englishman, and one whom I was proud to serve with; the mainspring of his activities was his ardent desire to do all he could to win the war for England. I, myself, would have followed him anywhere, into the grave if need be.

His coming gave immediate strength and purpose to the Arab revolt. He was not fighting a lone battle; he had, as I said, been sent to the Arabs by the top brass in Cairo, but you cannot expect generals and politicians and staff officers sitting back in a great city to assess the needs of an army of irregulars out in the desert. There were some, however, Sir Reginald Wingate and Sir Ronald Storrs to mention but two, who listened to the advice that Major Lawrence offered, so that supplies and material started to flow from British arsenals, escorted by the British navy up the Red Sea coastline.

Major Lawrence was also responsible for moving the Arab base up to Yenbo, to the west of Medina, from where raiders could effectively cut the railway to the north, instead of expending life and energy on futile attacks against the town itself, a policy which those who should have known better still urged upon them. Furthermore, with the base at Yenbo the battle for the Hedjaz was virtually won so that all eyes then turned further north.

The Major's clear and logical mind also came into play as he worked out the strategy and tactics to be employed. He looked at the enormous area over which we had to fight our battles, an area of at least one hundred and forty thousand square miles. We had the means to move anywhere over this immense wasteland, means provided by our hardihood and by the camel; the Turks had no such assets, tied as they were to fortifications. He worked out, mathematically, that provided we were prepared to discard proven ideas of fronts and lines of supply and to attack anywhere at any time, the Turks would need six hundred thousand soldiers to retain control of this territory from within fortified posts.

Major Lawrence realised that the Turks, in this arid wilderness, depended for their army's survival less on men than on material, ranging from food and small arms to engines and armoured trains. He therefore decided that we should attack not Turkish soldiers but their transport and provisions. Furthermore, all these provisions had to travel down the one long and vulnerable railway from Turkey to Medina in the Hedjaz, and along the offshoots into

Palestine. This railway would be the focus of our assaults, but in order that it should serve our purpose, its termini had to be left in being. Medina, far from being taken, should be allowed to remain in Turkish hands for so long as their pride demanded.

In order successfully to play this unorthodox game we had to know when and where the enemy's materials moved or were stored, and where he was posted, and in what strength, so that we could avoid him or attack him only in overwhelming strength. In space of time Major Lawrence saw to it that almost every Arab in the area was a source of information.

Then, finally, he foresaw the value of psychology in war of this nature; he reckoned that if sufficient ill-will towards the Turks could be generated in the minds of the Arab tribesmen, whether in their settlements or wandering as nomads over the desert, then we must win the war. Two per cent in active support were enough for victory, he thought, provided the remainder gave us their sympathy.

I have written down his arguments only briefly, but I have heard the Major talk at length on the subject and, despite my regular training, it did not take me long to see that this was the way that we must fight, with the people we had to fight with, with the light weapons at our disposal and in this great waste of sand. There was one point, though, on which I could never agree with him, and that was his reluctance to shed blood. He was sure that our best means of victory was to destroy enemy material, not enemy soldiers, and it drove me mad when we had chances of wiping out small Turkish posts with little loss, and failed to do so. To my mind you cannot win wars without shedding blood and there is nothing more distressing to an army of occupation than constantly to have its men hacked to death. However, he had a proper bee in his bonnet that an Arab life lost in battle was a life wasted, and this in the main was the buzz we followed except, of course, on those few occasions when the Arabs had their blood up and killed and slaughtered no matter what he said.

Major Lawrence had not long been with the Emir when, at his instigation, the Arab base was moved from Yenbo yet further north to Wejh, and then north again to Akaba. In order to capture this place the Major rode for six hundred miles across the desert, with a tough old warlord, Auda abu Tayi, recruiting from the tribes as they went. They fought and beat the Turks outside

Akaba, then, on the 6th day of July, 1917, galloped through a driving sandstorm into the ruined town; an incredible feat of arms.

While the Major was away Emir Feisal, with a force from Wejh, cut the Turkish railway north of Medina and tried in vain to hold a position across it. The Arabs had not yet learned that they were no better trained nor equipped successfully to hold a defensive position than they were successfully to attack one.

Only one month after Major Lawrence's dramatic capture of Akaba I was myself in the place, teaching the Arabs how to handle the mortar. I could not speak their language, nor they mine, but after only one month they were able to fire with reasonable accuracy. After that I thought that I should go out into the desert with them, and on the 7th of September, 1917, I set out for my first long ride on a camel, my first trek into the great unknown.

We rode north to Guweira, taking it fairly easily, and thank God we were in no hurry because I was retching at every movement of my horrible beast. At Guweira we collected a number of Howeitat tribesmen; these were Auda's men. This was my first experience of raising an army on the way to the objective, but that was how we operated in this campaign, the tribesmen often being warned of our coming only by Emir Feisal's propaganda. I discovered later that we seldom knew how many men we would have to fight with because tribal squabbles and ingrained jealousies could deplete our force even more quickly than we were able to raise it.

It was at Guweira that we suffered minor inconvenience from a Turkish aeroplane which dropped a few small bombs. However, we spread ourselves among the rocks and the bombs did no harm, the Arabs looking on as though watching a show for their amusement.

On the 11th day of September, after two more days of hard riding which numbed my arse and turned my stomach inside out, we came to the fantastic tamarisk-covered valley called Wadi Rumm, nestling beneath towering sandstone crags and cliffs. Here, in this awe-inspiring place, we met more trouble, not from the enemy this time, but from the tribes themselves. I could not understand what it was all about, but it was typical of the quarrels which beset the Arab revolt, one tribe set against another with others taking sides; pride counting before loyalty; selfish interest before a cause which was by no means common; all showing a lack of appreciation of the task ahead, or of the enemy before us or why we were fighting him.

In Rumm there were men of the Dhumaniyeh, Darausha, Zelebani, Zuweida and the Togatga clans, in addition to our own Howeitat. All suspected the old warrior Auda, while the Dhumaniyeh threatened to withdraw their support and even to go over to the Turks.

Major Lawrence, after much argument, had to ride back to Emir Feisal in Akaba to try to sort the muddle out, but despite his efforts we left Rumm with an uneasy band of only one hundred and sixteen men. Throughout the journey to our objective, the Turkish-held railway station at Mudowwara, the Major worked to hold the force together and to obtain agreement to some sort of plan.

Late on the afternoon of the following day we came to a stinking water hole into which the Turks had deliberately thrown dead camels, but nonetheless, we filled our skins and later, at dusk, Major Lawrence and I, with the Arab leaders, crept forward to the last crest overlooking Mudowwara. At first we were content to look down upon it through the gloaming, but so peaceful was the scene that we edged nearer until we could hear the enemy talking.

Then we moved back over the crest to consult in whispers; what we had seen was not in the event reassuring and the Major decided that the garrison was too well protected and too large for us to attack, even with the certainty of surprise to help us.

So we returned to our camels by the filthy water-hole, and there we slept until next morning when we marched south, looking for another place where we might blow up the railway. We were soon in luck, for we found a place where the track crossed a dry wadi by a two-arched bridge, and here we quickly laid the charges, set up the Stokes mortar and the Lewis guns on a ridge above the hollow, and, so we thought, disposed the Arabs in ambush.

However, when all seemed ready we looked up to see that a number of the tribesmen had climbed up on to a high ridge and were sitting in full view of the Turks both in Mudowwara and in another post further south. Make no mistake but these Arabs were first-class at using ground, yet, in the face of the enemy they were so cocksure of their fighting prowess as to be both stupid and careless. I reckon we were saved from discovery only by the darkness and by Turkish disbelief that there could be an enemy force within their domain. A small patrol came to look for us the following morning, but we sent out a party to draw them away from our ambush.

The burning heat of noon brought with it plenty of excitement as a hundred Turks set forth from Mudowwara heading straight towards us, though slowly, as if they had been roused from a mid-day sleep. We began silently to pack up, preparatory to moving off for, mobile as we were, we could escape them at will, but at that moment the watchman cried out that a train was approaching.

We yelled at everyone to take up position, and there was a wild scramble over the rocks and sand in which I was left well behind, but made my position in the nick of time.

Then the train came into sight, two engines and ten carriages, crowded with soldiers, all with their rifles poking out of the windows and firing wildly into the desert. When the rear engine was on the bridge the Major gave the signal and a terrific explosion shook the air; chunks of steel and lumps of iron and plate shot up into the sky, and a cloud of black smoke billowed up to shroud the scene. There was one brief moment of silence, then the Bedouin went mad, rushing forward pell-mell to close with the enemy. Shots rang out in all directions; battle-cries, oaths and screams rent the air; pandemonium took over where before had been the silence of waiting men. I could see little until the smoke cleared to reveal a number of Turks behind a bank, shooting into the Bedouin only twenty yards away.

I brought the mortar into action and the Turks, in terror, fled into the desert; then the Lewis gunners took over, shooting them down one by one, strewing the sand with writhing bodies.

Meanwhile, Bedouin were rushing about here and there, killing anything that showed signs of life, dragging loot out of the train and loading it on to camels, casting aside what they did not want. There was no discipline, none whatever, and they even fought each other for bales of material, for boxes of food, for anything which they thought was rightly theirs.

Only the Major kept a cool head, and a few men around him. They blew up the remaining engine, but even the blast of these new explosions failed to disperse the looters.

All around was the noise of shouting and shooting, whooping and shrieking. Women from the train begged for mercy, wounded soldiers for succour, but none heeded them: rather the wounded and those who sought capture were stripped almost to a man. I swear that even myself, and the Major too, would have been set upon had we had anything of value on our persons.

Then suddenly, with no signal given, and while the Turks from Mudowwara plodded cautiously towards the scene, we rode fast away, first to the old well to refill our skins, and then for ten miles out into the desert beyond reach of vengeance. Our going was faster than the Turkish pursuit, even though each camel was weighed down with loot and even though we had to mount ninety prisoners who had survived the wrath of the Bedouin. Safe in the desert we slept until morning, then were away again to the Wadi Rumm. Two days later, on the 20th September, we entered Akaba in glory, claiming that the Turkish life-line to Medina was at our mercy.

For myself, I was glad that I had learned to endure, as the Arabs endured, while riding for fifty miles a day on camel back.

This attack near Mudowwara set the pattern for hundreds more which we made against that long stretch of railway between Damascus and Medina. And yet I often thought how much more successful they might have been had the Arabs put an end to their tribal feuding, and had their discipline on the march and in action, and also after action been better; but they were what they were and with them and for them we had to do our best.

I should say, here and now, that despite our weaknesses, by making use of our extreme mobility and hardihood, our sorties in the four months between October, 1917, and January, 1918, from Akaba alone destroyed seventeen locomotives, made travel a nightmare for the enemy, caused engine drivers to strike, stopped all civilian traffic and forced the enemy to bring troops from Palestine to protect their precious railway. While we left the Turks in their pride in Medina, we could force them to draw off yet more men to guard their lifeline.

While they were unable to assess the strength of our fleeting raids we knew exactly the strength of their static posts, so they could gain no marked success against us. We needed only a secure base from which to operate, and this we had in Akaba, secured on three sides by our mastery of the desert, and on the fourth, the sea-ward side, by the British navy. In addition we had other bases, at Wejh and on the Wadi Musa, and elsewhere in the desert from which we threatened the Turkish positions throughout the area.

At this time General Allenby was in command of the British forces in Palestine. In the few months since his arrival in the Middle East he had already made felt, even to the Arab movement, the force of his personality and determination. From all reports he had also put new heart into his army, had obtained the reinforcements and equipment they needed, and all in all had the lads eating out of his hand. In his plan for an early attack against the Turks on the Gaza-Beersheba line, General Allenby intended that the Arab force should attack the Turks on the inland flank, on the right of the British army.

I had been with this mob long enough to know that it is wrong tactics to launch a crowd of amateurish irregulars against a regular army in prepared defensive positions, thus pitting the irregulars' weaknesses in fire-power and in lack of battlefield discipline against the enemy's strength in these very departments. Major Lawrence felt the same, I know, and he was further bedevilled, as always, by never knowing how strong his force would be at any one time, or for how long this tribe or that would stay with him.

There was much discussion between the Major and the General's staff until it was finally decided that we should first act as an intelligence service for the regular army and, secondly, that we should destroy the railway in the Yarmuk Valley, a key point on the route between the Turkish supply bases and their front-line troops in Palestine. These roles seemed good ones to me, although I do not suppose that I would have thought so at the time had I known what they were letting us in for.

We had already established an excellent intelligence service, with eyes and ears all over the desert, among the nomad tribes, among the settled tribes and in every mud-and-stone-built town and hamlet; we knew what the Turks were going to do almost before they knew it themselves. We gave this organisation fresh tasks and passed the news across to the British army.

The plan to smash the railway into the Yarmuk Valley presented different problems. We thought that we could cut the line almost anywhere we chose, and it was tempting, for instance, to look at Deraa, a communications centre well north of the main fighting front. Here were tribes who would rise with us to the attack; the Rualla – if not away in their winter quarters – the Serahin, and with them the peoples of Hauran and the Jebel Druse; but if we took Deraa we could not hold it, since we were neither constituted nor equipped to hold ground. Damascus, further north, was another tempting target, but to go there would involve us in the same risks and drawbacks as at Deraa. So we decided to operate against the Yarmuk Valley bridges, an operation which was to test our powers of endurance to the uttermost and was to end in bitter failure.

We collected a small force in Akaba; a loyal bodyguard for Major Lawrence, a handful of regular Indian machine-gunners who had for months been riding in the desert, rail-cutting from Wejh, and the leaders who were to raise the tribes on the way. Two of these I remember clearly: Ali Ibn Hussein, a man of enormous strength and agility who could outstrip a trotting camel on his bare feet for half a mile, then leap into the saddle, a brave and reckless man in battle; and the Emir, Abd El Kader El Jezairi (whose grandfather, I was told, had spent some years fighting against the French in Algiers), a man whom I did not trust one inch further than I could see him.

On the 24th of October, 1917, we set out with this small party on a ride which was to take us for four hundred miles through the torrid heat of the desert, to the high cliffs of Rumm, to Batra, North-East into Bair, through the distant waste-lands, and then on again to Azrak, our base for the attack on the Yarmuk.

This terrible journey lasted for eleven days of jolting and swaying through the suffocating, dust-laden air; eleven days of moving from horizon to horizon with a vast area of nothingness all around, and with no thought but of the last mile put behind us; eleven days of thirst and hunger, of all kinds of physical torture. We were filled with relief, as at the lifting of fearful pain, when suddenly we came upon Azrak, a small township built upon green meadows among clear springs of life-giving water. We viewed it first from a stony knoll, then dashed down and threw ourselves upon the grass.

But we were to enjoy this beautiful place for no more than one brief night. The raising of the tribes had not progressed as well as we would have wished, so that we were weak in numbers. But worse, Abd El Kader had left us, perhaps to take to the enemy news of our attempt and details of our plan.

So we broke camp next morning, moving at first along a rock-strewn valley on to a high ridge, and then for miles over perfect camel country to Abu Sawana, our last water point. Here we missed by a few minutes a patrol of Circassian horsemen, a reminder that we were nearing territory held by the Turks.

We rode on again through the next long day, to wait until dusk at the edge of the flat plain across which the railway ran. We crossed it in darkness, then disappeared into the foothills below Deraa where we sorted our men and kit. For the final approach to the target we had to reduce the Indian machine-gunners to only one gun and crew, for the remainder, bad riders as they proved to be, had broken up both themselves and their camels on this punishing journey. We took fighting men of the Beni Sakhr for our storming party and the Serahin as porters and as escorts to the baggage camels.

We left the shelter of the hills only one hundred men strong, planning to ride eighty miles in the thirteen hours of darkness, with a difficult demolition thrown in. As we left I could feel apprehension throughout the column, a state of unease induced by Abd El Kader's defection. Almost at once further incidents disturbed the Arabs, already overwrought: a startled shepherd firing his rifle and screaming in terror as he fled; a barking dog; a stray camel rising unexpectedly in our path. But we soon looked down upon the lights of Deraa and of the villages scattered in the plain below, and pressing on relentlessly, came out of the hills on to land half-ploughed so that the camels sank in to their fetlocks, making every step a slow agony.

Before midnight rain came, a steady drizzle, and at once the surface of the land grew slippery; camels fell and rose; men hissed and slashed and cursed in an effort to maintain the pace; the Indians dragged behind. Major Lawrence seemed to be everywhere, urging, hustling, belabouring men and beasts alike.

After a space of time which seemed endless, we came to our journey's end, the black edge of the Yarmuk gorge, with the bridge, our target, lying right beneath us. We crept around on the dark slopes to take up positions, my own with the Beni Sakhr, while the porters and the demolition party crawled down to the bridge on which we could dimly see the guard tent and the sentry, both revealed by a single, flickering light.

I lay in the darkness musing over the rigours of the long ride, marvelling at the exertions which had brought us successfully to our objective and at the determination of our great leader. All would be worthwhile when we saw that long span of bridge-way crash down into the valley below. Then all at once a rifle clattered down the rocky slope. The sentry, alerted, shouted out, then fired; instantly, all was confusion.

The Beni Sakhr fired repeatedly into the darkness, but hit nothing; the Indians, whose task it was to riddle the guard tent before the guard deployed, failed to bring their machine-gun into action; the Serahin porters, carrying the explosives, dropped their loads and fled. No orders were issued, none could be, yet we knew that the enterprise had failed, that we must flee at once for the safety of the desert.

I scrambled over rock and shale to the rendezvous where we had left the camels, to find the Serahin already mounting. In a few moments we were away, trotting off at speed, with rifle-fire still cracking behind us, deep down in the valley.

No sooner were we free from danger than the Serahin set upon a party of peasants returning from Deraa. The ear-splitting shrieks of the engagement alarmed all the settlements, so that we were again urged on by shots and shouts from all around. We rode miserably through the night, accompanied only by the haunting sense of failure, reminded of our futility by the sound of General Allenby's guns reverberating away to our right.

Throughout the following day we plodded in the drizzling rain towards Abu Sawana, where we arrived at sunset, exhausted after a ride of one hundred miles over bad country in the short space of only twenty-four hours.

We had brought with us from Azrak only three days' food so that we were now without any, but even so, Major Lawrence led sixty Arabs away to blow up a train further down the line; the rest rode straight for Azrak. The Major returned three days later, having destroyed his train, but it was small compensation for the failure of the Yarmuk operation. Furthermore, we had to set against it the overwhelming success of General Allenby's army, which had broken the Gaza-Beersheba line, a victory which was to lead to the capture of Jerusalem itself on the 11th of December, 1917.

We were now asked to drive the Turks out of all the country to the east of the Dead Sea, right up to its northern shore, in order to conform with the British advance. As a preliminary move the tribal leader Maulud, who had a few weeks previously repelled an attack on his base on the Wadi Musa, drove the Turks back into Ma'an from their forward dominating positions at Aba El Lissan, thus opening the way to Tafileh.

We took Tafileh on the 16th of January, 1918, and then, when they counter-attacked, gave the Turks a bloody mauling on the Wadi Hesa. In this engagement Major Lawrence displayed an amazing grasp of military tactics, outwitting the Turks at every stage.

To underline our success at Tafileh we sent news of the victory to Abdullah El Feir which sent him raiding to the south coast of the Dead Sea, with seventy horsemen of the Beersheba Bedouin. There they destroyed the best part of a Turkish fleet of motor launches and supply lighters, returning with sixty prisoners and without loss to themselves.

There followed a wretched winter in Tafileh, a poor village of stone huts on a plateau five thousand feet up; a plateau swept by bitter winds and driving snow. We huddled in the huts, ill-equipped and ill-clothed for such a climate, our minds and bodies dead to all but the cold. During these months the inevitable inter-tribal disputes arose and the force slowly melted away so that we were unable to complete our main task, the advance to the north coast of the Dead Sea.

The winter ended, we withdrew to the base at Akaba, leaving an outpost in Aba El Lissan, to while away the hot summer planning for an autumn offensive.

The plan of campaign for the autumn of 1918 was designed to break the Turkish hold on the Arab countries. General Allenby aimed to break through the Turkish lines, now reaching from Jericho to the coast, and then to pursue the enemy right up to the gates of Damascus. The role given to the Arab movement was to ride through the desert to Deraa, and there cut communications leading down into Palestine.

This plan called for precise timing, and for the use of deception. We had to deceive the Turks as to our strength, but at the same time maintain the threat to their railway, in order to prevent them releasing guard battalions for the main front. While keeping their attention on the railway we had still further to deceive them as to where we proposed finally to destroy it.

General Allenby insisted on exact timing for our operations at Deraa; as he put it to Major Lawrence – three men and a boy with pistols in front of Deraa on September 16th would fulfil his conception, and would be better than thousands a week before or a week after. Planning so precise a manoeuvre presented difficulties, since the plan involved a fortnight's approach march from Aba El Lissan to Deraa in a great sweep to the east through the barren desert, taking with us every item of supply.

The plan which Major Lawrence finally decided upon looked simple enough to the untutored eye. A detachment of the regular camel corps, which had been loaned to us from Egypt under an officer whose name, I remember, was Buxton, would ride to the railway bridge near Kissir during August and persuade the Turks that we were reconnoitring for an attack on Amman. At the beginning of September a force of five hundred mounted infantry, supported by mountain guns, machine guns, engineers and by two armoured cars, and including camel scouts and two reconnaissance aeroplanes, would take the long route to Deraa, accompanied by two thousand baggage camels. They would reach Azrak on September the 13th; on the 16th they would envelop Deraa and cut its railways; two days later they would fall back into the desert and await the results of General Allenby's attack.

It seemed impossible that this column could be fed, watered and supplied over the immense distances involved, but Major Lawrence knew his camels and his men, and he understood the desert. He reduced camel fodder to a minimum; they could feed off the pastures around Azrak which this year were particularly good. He took no food for the men's return journey; they could live off the country or by eating the camels (I discovered later that, in any case, he did not plan to return), and he reduced petrol, ammunition and all else to only the barest minimum necessary to meet the plan. The only reserve against the unforeseen was the purchase of barley in Jebel Druse for storage at Azrak.

As planned, on the last day in August we rode out from Aba El Lissan on the last long journey of the campaign. There was a difference between this and the many other rides I had undertaken during my time with the Arabs, a difference in the size of the force. As we headed out towards the distant horizon the whole desert was filled with plodding camels; on all sides one saw these patient creatures holding to their given courses, the whole great cavalcade covering the ground as far as the eye could see, there to be absorbed by the mirage. Movement appeared unhurried; time passed us slowly by; yet we were marching forty miles each day.

At night we would dismount from our weary beasts and sleep

where we lay until it was time to move on again into the burning dawn.

On the 12th of September we reached Azrak, and there the army assembled under the leadership of Emir Feisal and Nuri Said. In the afternoon other Arab leaders joined, Nuri Shaalan, the tough warrior Auda Abu Tayi, Fahad and Adhub the Zebn leaders, with chiefs from the Serahin and Serdiyeh. Later still, with a rattle of rifle-fire, came yet another, Talal El Hareidhin with forty mounted peasants behind him. Druses, Syrians, Isawiyeh and Hawarneh added to the force. The barley from the Jebel Druse began to arrive in steady convoys. Everything was going according to plan.

While we assembled, we heard that the camel corps' attack on Kissir had been a complete success.

At dawn on the 14th the column marched again, three thousand three hundred strong, including three hundred of Nuri Shaalan's nomad horse. We camped that night below the high ridge which concealed Umtaiye from the railway. There was an air of happy purpose among the Arabs, and those allied to them, as we lit our fires, made our bread, drank our coffee and watered our noisy beasts.

At dawn we moved off in the early sunshine, across rough flinty ground, circling Deraa to the east, heading for the guard redoubt on the railway near Tell Arar, four miles north of the town, meanwhile casting off the armoured cars to raid the line to the south.

As we reached the slope overlooking the railway the Rualla horsemen dashed headlong for the line, but on reaching it, stood there, wondering what to do. The Turks fired from the redoubt until we moved up Pisani's guns to silence them. Then the Rualla charged in and captured the place.

Upon this the Arabs rushed down from the ridge in an avalanche of men and beasts, spreading on to and over the railway. They crowded on to the mound of Tell Arar, from where they could see Deraa to the south, Mezerib to the west and Ghazale to the north. The plan had worked almost beyond our wildest dreams and here, within our grasp, lay the only railway down into Palestine. We set about its methodical demolition, hindered only by Turkish aircraft which dropped their bombs with uncertain aim. We then moved across at leisure to Mezerib, and captured and destroyed the station there.

The happenings at Mezerib, and after, illustrate the devastating effect of a force such as ours appearing at a place where the enemy least expected. We fired the railway station; we looked at the bridge beyond and decided that it would cost too many lives to capture and destroy, so we left it. We blew up the water tower at Mezerib; then marched down to Nisib, south of Deraa, thus completely encircling the town; from guns and machine-guns we poured shot and shell into the station there. While engaging Nisib we seized the great bridge north of the village and blew it up. Major Lawrence himself laid the charges against the redoubts, his seventy-ninth bridge, he reckoned. Then we made off, back towards our base at Umtaiye. From there we kept the railways out of action for as long as was necessary.

Meanwhile, General Allenby's armies, nearly one hundred miles to the south-west, had gained a crushing victory over the Turkish main forces. Attacking on the 19th of September, they had burst through the main positions between Jericho and the coast. Rushing north they swallowed up Nablus, Beisan, Afuleh and Haifa and were now pursuing the remnants of the Turkish army, remnants which were never again to be gathered into a co-ordinated fighting force. On the east side of the Jordan the residue of the Turkish Fourth Army were staggering north from Amman; as they came the Beni Hassan harassed them day and night, cutting off stragglers and weak detachments. Such was the panic which we instilled into these ragged, thirsty, ill-armed and ill-equipped soldiers that they threw away what little they held in their hands or knapsacks and fled for the supposed safety of Deraa.

News of victory brought thousands more Arabs flocking to the colours until, before the end of the month, we were at least sixty thousand strong. The infamous crimes committed at Tafas, where fleeing Turkish soldiers and police had flung babies to the ground, smashing in their heads, had thrust lances through the bodies of young children and had crucified to the low mud walls the women of the village, each with a bayonet nailed between her naked thighs, drove the Arabs beserk and intent only on wreaking a terrible vengeance.

I have never seen such slaughter, such shedding of blood, such wanton cruelty as ranged over the desert around Deraa on the afternoon of the 27th of September, 1918. The fleeing Turks were cut down on all sides and either shot or hacked to pieces where they lay; only the few German detachments with them fought as soldiers should, but even they fought in vain. A lake of blood soaked into the shifting sands while no single Turk was safe from the death-lust of the Arabs. No orders from their leaders, however sternly given, stopped them until they had stripped and plundered and killed every Turk in sight. Crimes of cruelty and improper behaviour, as at Tafas, are nowhere more severely punished than in the homeland of the victims.

Tirad rode into Deraa, and after him his brother Khalid with hundreds of Rualla horsemen, to continue the slaughter. Nasir followed, to set up a military governorship. Twelve hours later General Allenby's forces arrived in the town and there went Major Lawrence to explain to the Commanding-General, Barrow, what the Arabs had achieved and how they should best be met.

During the long rides through Azrak to the railways at Deraa one saw these Arab irregulars at their best, mobility their greatest asset, the desert their refuge, as they cut and thrust at the Turks' material support, their activities concerted with those of a regular army many miles away. In pursuit they were devastating. Despite the utter lack of discipline and the poor direction of their efforts, the presence of their flashing swords and barking pistols, of the rifles and explosives in their hands, behind and among the enemy lines, ensured that the Turks would never again stand and fight.

But even in the moment of victory the old weaknesses started to reappear, leader turning against leader, tribe against tribe, as they fought over the pickings of a defeated army, as they strove to outshine each other in the light of glory. As the discipline previously imposed by responsibility and hardship, loose as it was, deserted them, old jealousies were at once renewed.

It was well that before dissensions broke loose the Turkish army had been destroyed. It now remained for us only to prepare the approaches to Damascus, and indeed Damascus itself, for the coming of General Allenby's armies; and this we did, so that the land through which they passed, and the old and famous town into which they entered on the 1st of October, 1918, received them as friends.

Chapter 5

Introduction to Communist Guerilla Warfare, leading up to Russia, World War II

The preceding short account of the Arab revolt is sufficient to demonstrate that T. E. Lawrence provided the motive power behind the military techniques adopted by the Arab guerillas in support of General Allenby's armies in Palestine and Arabia. He it was who discarded the formal attacks on Turkish defensive positions, such as at Medina, who deliberately applied irregular warfare as a form to the country in which he fought, to the people with whom he fought and to the circumstances in which his enemies were placed. He it was who saw that the true object of the guerilla is not necessarily to fight; 'In the Turkish army,' he wrote, 'materials were scarce and precious, men more plentiful than equipment. . . . The aim should be to destroy not the army but the materials.'[1]

That his ideas were embraced by other military commanders in the area is proven by the fact that the movement he inspired was looked upon, at each stage, as an integral part of the strategical plan for defeating the Turkish army, a strategy which led to ultimate victory.

After World War I, Lawrence published his views on guerilla warfare, reducing them to final form and almost converting the tactics of the guerilla into a science. His work was appreciated not only in his own country, but also in Russia and China, where the spread of Communism saw his methods copied and expanded upon in two major theatres of war.

Lawrence's views were, however, confined to a military system;

[1] T. E. Lawrence – *Seven Pillars of Wisdom*.

to this the Russians and Chinese grafted economic and political concepts which fundamentally altered the nature of guerilla warfare.

Following the precepts set down by Karl Marx, Lenin, in an article entitled 'Partisanskya Voina' and published in his newspaper *Proletaria* in October, 1906, points the way to the form which Communist guerilla warfare is to take, although the article itself covers no more than the initial stages of revolution. His use of the word 'partisan' stands for terrorism, hold-ups and robberies rather than for the full scope of revolutionary warfare.

In the event, the Bolsheviks seized political power in Russia, in 1917–18, without the need for extensive military activity, either regular or irregular, so that it was not until shortly after Lawrence's experience that Lenin's writings further developed the theme and fully adapted guerilla warfare to the business of revolution.

From a mass of verbiage and tortuous phrases it is possible to extract the basic principles laid down by Lenin:

1 Intelligence of enemy movements, while keeping your own plans hidden, is the prime tactical secret.
2 Avoid the enemy's strength. (It is worth noting that within this formula Lenin adopted one half of the motto of the Jeune Ecole, the initiators of the *guerre de course* – 'Shamelessly attack the weak; shamelessly fly from the strong.')
3 By employing rigidly controlled units, the Communist leaders can out-manoeuvre larger, less mobile forces.
4 By concentrating on vital objectives the revolutionist weakens the enemy while encouraging his own people.
5 By physically attacking the enemy one slowly weakens him by creating disunion, distrust and loss of morale within both his military forces and civilian administration.
6 Among civilians the emphasis is on talk and discussion rather than on physical action.
7 Deliberate use of terror is a means of breaking down resistance while keeping your own people under control.
8 A flexible attitude must be maintained. The weapon chosen, e.g., the strike, insurrection, robbery or military action, must suit the circumstances.

In the light of such guidance given by one of their most eminent leaders, it is on the surface surprising that this Communist concept of irregular warfare had not been fully developed by the opening of World War II; that it had not was due to two main factors. The Bolsheviks, once in power, had to maintain their position in face of opposition from irregular organisations, particularly in the Ukraine where the peasants took up arms, chose a local *ataman* and established a power of their own, paying no heed to the central government. Furthermore the central government was more anxious to establish a regular army than to develop irregular forces; existing irregulars received temporary recognition so long as they accepted the authority of the central government.

Lenin was not the only Communist leader to write on guerilla warfare. In 1937 Mao Tse-tung wrote a dissertation on the subject, after fourteen years of experience as a leader of a Communist revolutionary and guerilla movement. His writing blends the Communist party line with his own field experiences, taking note of the lessons of history. The main points which he makes in his work, a modern classic, are these:

1 Guerilla operations are a necessary part in a war of revolutionary character. . . . They must not be considered as an independent form but as one step in the total war, one aspect of the revolutionary struggle.
2 Without a political goal guerilla warfare must fail, as it must if its political objectives do not coincide with the aspirations of the people.
3 Because guerilla warfare basically drives from the masses, it is supported by them and can neither exist nor flourish if it separates itself from their sympathies and co-operation.
4 All guerilla units must have political and military leadership.
5 Guerilla strategy must primarily be based on alertness, mobility and attack.
6 During the progress of hostilities, guerillas gradually develop into orthodox forces that operate in conjunction with units of a regular army.
7 An opinion that admits the existence of guerilla war but isolates it is one that does not properly estimate the potentialities of such a form of making war.

Mao Tse-tung held a different attitude towards his guerillas from that held by the Russian leaders. His coming to power depended upon their broad shoulders and strong legs, upon their stamina, hardihood and loyalty. Secure in the knowledge of their support, having devised a strategical plan to fit the Chinese topography and his solders' fighting capabilities, he introduced a new concept, one only partially developed by previous strategists. Guerilla forces would eventually grow into a regular army and it was only when this regular army had defeated the armed forces of his opponents that victory would be won.

The Russians, on the other hand, although recognising that guerilla tactics were necessary to a revolutionary struggle, looked upon the guerilla himself as too individualistic to take his place in a Communist state. None the less, certain cautious steps were taken to prepare the country for the catastrophe of World War II.

'The Russian Partisan Directive of 1933' laid down the general plan for partisan warfare in the event of an invasion of Russia. It is clear that the Soviet leaders were as much concerned with the political reliability of the partisan as with his military capability; a nucleus of potential guerilla leaders was trained accordingly. Some of these men, together with officers of many other nations, received a baptism of fire and acquired practical experience of guerilla warfare during the Spanish Civil War between 1936 and 1939. To the detriment of the Spanish people, the International Brigade provided a splendid training organisation for the guerillas of World War II.

During the years 1940 to 1945, the German jackboot inspired a large number of guerilla movements as the undaunted peoples of Europe rose up against their cruel oppressors. In Norway, Holland, Belgium and France, in Denmark and Italy, in Poland, in the Balkans, in Greece and in Russia, despite an almost complete lack of preparation, armed men came to infest the towns, to haunt the countryside or to take to the hills in occupied countries, the strength and scope of each movement reflecting the moral strength of the nation which gave rise to it and the skill and determination of the leadership available. All cried for help from outside and all were provided for, the Russians by their own people, the remainder at first by the British, later by British and Americans together.

But not one of these guerilla movements was able of its own volition or physical effort to throw off the yoke of German occupation, although all made a significant contribution to final victory.

It was not until the allied armies crossed the Continent from east and west, to defeat the German armed forces in the field, that the countries of Europe were freed.

Japanese conquest and Communist ambitions in Asia also gave rise to a number of guerilla movements. In China, from 1937 onwards, Mao Tse-tung turned a proportion of his guerilla strength against the Japanese, while the latter's forces were engaged by the regular Chinese armies of the Kuomintang, under General Chiang Kai-shek. In the Philippines the Hukbalahap, supported by the Americans until political differences separated them, made feeble gestures against Japan's occupying forces. In Malaya, a 'Liberation Army', supported throughout by the British, made sufficient show against the Japanese to retain its identity. In northern Indo-China, in the latter stages of the war, the irregular forces of Ho Chi Minh first appeared.

All these movements in Asia were Communist-inspired; all had only one aim in mind throughout the Japanese occupation, namely, to take over the governments of their countries once the Japanese had been defeated by American and British forces. Waving the banner of patriotism they busily recruited for the Communist parties, while deploying a minimum effort against the invaders.

In Burma the British Fourteenth Army instigated its own brand of guerilla warfare far behind the Japanese lines, under the leadership of the controversial figure of Orde Wingate; on their left flank the American Merrill's Marauders dug deep into the Japanese rear areas.

It is beyond the scope of this one volume to discuss in detail all the guerilla actions of World War II. In Europe those movements which were not Communist-inspired followed much the same course as had the Arab revolt, differences in method arising from varying political and topographical environments, racial characteristics and from the more modern means of communication available to the World War II contestants. These movements were solely concerned with ridding their countries of the foreign invader.

However, there were three Communist-inspired guerilla movements in Europe which merit detailed discussion; they were mounted in Greece, Yugoslavia – and in Russia.

In June, 1941, the Germans invaded Russia with three million of the best-trained and best-equipped troops of that time. Aiming at a blitzkrieg victory so vital to the success or failure of the enterprise, the Germans launched ferocious assaults on a front of two thousand miles. Within a few days the Russian Marshal Timoshenko's army groups lost 640,000 men. German panzers operating on the left flank under Colonel Erich Höppner penetrated as far as Kalinin in the face of light opposition. On the right flank, Colonel-General Heinz Guderian's forces struck through Orel to Tula. In the centre Colonel General Günther von Kluge's armies advanced to within fifteen miles of Moscow. But on the 18th of October these massive forces were held by determined Russian opposition, and by rain and mud which brought mobile operations to a standstill.

Russian units overrun by German formations took to the forests and swamps, some retaining unit identity but most breaking up into small groups; from these refuges they continued to resist. The Russian High Command were not slow to exploit this situation by sending political and military leaders through the thin screen of the German lines to join these desperate units. Thus began a partisan movement which was to build up into a terrifying and effective weapon of war and one which, in co-operation with the Red Army, brought about the eventual defeat of the Germans and drove the invaders from Russian soil.

The story of the partisan movement in Russia is told by a soldier of the Red Army turned guerilla.

Narrative 4

Russia — 1941 to 1944

'Oppress not the cubs of the stranger,
But hail them as sister and brother,
For though they are little and fusky, it
May be the Bear is their mother'.

MAXIMS OF BALVO

This small plot of Russian earth, that strip of sky, the trees around
me, they were still mine; I might as well delight in them before
leaving them forever.

What a thirst, what a hunger I had! The Germans were everywhere. I threw myself on all-fours and began to crawl from tree
to tree, from thicket to thicket. To my surprise I came upon six
men from my own unit, crouched round a spring in the bushes.
I drank, but we had no food. The Fritzes searched and searched;
I decided if they found me that my life would cost them dear. I
cradled my tommy-gun in my right arm.

How many days, how many nights were we in the thicket? An
old peasant woman came upon us while gathering fire-wood, a
simple soul. She put us in contact with the collective farm nearby.
They told us that other Red Army men were in the woods – six
husky lads under Corporal Tyukhov.

September 10th, 1941; a new beginning to life. I went scouting;
suddenly a yell: 'Halt! Hands up!'

'What's the joke?' I answered, 'Friend'.

'Your papers,' said my new acquaintance, a revolver in his hand
pointing at my heart. He stepped forward; tunic neat and tidy, face
clean, hair washed and combed. His army card was inscribed
'Junior Political Instructor Peter Derevyanko'. A Red Army
leader; it was good to find someone to obey.

I told my story.

'You – – !' he spat out a foul, insulting word. 'Here you sit like

70

old women, gossiping for a month in the bushes, doing nothing, nothing. Here, see this'.

He pulled a tattered piece of paper from his tunic pocket. I read to the others who had by now collected: 'In the area occupied by the enemy, partisan units on foot and horseback must be established. Moreover, bands of saboteurs must be organised to fight hostile detachments . . . to blow up bridges and roads, to interrupt telephone and telegraph communications and to set camps and depots afire. In the occupied areas insufferable conditions must be created for the enemy; you must follow him everywhere and annihilate his forces.'

'By order of Josif Vissarionovich Stalin, the Great Leader of all mankind. Dated July the 3rd,' said our new leader.

We were ashamed to look each other in the face. How could we ever redeem ourselves in the eyes of the people? One month of idleness!

Peter Derevyanko had been despatched through the German front lines to contact the partisans. He had been captured, but after two weeks of hideous torture, he made his escape; later we saw the marks of torture on his body. He had at last found the nucleus for a partisan force and he stayed to guide us.

We established a base in the forest, digging dugouts in the soft ground, covering them over with trunks of the great fir trees and spreading branches and brushwood. We made camouflage so that from only one metre away a man could not say that partisans were hidden there. Down in the dugouts we made seats and tables of rough wood. Tyukhov went to the farm and stole a lamp which we placed in Derevyanko's hideout.

Every day our numbers grew as the news of our presence spread over the Russian countryside. Young boys and girls, women, old men, all aflame with a burning passion to drive the fascist invaders from the soil of the Motherland, came into the forest. Peter carefully checked everyone, testing and probing, in case a traitor might find his way into our midst. Those whom he turned away as too young, or too old, or unfit for the challenging dangers and hard life of the partisan, were told to collect information. We were to be told of all enemy movements, of the whereabouts of enemy stores of arms and ammunition, of every thought and action of the brutes who had brought destruction and devastation to our country. All agreed to give the help we asked of them.

The speed at which our small force grew was not quick enough for Peter. He called me. 'Pavel Dmitrievich, you know the district, you know the people'. Before joining the Red Army to fight for the cause I had been a member of the district committee of the Young Communists. 'Go out into the villages; bring in those whom we want – the young, the brave – yes, and the middle-aged – we need some level heads.'

I set off at once. The forest was beautiful in its autumn sheen; the firs dripped music on to the soft ground. I was going back to my village for the first time for more than one year.

The shock hit me like the blast of a winter storm, freezing my belly with a cold anger. Where were the slaughter-house, the school, the hospital? Why were the fields as black as night? Where were the horses, the cattle? The well – why did it stink of human refuse? Had they left my father's house standing? I rushed into my village like a madman. Yes, the house stood there. I battered on the door. My mother opened it. I fell in, weeping. My father lay on the stove, barely able to open his eyes.

'The Hitlerites came', he said. 'The filthy swine asked for you – we told them we did not know. They destroyed, they took everything.'

'But the well, father, the well!'

'They threw the corpses down there – men, women, children.'

'There are so many to mourn', added my mother.

'Make a bed for me near the stove, mother; in the morning we will call a meeting.'

The people crowded into my father's room. 'Who would avenge the desecration and inhumanity of the fascist killers and murderers?' I asked. All stepped forward in unanimous hatred; not one held back. I told them of our partisan group, of the dangers which attended our road, of the hardships we must suffer, of our thoughts and intentions, concealing only our whereabouts. None stepped back.

I chose three old friends, Nickolai, Koska and Alexandra Fyodorovna – Comrade Derevyanko had told me to find nurses. Before leaving I handed round copies of the leaflets which the comrades had given to me, all written in laborious hand by the partisans in the forest: 'Comrades, remember you are masters of your land; do not let the Germans trample your souls. Remember that the grain is your grain; the cattle your cattle; you are free people. Smite the invaders.'

I despatched my old friends into the forest. I travelled two hundred kilometres from village to village. In each one it was the same story – rapine, pillage, murder, robbery, the people crying out for vengeance, ready to take any steps, however dangerous, to drive out the marauding Hitlerites.

My return to the base was greeted by the partisans with rapturous joy. Next to Peter they looked to me for leadership, a trust I ill-deserved, but given perhaps because of my Red Army service.

The comrades had not been idle. Every day they had cut the telephone line from M . . . to D . . . , an important line for the invaders; one day they would cut it at thirty kilometres distant, the next at ten kilometres, each day in a different place. One party had ambushed three trucks on a nearby road, leaving eight enemy bodies on the ground with their lives oozing out. Another raided a secret arms dump in the village of B . . . . They surprised the sentries, cutting their throats, and burst into the store. They brought back twenty rifles, five tommy-guns and a load of ammunition. An old peasant had told them where to find the dump.

Peter sent for me and approved my efforts; I was proud of his confidence in me. He then said 'We must have a newspaper.'

I was aghast; a newspaper behind the lines?

'Yes, we must tell the people what the heroic partisans are doing for the Motherland.'

I asked: 'What shall we write on, the bark of the trees?'

To date we had written a few scribbled leaflets with much labour. If we were to have a newspaper we must do it in style. I sent a party to the nearest town, one hundred kilometres distant. 'Bring back a typewriter,' I told them.

They returned eight days later – bringing Katya. They found her behind a desk in the local government office. She brought her typewriter with her. A week later we brought out the first edition; we called it *The Herald of the Partisans*. Alexandra Fyodorovna was sent out to distribute copies.

Nickolai stopped eating, became nervous, always picking at his teeth. He was waiting for Alexandra who had been absent for one week. Three days later Nickolai brought her in, lying across his shoulders. Somehow he had found her wandering in the forest.

He laid her gently on the wooden bench, unbuttoned her jacket, loosened her blouse. 'Look what the brutes have done to her.'

Her body was bruised from neck to waist; a five-pointed star

73

was burnt into her right breast; blood still oozed from sores on her cheeks.

Alexandra had almost finished her task. She was approaching a large village when a shout came through the dusk: – 'Halt! Halt!' She stopped.

'Ah! A partisan,' shouted the sentry. 'What's this? The Herald of the Partisans?'

The traitor dragged her into a large hut where there seemed to be hundreds of the brutish invaders.

'Where are the partisans?' shouted one; she spat in his face. Again and again they shouted 'Where are the partisans?' She would not answer.

'Aha!' cried another, 'We know how to deal with obstinate *untermenschen,* especially beautiful ones!'

They stripped Alexandra and threw her on the floor. They tied her hands over her head. One after another they poked their horrid lustful bodies into her, the watchers drinking and shouting obscenities. Alexandra could not count how many had defiled her before she fainted.

When she came to only two of the pigs were facing her, half-drunk. 'Where are the partisans?' they shouted. She did not speak. One of the brutes picked up an iron and plunged it into the stove. He drew it out, red-hot, and brought it near to her flesh.

'Where are the partisans?' he shouted. She remained silent. He brought the iron down on her breast and she fainted again as the heat shot through her tender body.

When she awoke it was dark; the two pigs were asleep, snoring loudly. Her body was racked with pain, her right breast as though on fire. She loosened her bonds, groped round in the dark for her tunic, blouse and trousers and clambered out into the night through an unlatched window. She made for the forest and as she entered there was only one thought in her mind: 'In there are my people.'

Comrade Derevyanko called a meeting. 'It is not within the instructions from the Great Leader to avenge individual acts of wanton cruelty,' he explained, 'but to avenge Alexandra Fyodorovna comes within our orders. The enemy Commandant pitilessly oppresses the people; we must lift the burden from their backs. He has the face of a pig, the neck of a bull, the body of a flour-sack. He has the young women brought to his room and takes them, willing or not. He should no longer be allowed to plague the existence of our struggling people.'

While we were discussing what best to do, a sentry rushed in. 'Germans! Germans!' he cried. Quickly we took up our meagre possessions and rushed up above. Firing came from only one hundred metres distant. We fled in the opposite direction and the forest took us into its sweet embrace. Who had betrayed us? If I find out I will lay my hands round his traitorous throat.

We had arranged a meeting place fifty kilometres distant for just such an emergency. The comrades assembled, arriving in sad little groups of two or three; at the final count we knew that thirty of our heroic number we would never see again. Nickolai was missing, and Alexandra. They arrived a week later; he had carried her every metre of the way, a man with the strength of an ox and a heart worthy of his people's trust. The typewriter lay in his knapsack. Katya drew it out and immediately set to work.

We started building a new camp, this time of log huts, with double brushwood floors. We would need the warmth and the shelter, for winter was already laying its iron grip on the land. It was the end of October, 1941.

The sudden attack made us aware of our inexperience. We had remained for too long in the same place; our guard and scouting system was not secure. We became more cautious. We trained for two months in the forest, learning how to use the snow, how better to fire our weapons, how to place and ignite the explosives we had taken from ambushed Fritz convoys.

We continued to distribute our newspaper in the villages, telling the people stories of the partisan heroes and calling upon them to join the brave struggle against the fiendish aggressors.

January 16th, 1942. Comrade Derevyanko called a meeting. 'We will avenge Alexandra', he said. 'The Commandant drives out each Monday from the town of N . . . ., by one road only sixty kilometres distant. I have information of his every move. We will ambush his car'. We made a plan in military fashion and set off, thirty in number.

A grey dawn filters through the mighty trees. We wait at the forest's edge, buried to our necks in snow. One tree, half severed, will fall at the bursting of its necklace of dynamite. For three hours we lie in silence, sure that the enemy will come; the people have told us so.

The sound of engines; every body tenses. An armoured car trundles into view, passes by. The tree crashes down, the explosion throwing up a cloud of fine white powder. The German soldiers shoot into the forest. The Commandant's car stops only five metres from where I lie. Bullets spray the engine; the driver slumps over the wheel. I rush to the car, drag open the door. The pig is there just as Peter has described him. He waves a revolver. I knock it out of his hand and drag his shapeless form into the snow. There is firing to right and left as Koska's group shoots it out with the rear escort. In five minutes all are back in the forest, leaving ten dead Fritzes on the snow and an armoured car with the terrified gunners firing senselessly at the silent trees.

The Commandant collapsed after only one kilometre of marching. We lashed him to a tree branch and put him behind a horse which carried our supplies. Back at the camp the partisans showed their contempt for their would-be conqueror.

We tied him between two saplings, arms out-stretched. 'Spread wide the vulture's wings', shouted Nickolai. 'Take off his trousers', shouted another. 'The frost will see to it that he never again desecrates our women – but let his heart continue beating.'

As dusk fell we returned to our shelters. The prisoner, feeling the cold creeping up his naked legs, cried out for mercy but none heard him.

Later in the evening I rose from my bunk to inspect the prisoner by torchlight. He still lived, but the frost had done its work. I cut him down and turned him loose, blubbering and moaning, clutching at his parts. I had no fear that he would escape; the forest would swallow him up and lay his evil body in the snow.

I look up through the tree-tops where a million stars sprinkled the sky. How beautiful are the forests of the Motherland, how good the Russian winter!

In the tunic pocket of the fascist criminal we found the Hitler-ites' latest instruction about the treatment to be meted out to our toiling peoples; 'Wherever the population makes the situation difficult, act mercilessly. The man who totally ignores personal feelings, who mercilessly and implacably kills all partisans and all persons suspected of aiding them, that man is acting correctly. Kindness and considerateness can become a crime and therefore all partisans and persons in sympathy with them should be shot. The enemy must be completely exterminated.'

News of our exploit spread far and wide. We gave it two pages in our next issue of the *Herald of the Partisans*. As a result many heroes came to swell our numbers. Peter had now made arrangements for them to report to centres established in the villages round about and he went to screen them on appointed days. We needed not only the strong and the brave but, more important, the reliable also. By this means our small *otrjad* rose to the size of a *polk* of six hundred men. Peter still retained charge of political instruction, organisation and discipline while I took charge of military activities.

As our numbers grew, so we needed more and more equipment. We secured this by daring raids on stores and arms caches, and by frequent ambushes on the roads. These became more difficult to accomplish as the enemy increased the numbers and vigilance of his guards, but the heroism and determination of the partisans defeated all his efforts.

February 10th. Today *otrjad* leader Gorazdykh was shot for leaving camp without permission.

February 11th. Today the spy Mozharova was shot for failing to carry out successfully her last two missions; her political reliability was, in any case, in doubt.

February 14th. Today two comrades, Fedya P . . . . and Sergie Z . . . . . were shot. The *otrjad* leader Klyuchin found them in a village drunk and exhibiting themselves in front of the people.

February 27th. Comrade Sidor, a Ukrainian, was shot for spreading reactionary political views.

One day early in March we captured a wireless set. In the morning we tuned in and for the first time for many months we heard the quiet, even voice: '08.10 hours, Moscow time'. Our hearts were filled with happiness; we were at last in touch with the 'mainland'.[1]

Eagerly we noted down every detail of the achievements of the all-conquering Red Army, of the magnificent efforts of the workers in Siberia, of the war material pouring out of the factories in the Urals, details which we would later publish in issues of the *Herald of the Partisans*. Only by means of the partisan newspapers could the

---

[1] The partisans referred to that part of Russia behind the Red Army's front lines as 'the mainland'.

villagers obtain the truth. Even in those few places where the invaders had not stolen every radio it was dangerous for the people to tune in to the 'mainland'.

It is good to be alive today. We are on the march. The snow has melted and the spring sunshine smiles down on the fair land, making every flower and blade of grass dance with joy. We sing as we march:

'To the storm of battle the Motherland sends us
For battle equipped her faithful warriors . . .'

Good as it is to be alive, we are yet ready to die as Komsomols should die.

We have two hundred kilometres before us, but our legs are strong and our hearts ready. To look at us on the march, what would anyone make of us? More than half the detachment are in German uniforms; others wear civilian clothes; others Polish and Hungarian uniforms. I am lucky in that I have retained my Red Army uniform, though it is tattered by now. Three farm-carts carry a few supplies and a number of disguises; horses drag two captured anti-tank guns.

Our objective is the district centre of K . . . . . Our spies, deliberately left behind to work for the Germans under the watchful eye of the secret Communist party organisation, have told us that there are fifty German soldiers in the place and seventy police, with rifles and machine-guns. The ammunition is stored in the police station.

Our plan is simple. We have one hundred men. We will attack the police-station at night – at dawn we will drive the traitors and fascists from the town.

It is two o'clock in the morning. We march silently through the black night. Like shadows, the members of one group surround the police-station. A dog barks. No-one stirs, except the heroes, creeping close.

At 6 a.m. a light shoots into the sky. Our tommy-guns and machine-guns blaze away into the windows where the enemy is billetted. Grenades burst everywhere. The comrades rush into the police-station. Anti-tank guns fire down the railway line, cutting off the enemy's retreat.

Dawn comes. The enemy have reorganised. They advance up the streets in little groups, dodging from house to house, from alley-way to alley-way. The police-station is surrounded. They set it on fire; the flames shoot high. There is a crackling, a roaring and a thousand detonations as the ammunition explodes. Forty of our brave lads are trapped inside. We are unable to go to their help for we ourselves are surrounded. We withdraw, fighting our way out of the encirclement, back into the shelter of the forest where the Germans will not pursue. Those who are left gather at a new meeting place.

The failure taught us many lessons; we will not repeat our mistakes. The fifty defiant warriors who died for the Motherland were quickly replaced as news of the affray spread round the district, encouraging the citizens. Three or four new comrades came in each day.

We decided to stay in the new place and concentrate our attacks against the railway, a main line for the invading armies. During the following six months we blew up eleven trains, destroyed 200 railway wagons carrying clothing, coal, ammunition and provisions. We brought down five railway bridges. We killed 65 officers and soldiers, five of them Gestapo agents, and destroyed five tanks and thirty lorries.

The detachment lost 25 comrades whose memories are cherished as sacred. The detachment recruited 96 new members.

We carried on our aggressive operations all through the winter of 1942–3, over an area 600 kilometres wide and 1,000 kilometres from end to end. Towards the end of this period, the partisans held the countryside in such firm grip that we were able to sleep in the villages in complete safety, and were able to move from place to place as and when we pleased. We had complete intelligence of the enemy, while they had none of us.

Spring, 1943. We were transferred to a new area. As we passed through the countryside we were surprised to see the farmers working happily in the fields with the villages unscathed and serene under the smiling sun. The people looked upon us with suspicion; there was no welcome in their eyes, nor apparently in their hearts. We were cast down to find this different attitude and wondered what lay in store. How could the partisans operate without the support of the people?

On arrival at the appointed place, a new commissar was waiting to greet us, a Major Galiullin, fresh from an *NKVD* training school near Moscow. He told us about the conditions in the district. The Hitlerites had established a *burgomeister* who had set up an administration which seemed to the people to be just and fair. There were to be no raids on the villages, no destruction, no killings, no unwarranted arrests. From the collective farms he had returned the land to previous owners. He had ordered that the people should run their own affairs, responsible to him only for matters directly concerning the war. Comrade Galiullin concluded: 'This man is as evil and as dangerous to our cause as any of the foul murderers who oppress our peoples. He is to be eliminated.'

It was difficult to obtain information. How low had our people sunk to be siding with the fascist aggressors? But at last the resourceful Nickolai, disguised as a factory worker, made his way into the district centre of Y . . . . . and frightened a chambermaid working in the *burgomeister's* house into telling him all that we wished to know. Six heroes entered by stealth one night and slew him in his bed.

The partisans then descended upon the villages. We pulled out the worst of the evil collaborators, destroyed their houses and hung them and their families on the trees; there was a gallows in every village for many kilometres around. Let the bodies swing there night and day as a sure sign to the people that the country is ours, if only we are bold enough to resist. We must never submit to the invaders.

July, 1943. The sun burns the fields but in the forest we are cool, comfortable, calm. In the evenings the sparks fly up into the dark sky. The news is bad but we are ready for anything that may befall.

After the killing of the *burgomeister* at Y . . . . the aggressors sent fresh units to hunt us down – the *Jagdkommandos*; we had not heard the name before. They burnt the villages, they killed all the people they could find or took them away for slave labour, although many escaped to join the partisans.

According to information received from scouts, the Germans were preparing an offensive against our territory. I was on look-out on a low hill. A runner panted towards me.

'The Germans are over there', he shouts. 'We have only two snipers there. Send a machine-gun quickly'. The runner crouches low and goes on his way; he is bleeding from the arm.

There are many Germans, a battalion in strength. They are all around us. Our detachment is weak, only fifty strong, men and women; many are away on raids and ambushes.

'Russians, surrender, Russians', cry the Germans.

How they come on – quickly, relentlessly, using the hillocks and thickets and trees for cover. I run back. I give the order: 'Follow me. We must fight a way out of the encirclement.'

A shell kills three fellows by my side. The shock hurls me to the ground. I scramble up and run. The Germans are all round us. I shoot one, then another. I am free, with a dozen comrades. Natasha goes down; another falls, and another. The Germans pursue, moving as fast as we. I dive into a thicket and lie there panting, stifling my sobs. The Germans shoot into the thicket as they run by. A bullet passes agonisingly through my hand.

The firing recedes. Soon all is quiet. How many comrades have escaped? We were taken utterly by surprise. The Germans destroyed the source of our information – the people – then silently crept in upon us.

I must go to another detachment. I wait for darkness, then make my way through the forest. My hand burns like fire, but I go on. I come near to the new encampment; it is on high ground near the swamp. I wait for darkness before approaching. Fires burn, men and horses crouching round them. I creep closer. The men's voices are German. I lower myself into the swamp and sneak away. I spend the night cold and damp, eaten alive by mosquitoes. In the morning I hear the Germans marching away, singing their coarse songs. I return to the camp. Many comrades lie dead. The pigs have taken everything away but the corpses.

For two long weeks I wander from one desecrated village to another. All are burnt and empty. The *Jagdkommandos* have been busy. There is no living thing to be seen. Only the crops are standing in the fields; the Germans will come back for those when they are ripened. But I will not give in; one must never submit to the invaders.

I come upon a family of poor wretches who have escaped the slaughter. They live in the forest near their land for they cannot bring themselves to leave it. They tell me of a partisan group twenty kilometres to the west. Imagine my joy when I see their smiling faces; imagine my relief when I see my old friend Major Galiullin again.

He is questioning a prisoner by the light of a lamp, a scrawny little creature with the face of a criminal. 'Listen to the guns', he said. 'They are Russian guns.'

Why had I not heard the happy sound before? I had been too much taken up with my own survival. As each boom reverberated through the forest, the lamp burned brighter and another star came into the sky.

Major Galiullin now received his orders from the Red Army, and the Red Army, in turn, received information from us. Many heroic couriers found their way through the German lines with instructions for the partisans, and returned with details of enemy movements, locations and strengths. By radio we received not only details of the fantastic successes of the Red Army men but also coded messages for each of the groups. We knew what to do. The Red Army was advancing many kilometres each day; it was our duty to smash the invader's lines of communication, to interrupt his railways, his telephone and wireless traffic, to ambush the roads, to raid his headquarters, to secure bridges, wherever and whenever possible to make the way easier for the advancing formations. We must also give to the Red Army a ceaseless flow of information covering every aspect of the enemy's military and political manoeuvres.

November, 1943. The horse-flesh is cooked, the flat cakes baked, the equipment ready. The partisans go out on a mission. Comrade Galiullin has planned to call Soviet bombers down on to the railway junction at O . . . . . We will light fires all round the target to show the way to the immortal pilots of the Soviet Air Force. As the Germans flee in panic, groups are to dynamite the railway line in six places along a stretch of fifty kilometres.

The partisans arrive at their appointed places. The Germans have put up barbed wire entanglements along the whole length of the railway line; but no obstructions can halt the brave.

The Germans have constructed machine-gun emplacements at every two hundred paces; but no obstructions can halt the valiant.

The Germans have brought up mechanical saws and cleared a space 400 metres wide on each side of the line; there is not one stick of cover; but no obstructions can halt the courageous.

We hear the bombers overhead, and rejoice. The bombs rain down. The groups rush forward and lay their mines under cover of fire from their comrades. Hundreds of metres of tracking shoot up into the sky; two trains are completely wrecked; one bridge blown up.

On our return we see a light civil aviation plane standing at the edge of the forest. The pilot, a young, earnest boy with sad eyes, holds back a crowd of partisans from his glittering machine, for they would have torn it to pieces in their joy. On the ground nearby are a number of small, square cases, together with sacks of uniforms and bundles of newspapers. After a while the partisans pick up the bundles and carry them into the forest. The pilot climbs into his aircraft and taxies away over the rough field; we all wave heartily as he disappears into the grey sky.

Back at the encampment. We sip hot water flavoured with rowan-berries. The evening draws down, the snow falls, the angry wind tears at our clothing, but we can take it. To the fascist bandits, on the other hand, the winter spells death.

'Hullo to you, Russian winter', sings out one comrade:

'You for us are splendour, glory;
You our fortune and our strength;
You our Russian joy and laughter;
Winter, young and bright and blithe'.

In the evening we gather round the wireless set. A calm paternal voice fills the cabin. We hang breathlessly on every word; even the trees cease to rustle and the snowflakes tremble as Stalin speaks. His last words are addressed to us personally: 'Glory to our men and women partisans'. We embrace each other, shake hands and dance up and down in our joy.

We passed the winter among further joys and hardships of campaigning. No matter which way the brutish invaders turned, they could not escape the attentions of the partisans. They had their victories as experience taught them how to cut off our sources of information, how to track us down and trap us in a net, and in particular we avoided whenever we could the *Jagdkommandos*, but no number of losses or defeats, no threats of reprisal, torture or death dampened the ardour of the partisans. We were no longer alone; the Red Army told us what to do and every day brought nearer the massive strength of their mighty formations.

February, 1944. The most glorious day of the war! The tanks of the invincible Red Army roared through the forest. We lined the roads and trails, dancing, laughing, shouting. Clambering on to the armoured monsters and into the accompanying trucks, we were swept forward on the wheels and tracks of victory. Very soon we were absorbed into the units of the Red Army and went forward into the battles which were finally and forever to drive the Hitlerite bandits from the Motherland.

I have been asked how many were the partisans. People tell me in the region of 1,500,000, but I would say that we were as many as the trees in the forest, as the snowflakes which fall on a winter's day, as many as the stars in the sky on a summer's night.

Chapter 6

Summary of the Russian Campaign and introducing Yugoslavia

The final paragraph of Chapter 5 gives a somewhat romantic assessment of the total strength of the Russian partisans; no accurate figure is known, the nearest estimate of one and a half million being only an approximation, but there can be no doubt that their numbers were enormous. This phenomenal organisation was controlled by the Russian High Command, the Central Staff of the Partisan Movement being directed by Lieutenant General Ponomarenko.

Under the Central Staff were regional staffs at the higher head-quarters of the Red Army in the field, which directed the strategy of the partisans and the co-ordination of their activities with the Red Army's operations through Operational Groups established in various regions behind the German lines. Group headquarters not only interpreted instructions from above but also dictated the general tactics to be adopted in each region. In the lower echelons organisations varied widely; divisions and brigades existed, although the numbers of formations and units within them bore no relation to those in regular formations of the same designation. The basic fighting unit was the *otrjad* – the section. In addition to these fighting units peasants and townsfolk, while still retaining their normal civilian jobs, temporarily fought with the partisans and helped them as scouts, couriers and agents.

In most units the leaders were officers specially trained for guerilla fighting; in almost every unit there was also a commissar who was responsible for political instruction, for the iron discipline at all times maintained, for morale and for keeping an eye on military activities.

Looking at the Russian partisan movement as a whole one can see the precepts of Karl Marx, as embraced and expanded upon by Lenin, put into practice by Stalin, after no very thorough preparation and under the most difficult physical circumstances, with a speed and fervour which took by surprise both the German High Command and the invading armies.

The Germans started preparing for war with Russia in the autumn of 1940. At the beginning of 1941 the German authorities had made elaborate plans both for the defeat of Russia and for her subsequent economic exploitation. Thorough as these plans were, neither the German General Staff, nor Hitler and his henchmen Goebbels and Himmler, had given due thought to the implications of guerilla warfare. The General Staff believed that guerillas could be dealt with by Himmler's infamous Security Service; Hitler reckoned that they could be 'ruthlessly liquidated'.[1]

It was not until March, 1942, that German records and diaries began to show concern in high places for the situation in occupied Russia. To quote from Goebbels' diary:

'March 6th, 1942. A SD (Security Service) report informed me about the situation in occupied Russia. It is after all more unstable than was generally assumed. The partisan danger is increasing week by week.

April 25th, 1942. The inhabitants of the Ukraine were at first more than inclined to regard the Fuehrer as the saviour of Europe and to welcome the Wehrmacht most cordially. This attitude has changed completely in the course of months.

May 22nd, 1942. Personally, I believe we must change our policies essentially as regards the peoples of the East. We could reduce the danger from the partisans considerably if we succeeded in winning some of these people's confidence.

December 4th, 1943. I received a more detailed report about the situation in the East. . . . We made a big mistake in not evacuating the male population in time from the regions about to be abandoned (by the Wehrmacht).'

In these short entries we see concern for the problem but inconsistency in suggestions for its solution.

The German army – the Wehrmacht – whose task it was to

[1] The Fuehrer Decree of the 13th May, 1941.

defeat the Russian armed forces in the field, was the first to feel the full effects of the partisan movement. Their efforts to combat it were, however, hampered by the Wagner-Heydrich agreement, concluded on March 26th 1941, which laid down responsibilities for dealing with partisans. The army was made responsible for the front line which was considered the main hunting ground for partisans – their method, ruthless extermination. The Secret Service was made responsible for the Russian hinterland once it had come under civilian control – their method, liquidation of individuals before the partisan groups started up.

In the event an enormous operational area developed between the front line and the hinterland in which the army was nominally in control, but for which no responsibility for counter-guerilla operations had been laid down and no specific units earmarked. When partisans appeared in this area the Germans tried to meet the danger in three ways; they moved a part of the Security Service into the area; they consigned army units to it; they applied more ruthless methods.

From this time onwards, both the Wehrmacht and the Secret Service acted with increasing ruthlessness and military efficiency against the partisans and their civilian supporters. The Secret Service, assisted by the *Einsitzgruppen*, murdered two million defenceless men and women in the rear operational areas and in the hinterland. The Wehrmacht, fast gaining experience, improved its military techniques and turned on the partisans with ferocious determination. The formation of the *Jagdkommandos,* specially trained guerilla-hunting units, further added to the Germans' counter-guerilla military capability. The techniques evolved by the Wehrmacht were detailed in the pamphlet 'Warfare against Bands' dated the 1st April, 1944, a document which set out a number of most effective counter-guerilla tactics.

However, these new methods were adopted too late and were in any case doomed to failure because the psychological battle had already been lost; in this, the most important aspect of guerilla warfare, the Russians defeated the Germans at every stage.

Prior to August, 1941, Russia did not consider herself bound by the Hague Convention of 1907 governing the 'Rules and Usages of Land Warfare'. Even at this late date she acknowledged herself bound by the Hague Convention and the Geneva Convention concerning treatment of wounded and sick in the active army only in so far as they were observed by the Germans; this conditional offer was not, however, extended to the Geneva Convention of 1929 for the treatment of prisoners of war. Thus the Russians were free to fight the war to whatever rules they chose.

In the pre-war years Russian authorities imposed the iron discipline of Communism upon their people, a measure demanding blind and unquestioning obedience. They also inspired in the people the 'spiritual idea' which justifies the use of trickery, deceit, law-breaking and the withholding and concealing of truth, etc., in the cause of Communism.

With a free hand in interpreting the rules of war, with a disciplined and amoral people, the Russian leaders held two strong cards by which to gain psychological ascendancy over the Germans, in the fight for a people's hearts and minds. The Germans, suffering already under the handicaps of lack of forethought and preparation for guerilla warfare, entered the fray with yet one other notable disadvantage: they were the invaders; the Russians the defenders of the Motherland.

The Soviet leaders capitalised on their advantage by unleashing upon the Germans a warfare without rules. Prisoners of war, wounded and sick who fell into the hands of the Red Army were either shot or enslaved; those captured by the partisans tortured and killed. Stories of these atrocities ran like wild-fire through the German army resulting in reprisals of the most violent and indiscriminate nature. In this way the Russian leaders incited the German soldier to a ruthlessness which alone could, and did, kindle the flame of resistance all over occupied Soviet Russia. The excesses of the Secret Service in the rear areas cannot be attributed solely to this psychological strategy, but it served to aggravate them and to excuse them in the minds of the perpetrators whenever excuse was needed.

The vicious circle grew in scope and effect as the war proceeded. The more atrocious the Russians, the more ruthless the Germans, the stiffer the resistance in occupied territory, the more effective the partisans. The Russians carried this policy through even to the extent of murdering the few German commandants and *burgomeisters* who showed consideration to their people.

The success of Russia's policy was particularly to be noted in the Ukraine where the people initially welcomed the Germans as liberators from a harsh regime. By Russian instigation and due to the Germans' behaviour their amity quickly turned to bitter hostility. To conclude Goebbels' comment on April 25th, 1942: 'We have hit the Russians, and especially the Ukrainians, too hard on the head with our manner of dealing with them. A clout on the head is not always a convincing argument – and that goes too for the Ukrainians and the Russians.'

The Germans failed to appreciate the full meaning of the Russian concept of war in depth, a concept which extends the war, from the outset, to the whole of the territory available to the defenders, whether or not occupied by the aggressors, and which looks upon the contest between the regular armed forces as only one part of the total struggle. Thus they failed to equip themselves with certain vital weapons, namely, a propaganda based on an understanding of the Russian people and their political strengths and weaknesses, a military capability for dealing with armed guerillas and a policy of administration in occupied territories, to be pursued if necessary in the face of extreme provocation, which the indigenous people would recognise as being effective, humane and just.

While the people in occupied Russia were straining every nerve to free themselves from the German yoke by means of irregular warfare, a similar form of struggle was developing in Yugoslavia, under the famous Communist leader Josip Broz, Marshal Tito.

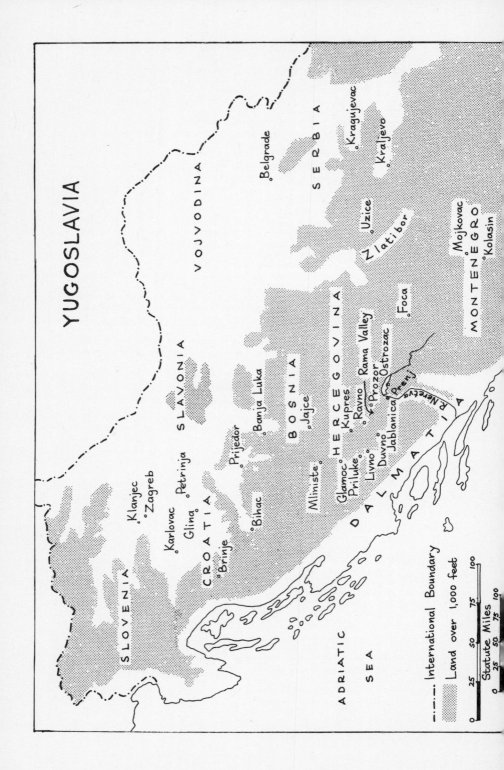

YUGOSLAVIA

SLOVENIA

CROATIA

SLAVONIA

VOJVODINA

Belgrade

SERBIA

Kragujevac

Kraljevo

Uzice

Zlatibor

MONTENEGRO

Mojkovac

Kolasin

Foca

HERCEGOVINA

BOSNIA

Banja Luka

Prijedor

Bihac

Brinje

Glina

Karlovac

Petrinja

Klanjec

Zagreb

Jajce

Mlimiste

Glamoc

Priluke

Kupres

Livno

Duvno

Ravno

Prozor

Jablanica

Ostrozac

Rama Valley

R. Neretva

Rama

DALMATIA

ADRIATIC

SEA

..—.. International Boundary

Land over 1,000 feet

Statute Miles

0   25   50   75   100

0   25   50   75   100

Narrative 5

Yugoslavia — 1941 to 1944

'He stopped the fliers
And, by his rare example, made the coward
Turn terror into sport; as waves before
A vessel under sail, so men obey'd
And fell below his stem.'

SHAKESPEARE

Marshal Tito's aim throughout World War II was to throw the German and Italian occupying forces out of Yugoslavia and to ensure that, once they were removed, the loose federation of states which had before the War constituted Yugoslavia should become a tightly-knit nation under Communist rule. The way in which he brought this dream to reality in the face of almost insuperable odds was a marvel of leadership, determination and *ad hoc* organisation.

Prior to the outbreak of war, the nine states of Yugoslavia – Serbia, Montenegro, Hercegovina, Bosnia, Croatia, Vojvodina, Dalmatia, Slavonia and Slovenia – were ruled by a royalist government which had driven the Communist Party underground. Many of the Party's leading members, including Tito himself, had spent terms in gaol as a result of subversive activities against the regime. Each of the nine states, although offering general allegiance to the central government, had its own proud heritage, its own separate history and peculiar interests and its own different religions, either Orthodox, Catholic or Mohammedan; to each of these religions Communism was anathema.

The Germans and Italians invaded Yugoslavia on the 6th of April, 1941; ten days later the country had capitulated, the central government escaping to Cairo and London where, with vocal support from a large number of royalist refugees, they held the attention of the British government. The axis powers had no sooner conquered the country than they set up puppet regimes, both in Belgrade and in the state capitals, under such men as Acimovic, Nedic, Pavelic and Novak. These quisling authorities raised their own armies and police forces to assist the Germans and Italians in holding down the Yugoslav people; these traitors were known to the partisans as *Ustasas*.

After a short time two irregular forces were thrown up by the people of Yugoslavia to oppose the occupation, the one a right-wing organisation directed and commanded by General Drasa Mihailovic who received immediate support from the refugee Yugoslav and the British governments, the other a Communist organisation led by Tito receiving, from 1942 onwards, only moral support from the Russians and from 1943 limited moral and material support from British and Americans. Many of the battles fought by the Communist partisans were fought not against German and Italian troops but against the Ustasas and General Mihailovic's Cetnics. In addition the Domobranci, and later the followers of General Rupnik clashed arms with Tito's partisans.

Tito had therefore to pursue his course in the face of opposition from occupying armies numbering up to twenty divisions, against the puppet regimes which employed as soldiers, police and spies thousands of Yugoslavians, against Mihailovic's force of Cetnics, against the Domobranci and Rupnik's followers, and against the religious convictions of his own people; and this with negligible support from outside the country.

The beginnings were small. The swift collapse of the royalist regular army came as a terrible disappointment to the Yugoslav people who accused both the army and the central government of weakness and moral decrepitude. But without guidance or preparation, with the armies of the occupying powers all around, with police spies arresting in large numbers all those who might organise resistance the bewildered people of Yugoslavia appeared to be in a hopeless situation.

They nonetheless took the answer into their own hands. In early May nine patriotic men slipped out of the city of Karlovac armed with one rifle, two shot-guns and a revolver. They took up a position in Babina Gora, a wood to the south-east of the city, and there vowed to see their country freed or die in the attempt. This was one, and probably the best-known of many such incidents which took place all over the country. Small groups of men, sometimes no more than two or three in number and armed only with fists or sticks, would stand concentrated behind a bush or thicket and shout '*Stoi!*' to some lone German or Italian soldier. The victim would surrender, whereupon the patriots would strike him down, remove his arms and uniform and bury his body. The example of these brave men was followed by others from the same or adjacent villages, the numbers and incidents growing in scope and frequency until the invaders' position in that area became untenable. The Montenegrins succeeded in freeing their state from initial occupation as early as July, 1941.

The people soon found that they had a leader, for Tito was immediately in action, setting up his headquarters in Belgrade, despite the daily arrests of his comrades and constant danger from quisling police and spies. With him were a number of dedicated men – Djilas, Colakovic, Balovic, Popovic, Dedijer and others – who were soon working together under the familiar Communist abbreviations Agitprop and Politkom. These men took a formal decision on the 30th of June to start an open struggle in order 'to destroy bridges and railroads and to conduct sabotage.' Their venue was the Ribnikar Villa on the outskirts of the town.

While Tito was building up his headquarters in the national capital, Communist committees were taking similar action in the various states, and communication between these outposts and the central authority was quickly established.

The occupying forces and their local henchmen were quick to lend inspiration to the partisan movement, in the same way as that by which they were inciting resistance in many other countries in Europe. No sooner had the small groups of partisans started activity than the enemy resorted to atrocious reprisals. Here are two particularly heart-rending eye-witness accounts:[1]

'I was following an ordinary village road on an ordinary summer morning, rather clear because of the gentle rain which had fallen during the night. First, beside the road under the broad branches of a huge pear I came on two peasants. They were lying in the shade on the grass, in the sort of shade that village mowers choose for resting in. They had been killed in the back of the head, the bullets coming out under the right ear opening huge wounds. Nearby were six more peasants, murdered. A little distance on in the middle of the road were ten or twelve corpses; I think there

[1] For these, and for other quotations in this chapter, see *With Tito through the War* by Vladimir Dedijer, published by Alexander Hamilton.

were two middle-aged men – the remainder were women, girls, children, babies. Three or four paces from this heap of blood and flesh was an empty cradle . . . the child was lying in the heap of corpses but its head was completely smashed with no top to it and not a drop of blood in the empty skull. It was a girl child and one day, perhaps just such a lovely day as this, and many such a day rich with sunlight and verdure, it was to have delighted in all this – in life, happiness, love, youth, and in those about it. The remaining corpses too were disfigured . . .

We went on further. At a cross-roads just outside the town were some two dozen or more corpses, a hill of male, female and children's bodies limbs and heads. A dark woman's plait, with red ribbon worked into it at the end, was tangled with the mournfully dangling moustaches of an elderly peasant. The road at this point was broad but the corpses were all slaughtered on the edge of the road, up against the fence, as if a hurricane had swept them there.

Among them were two mothers and their infants . . . one, young and dark-skinned, held her child in her arms and as she had fallen forward had almost crushed it with her body as if wanting to protect it, while the baby had gripped its hands in her breasts.

I entered a house. A seventy-year-old man was wandering about the rooms . . . He had the air of looking for something but he was only wandering aimlessly about the devastated house. In one room were two dead sons and an old woman – his old woman – dead, bent beside an empty chest.

In another house everything upside down; beside the hearth was a peasant woman, her throat cut; she was a young woman of thirty.

Thus house after house. There had been no living to bury the dead. In all truth there is one thing only in my brain and heart, in my whole being: life is not worth living in this world while there are men who commit such inhumanities. There is no other solution – we or they . . .'

'All the people of the village were assembled in our school. They bound us with ropes and divided us into three groups: those to be slaughtered with the knife, those to be killed with the beetle and those to be cast into the pit. They took the first group into a room in the floor of which there was a hole for the blood to run away into the cellar. The first stream of blood ran among some cattle and they began bellowing frightfully, so they took that group out in front of the school and slaughtered them there, then piled their bodies into a pit. Three times during the day the blood soaked out through the soil and was covered with sand. They also killed the children.

The rest of us were thrown into the pit alive. Grenades burst over us and rocks were thrown in. Those who were not killed only succeeded in escaping some days later. One little girl got out after seven days – one woman was in the pit for days and gave birth there. Two Ustasas kept four girls out, then raped them and cut their throats. Some girls and women, after raping them, they took to the pool and pushed them under.'

These and other indiscriminate and revolting reprisals had the effect of stiffening the people's will to resist and of driving thousands out of their villages to swell the ranks of the partisans as a means of escaping the terror. At first the Communists were rather slower to capitalise upon these numbers than General Mihailovic, who claimed to have fifty thousand men under arms as early as August, 1941.

However, Tito set about organising detachments in all parts of the country, each detachment based on a hard core of Communist Party members, carefully selected men and women who were to provide the motive force of the people's liberation struggle. The detachments were sub-divided into sabotage groups and into companies and platoons, their tasks to destroy or disrupt the adminstrative machine of the invaders and at the same time to conduct political work in the field so as to undermine the vital forces of all those opposed to Communism.

These initial tasks completed, they were then physically to protect citizens from enemy attack and terror and so enlist their sympathy, thus increasing the size and scope of the Communist Party until it embraced all the people in the district. The people were then to purge the district of invaders and quislings, thus establishing liberated areas within which other forces could be mobilised and given both political and military training.

One such area, centred on Kragujevac, was liberated in September, 1941, by an initial partisan force of five companies of fifty men each. No sooner had they cleared the district than the Cetnics appeared. There was an effort here, as in other places, to try and bring together the two forces of resistance, but political differences led to complete failure in co-operation.

While Communists and Cetnics were squabbling over principles, the Germans returned bringing terror to Kragujevac. The Gestapo kidnapped citizens who would never be heard of again; one hundred persons were killed in Grosnica; a priest and his household shot during a religious ceremony; villages were ravaged. All men from sixteen to sixty who could not escape the horror were arrested and mown down by machine gun-fire; over three hundred Communist Youth and over one hundred Party members were slaughtered, the best worker leaders gone. In all, in this counter-attack it was estimated that some five thousand defenceless men, women and children were killed.

After this particular disaster, Tito and representatives of Mihailovic's Cetnics met in conference, but to no avail. They were unable to arrive at a common policy regarding the enemy and from this time on there was constant warring between the two.

Meanwhile Tito and his Supreme Staff had moved from Belgrade to Uzice, but, with the Germans close on their heels, the situation soon became so critical that Uzice, too, had to be evacuated. The printing presses and the *History of the Communist Party* were first loaded as the Germans moved in from all quarters. The leading column hurried out towards Mount Zlatibor; on reaching the mountain the men trod the first snow, thinking of what awaited them – fighting, mountains, winter, hunger.

On the following day, November the 29th, 1941, disorder prevailed on the mountain, but radio and press were set up and the mid-day edition of the partisan newspaper produced. Meanwhile, Uzice had fallen.

While escaping, Tito himself was fiercely machine-gunned when German armoured units rushed straight through the town and up the Zlatibor high road. He was rescued by an escorting battalion which turned against the pursuing tanks and motorised infantry, but while saving their leader the partisans were terribly mauled by the superior armament of the enemy.

On the following night Tito and his staff moved across the mountains, nobody knowing the exact way to go. The Germans pressed on in pursuit, reaching a point only three miles from a house in which they were temporarily resting. The printing press and the *History of the Communist Party* (three hundred pages in an edition of five thousand copies) were again the first to be evacuated. Tito followed and he and his headquarters made away into the deep forest.

But there was no shelter there; they were forced to march on without sleep, with oxen pulling their munitions, their documents loaded on carts, with machine-gun fire harassing from left and right and gunfire from overhead. From one lofty peak to another, across frozen valleys and ice-bound streams they struggled forward, always with the Germans only one move behind. As the first snow of winter fell they escaped the immediate threat, but only to be faced by another as Italians were sighted to their front.

From this day onwards Tito and the dedicated men in his Supreme Headquarters controlled the political and military activities of a partisan movement which finally amounted to 300,000 men and women, from a headquarters which was forever on the move. Never were they in the same place for more than three months, seldom for more than two nights. His staff were able to move without warning in fifteen minutes, taking everything with them, a manoeuvre known in Slovenia as the 'hika', in the rest of the country as the 'pakret'. Their rate of marching tested the endurance of the fittest among them; they would often continue in march route for twenty-eight hours over mountains and valleys resting for only five minutes in each hour. Whenever it was safe to do so, they would sing as they marched.

They seldom had sufficient to eat and were often on the point of starvation. They suffered the intense cold and violent storms of the long winters in the mountains, yet rarely was Tito's 'office' under any other cover than that provided by a tent or a hut hastily thrown up in the forest. He never possessed the normal necessities for office work – secretaries, typewriters, lights, telephones. His headquarters was at all times liable to attack from air or ground forces and was seldom guarded in sufficient strength.

Tito was compelled by his lack of rapid means of communication to delegate authority. He established in each state an 'Anti-Fascist Committee of Liberation', consisting of a President, a Secretary and a number of trustworthy Party men. They in turn delegated responsibility to unit headquarters and district committees, but the state committees themselves were responsible directly to the 'Anti-Fascist People's Liberation Council of Yugoslavia' whose president was Tito.

The state committees' main responsibility was recruiting for

'The National Liberation Army and Partisan Detachments'. The term 'partisan', strictly applied, referred only to those small bands who acted as scouts and saboteurs in close proximity to the enemy. The organisation overall aimed at three distinct elements – the partisan detachments, a regular army and supporting echelons for both.

Methods of recruiting varied greatly. The most prolific source lay in the large numbers of refugees who were to be found in the depths of almost any forest in the country, adjacent to razed villages and de-populated towns. Thousands of men and women, driven from their homes by a reign of terror, were collected and carefully reorganised to suit the requirements of the partisans. Both men and women found places in the armed units and fought on the field of battle. The remainder were drafted into units which carried out adminstrative work of every description, many being sent back to farms and villages in both liberated and occupied areas to supply with intelligence, food and clothing any armed guerilias who might be fighting or training in the hills around.

In those towns and villages which still retained some element of the population, the most unorthodox methods were used for recruiting. In Kraljevo, for example, the partisans went to the fire-station, dressed out in fireman's uniform and, with the fire brigade band at their head, paraded the streets. As they went by the Germans saluted. When the comrades had passed out of the town they struck up the Partisan March and it was only then that the Germans tumbled to the ruse. A detachment soon formed in the countryside around Kraljevo.

But while recruiting, the state and district committees had to take care not to denude of vital personnel the 'rear areas', a somewhat fallacious expression the partisans used to denote those parts of the country in which fighting was not in progress. In the Piva district, for example, 188 Communist Youth, including 11 girls, joined the shock battalions, thus denuding the area of active party workers and leaving an open field for quislings and anti-Communist elements.

Recruiting for fighting formations was directed at the youth of the nation. The young people were considered the best material because they would most readily respond to the call to fight and because they had not been under 'fifth columnist' influence. The older peasants were considered as good partisans so long as they were defending their own villages, but as soon as they were away from home they would weaken in both political and military zeal.

As with other guerilla armies, so in Yugoslavia, one of the greatest problems in promoting efficiency was presented by the matter of communications. A commander or leader could only be in one place, yet his units were frequently spread over enormous stretches of territory. Similarly, state committees were widely separated from subordinate headquarters and from Tito's Supreme Headquarters. Yet information had to be passed quickly as in any army at war. In some liberated areas the partisans were able to use the telephone, but seldom were they prepared to accept the insecurity of this means. For the same reason wireless was eschewed as a means of communication other than for the dissemination of news and propaganda.

Tito solved his problem by developing an elaborate and supremely efficient courier system. The whole country was traversed by a network of courier routes; intersection points were arranged in the most unlikely places where messages would be sorted and directed on to their proper routes; courier posts, where letters would be deposited, were maintained at convenient places. The whole service was similar to a telephone system with its exchange and branch lines, but the information was carried not along wires but by sturdy legs, by motor-cycle, bicycle and on horseback. No matter how the army manoeuvred it was always within the network of the courier service. Reading accounts of the rapid and often unplanned movements of the Supreme Headquarters one invariably comes across the comment – 'The courier arrived at . . .' and this no matter to how remote a place the headquarters had been compelled to retreat.

Almost every courier in this marvellous service was a girl, many only fifteen or sixteen years old. These young girls, who only a few months before might have been afraid of the dark, were to be found at any time of day or night trailing the mountains alone or treading warily through the darkened streets of a town, with a rifle or sub-machine gun on their shoulders and mail in their knapsacks. Undeterred by deep snow, blinding blizzards, terrifying storms, by the heat of summer or by the presence of the enemy, often lost, always hungry, they had only one thought in mind – to deliver their message and to collect mail for the long and dangerous return journey. It is impossible to overrate the vital importance of this courier system to the success of the partisan movement, nor is it possible to set too high a value on the dedication of its members.

As an example of the working of this system we should look at Slovenia which was, in 1943, completely overrun by the enemy. The members of the People's Executive were forced for ten days to hide in an underground cave, while the partisan units had to move about so rapidly that no one unit was ever in the same place for more than a few hours at a time; administrative units had also to move about continuously or go into hiding. So far as the People's Executive was concerned there was not one day that the President and other members did not receive in their obscure hiding place quantities of letters from all parts of Yugoslavia, as well as from different units of the Slovenia forces. They knew each move of the enemy from day to day and the approximate daily positions of their own forces. The courier turned up punctually, and without fail, at midnight.

Operations, sometimes lasting for days and involving the co-ordination of thousands of troops in very large areas, were timed and calculated with great accuracy, although the only means of communication was the courier system. The system was of necessity slow, and serious gaps would occur, but it served the partisans well.

Couriers were purveyors not only of military information and instructions but also of propaganda and news. In common with other guerilla organisations the Yugoslav partisans maintained morale largely by dissemination of news both of local interest and of world affairs. The news of the Russian victory at Kharkov would be read with as much rejoicing as the announcement of the liberation of a Slovene town; the Beveridge Report was discussed with as much interest as the achievements of an agricultural brigade in a liberated area in Bosnia.

Newspapers were produced and circulated under conditions which would appal the newspaper men of today. In Drinici, a place at all times under threat from ground or air attack, the following newspapers and pamphlets were produced in a period of six months, from a press which involved making two machinings for each page produced:

54,000 copies of *Borba*, 6,000 copies of *People's Liberation*, 3,000 copies of *The Struggle of Youth*, 1,200 copies of *Women Today*, 2,200 copies of *Foundations of Marxism*, 2,000 copies of *The Jasenovac Camp*, 12,000 copies of AVNOJ Loan Bonds, 200 copies of Stalin's picture, 3,000 copies of Stalin's speech, 3,000 copies of a map of the Russian front, 10,000 partisan identity cards, and many thousands of other forms of stationery, altogether totalling 2,001,368 octavo pages of printing.

When Drinici finally fell to the enemy, the press was dismantled and moved away in a space of two hours, at night.

The administration of the National Liberation Army provided almost insoluble problems. The partisans' main requirements were food, arms and ammunition and medical facilities.

The fighting men were at all times hungry, as indeed was the majority of the population of Yugoslavia. The Germans and Italians pursued a policy of laying waste large areas, burning villages, destroying crops and carrying off all livestock. Reports of resultant poverty and difficulties in feeding large forces from a barren countryside make harrowing and startling reading.

Foca, February 1942. 'Hunger is tightening its grip. Comrades who have gone about in some parts of the town have found terrible poverty. One family had only rotted cabbage for food. There are very many refugees with nobody they know. One lad came in today having eaten nothing for three days. There are some walnuts and dried wild pears. Blacker days yet will come. There are four or five months to harvest.'

The Kolasin front, May 1942. 'The soldiers have been getting, and that irregularly, five ounces per day each of bread and a little lean mutton. For days some units have eaten nothing but herbs ... The Cetnics, on the other hand, have tinned food – Italian.'

May, 1942. 'Real summer heat. It will soon be a whole year since the war began. Here and there the uprising may grow weaker, but the people will rise again. We starve; we have no munitions; but we shall win through.'

At Tito's Headquarters, June 1942. 'We are peeling beech trees and drinking the juice. We are getting five ounces of flour each. We have had no bread for a whole week, only gruel. We are all exhausted. The men fighting every day on gruel, meat, gruel, meat ... fighting, cold, hunger, typhus, crossing the Lim in the middle of winter, and now starvation and scurvy. We shall indeed be steeled! A courier has just come in ... The Italians are only two hours' march away . . . start fixed for 2.00 a.m. It is freezing.'

The responsibility for providing food for the partisans was decentralised to the state committees and by them to district committees; no one could expect help from his neighbour. As a result there evolved an extraordinary system of communal living. In each town and village every item of goods, every possession, every grain of seed, every animal and piece of agricultural equipment was surrendered by its owner to town or rural committees. The people were told, down to the last small item, what they could and could not eat and how to deploy their meagre resources so as best to feed first the partisans in the field and secondly themselves. The women, and those too young to fight were regimented into an army service corps responsible both for supply and delivery. The organisation eventually developed into a number of agricultural brigades who turned each stage of food production and delivery into a separate operation.

On August the 15th 'the young fellows went into harvest action, with a hundred wagons and four hundred reapers, right under Glamoc, but did not succeed in saving the wheat, the Ustasas opening fire with mortars and machine-guns . . . The Dubica agricultural brigade in one night, close to the Jasenovac concentration camp, cut and harvested 800 acres of wheat, working within 150 yards of Ustasa pill-boxes. When the Ustasas saw the fields next morning they had a real shock. The youth of Kozara had taken it all . . .'

As the war progressed the problem of feeding became so acute that every brigade had attached to it a representative of the Supreme Staff without whose approval no food could be obtained. Only supply officers and properly authorised persons were allowed to enter a village.

For the first two and a half years of the struggle the partisans were desperately short of arms and ammunition. A report from Mojkovac illustrates just how short:

'We gave them a fair licking at Mojkovac – battle on impossible ground, all crevasses and cliffs. The partisans closed with the Cetnics and beat them with rifle butts when the ammunition ran out. Had they only had bayonets, many Cetnics would have been killed. We should have got into Kolasin easily had we but had reserves to follow up with. As it is we took two days rest – no food at all but meat – and again attacked Kolasin. Some of our units penetrated the town but had to withdraw as the enemy strafed them badly with two guns and with mortar fire.'

The only source of supply was the enemy and unit commanders were told to fend for themselves in this respect. As a result, many partisans' lives were lost in attacks which had no other purpose than to secure weapons. Attacking units were frequently accompanied by unarmed peasants, both men and women, in the hope that they would come away from the battle with a weapon or ammunition in their hands. Tito received negligible supplies of these two vital commodities from outside sources and the problem of properly arming his forces proved insoluble until the Italian army capitulated in September, 1943.

The partisans would go to almost any lengths to keep their wounded out of the hands of the enemy. An example of the lengths to which they would go is shown in the following report of an extraordinary evacuation which took place in February/March, 1943:

'*February* 16*th* – At Mliniste there are 100 typhus cases; on Glamoc 469 stretcher wounded, 245 horse-back cases and 350 typhus; on the Livno-Duvno line 169 stretcher cases, 608 on horse-back and 751 lighter cases which can march. These figures are approximate but we expect that there will be about 3,400 wounded.

They are to be organised as a division and divided into three groups – walking cases, horse-back cases and stretcher-borne cases. The first two must carry rifles and must be inspired with martial ardour because we are on the offensive. Groups will be organised under battalion commanders and political commisssars.

Under these conditions political activity will be of tremendous significance. Every wounded man must have a clear sense of the purpose of the whole manoeuvre and must know that the final success of the march will depend on each individual. 3,400 wounded must move through the mountain gullies in mid-winter, under enemy attack and through snow, with some 300 miles to go. Under the old rules we should never have begun this war – with no rear, no munition factories, no stores and against seven armies, but nothing is impossible – we are partisans.

Transport will be a basic problem. We have wagons, horses and three lorries only but the column will stretch over 60 miles. The only way out is to call the Party and the local People's Committee chairmen to mobilise horse-carts and anything else available.

February 18*th* – Left for Glamoc over the mountains – snow, hard frost, rock indistinguishable from ice, wolves around us; a thousand wounded wait in snow nearly waist-deep.

Mliniste reached. The typhus cases in carts – sunken faces, bones not arms, huge burning eyes, bare legs frozen and frost-bitten. Ten nurses in attendance.

February 19*th* – All typhus cases evacuated from Mliniste in weather in which a fit man if kept for twelve hours on a horse would be frozen stiff. The evacuation was only just in time, for the Germans were pressing very hard.

The whole bare mountain between Glamoc and Livno dotted with stretchers.

With one girl, herself ill but able to measure a pulse, I went through the whole column, holding the lass up as we went – she could hardly walk.

February 21*st* – A terrible wind blowing; it will kill our wounded men.

February 22*nd* – Evacuation proceeding according to plan. No wounded left on the Glamoc plain, the last now at Livno. Many typhus cases in Priluke, wrapped in rags.

February 23*rd* – By tomorrow not a single wounded man is to remain in the Livno or Duvno plains; the enemy may strike at any minute from Kupres. Over 1,000 men to be taken out in less than twenty-four hours. Some who should ride will have to walk. 250 horses have been collected so that the comrades will be able to take turns in riding. The wounded start out.

February 24*th to February* 28*th* – Battles develop all round the column of wounded as the Germans attempt to break through the partisan covering force. Meanwhile the wounded lie out on the mountain or are shunted from place to place in an effort to avoid the threat.

February 28*th* – The Germans come out on to Kobila, within shelling distance of the column. A most decisive battle develops. The partisans attack Kobila three times; three times the Germans get it back. Finally it belongs to the partisans, but the Germans continue advancing on the column like lunatics.

March 4*th* – The position somewhat stablised after Tito had taken personal control of the fighting. Seriously wounded and typhus cases now on the Ravno-Prozor line; light cases on the far side of the Prozor-Rama high road. 500 of the heavy and typhus cases at an altitude of 3,000 feet – terribly cold, wind whistling through every crevice.

March 5th – Number of wounded now risen to 5,000. Germans developing a new threat. Wounded given a new direction for evacuation, over the River Neretva. A bridge to be built at Jablanica and all wounded to be sent there.

March 6th – Wounded entirely hemmed into the Rama valley by the enemy, the canyon of the Neretva before them, the swift river 250 feet wide and beyond it the cliffs of Mount Prenj rising to over 7,000 feet. Lorries can drive down to Jablanica but not beyond; only goat tracks up the cliffs on the far side. The Rama valley has been badly looted leaving only 300 horses available for 2,000 men who should ride. The remaining 1,700 should be carried but with eight men to each stretcher, 13,000 bearers are needed and that in a depopulated area . . . Speed! – how did the Chinese partisans cross the R. Tata on their long march? The sky from dawn to dusk filled with enemy aircraft.

The Germans enter Ostrozac, not far from the bridge which will be ready at midnight.

March 7th – The sun breaks through, bringing more aircraft to attack the wounded.

March 8th – The enemy close in. German aircraft make a shambles of Jablanica but the bridge is not damaged. The 1st Proletarian Brigade and the 4th Montenegrin make a bridge-head on the far side.

March 9th – The decisive moment draws near. Will the wounded succeed in crossing the Neretva? The enemy has spotted the manoeuvre. More speed is needed, but more typhus cases arrive – nearly 700 in number. Italian prisoners of war put to carrying them.

March 10th – The Germans appear only 150 yards from the column. Tito orders another battalion to drive them off. The wounded must be taken across the bridge tonight.

Jablanica is full of human corpses, bomb craters, torn barbed wire, carcasses of dead horses; the whole Supreme Staff is there waiting to cross. The bridge is made only of basket-work and narrow planking. 25,000 soldiers and wounded men have to cross by it. The approach is terrible; even a healthy man would feel dizzy. The track is wet and full of holes. Wounded men are moving down it on all-fours; horses fall with their loads. Below the River Neretva foaming; from the hills all around mortars firing. A terrible picture.

Discipline among the typhus cases is breaking down. Some of the nurses have gone to pieces, so tired and hungry they can scarcely move.

March 11th – The wounded are to be got across today, but the aircraft give no peace, Dorniers and Stukas. We have to wait for dark to continue the crossing.

March 12th – Tito deploys all available forces to hold off the enemy from Jablanica. 'We are saved, it is true', he said, 'but we are occupying considerable fighting forces. But how else could it be done?'

March 13th – The evacuation continues by day and night, while the fighting units on both sides of the Neretva are steadily being bled defending the wounded. There is a steady flow of new wounded.

March 14th – The Neretva at last is mastered but the wounded have still to get away from the river. Above them is the Prenj, the most impassable mountain in Yugoslavia and 4,000 men have to be carried over it. There is no wheeled transport now but if we fail it would mean sullying our holy partisan principle: to fight to the last man to prevent a wounded comrade falling into enemy hands.'[1]

Initially the wounded were concentrated into central hospitals, but later the medical services were de-centralised, each division being made responsible for its own wounded. The new and smaller hospitals were erected to a standard type of about fifty beds each and scattered at wide intervals throughout the forests. They included provision for light and ventilation, a regulated temperature, concealment of smoke by day and good sanitation. Many of these hospitals survived as homes for the sick and wounded for over two years, but they suffered throughout from a shortage of drugs and medicines; operations were seldom carried out under anaesthetic.

Despite these deficiencies Tito continued to build up his Communist partisan forces with surprising speed. The scouts, raiders

[1] This description is an abridged version of a long and detailed account of this remarkable operation, written by the officer who organised and supervised the evacuation of the wounded – see *With Tito through the War* by Vladimir Dedijer, pp. 269 to 290.

and saboteurs were the partisan groups, operating in small, compact and mobile bodies; at the same time, with a view eventually to carrying the war to the enemy, he developed a regular army. The 1st Proletarian Brigade was formed in December 1941, the 2nd in February 1942, the 4th in June of the same year. On 7 November 1942, Tito formally handed their colours to the 1st Brigade at an impressive ceremony! The support units and the agricultural brigades similarly took shape.

Training schools for both political and military teaching were set up in liberated areas. When the areas were re-conquered by the enemy the schools were abandoned and set up elsewhere. Teaching of political affairs was carried out by Party members and commissars; military tactics were taught from British, Italian, German and Russian pamphlets. The training was hard and thorough; students worked from 7 a.m. to 7 p.m. each day of a seven-day week.

In order to promote uniformity of standards throughout all parts of the army a constant liaison was maintained between army commands, units and branches, as well as between political executives and committees. Liaison was achieved by literature and conferences, the literature distributed by the devoted girls of the courier service, the conferences held however exacting the conditions.

The tribulations of the partisans were manifold, but they never for a moment lost sight of the final political aim. Every partisan played his part in selling the Party line both to his comrades and to civilians. No opportunity was lost for bringing together Party members and leaders of the people, for holding elections to appoint committees or for tightening the Communist grip on the country.

By January 1943, Tito had sufficient forces under his control to engage in large-scale battles with his enemies. On January the 20th, 65,000 Germans, Italians, Ustasas, Cetnics and Domobrans began an offensive from all directions against liberated territory; 15,000 from Karlovac, 11,000 from the Lika, 3,500 from Prijedor, 16,000 from Glina and Petrinja, with a further 10,000 concentrated at Banja Luka.

The aim of the offensive was to mop up and consolidate the Balkans so that the Germans could turn against new threats to their southern flank from British and American armies poised in North Africa. The offensive was mounted with tanks, aircraft and all the weapons and equipment of a modern army. Tito was able to oppose them with regular divisions, brigades and battalions, and was eventually able to hold them off from their main objectives and more important still, to prevent them from depriving him of his means of making war.

By the late spring Tito and his Communists were firmly established in Yugoslavia, despite all the difficulties and dangers which had dogged their path.

On April the 27th an official British and American mission parachuted down to his forces at Brinje; on the 20th of May a second mission was officially attached to the Supreme Headquarters of the National Liberation Army. There started a regular air-delivery of British and American arms and equipment, in quantities too small to meet his material requirements, but a flow of immense political significance.

To peasants, with their memories of the horrible and bloody existence of the past two years, with their recollections of torture, mutilation and butchery at the hands of merciless foes, with their experiences of days and nights spent in the woods, in deep snow and with nothing but the scant clothing they wore, not daring to light a fire for fear of discovery, the contact with the outside world provided by the air-drop was the sign of a new life. Each drop became the occasion for a celebration.

There was no question of keeping the rendezvous hidden from the villagers. Each evening dark forms would approach the chosen dropping zone from all directions. They would light bonfires to mark the place for incoming aircraft and around each fire would assemble a dense circle of laughing, talking, singing folk. If the aeroplanes failed to arrive, they would make their way back to their shattered homes, disappointed but ready to resume their vigil the following evening. Night after night they would come in the hope of an aeroplane arriving.

When the aeroplanes were first heard, a dead silence would fall over the crowd and then a great burst of joy would go up as the first parachute descended. By daybreak all the stores would have been cleared and carried to appointed places.

In September 1943, the support given by the allied armies to the Yugoslavs bore first fruit when the Italians capitulated to the British and American forces in Italy. By intense and clever propaganda the partisans succeeded in persuading the Italians in

Yugoslavia to hand over their weapons and equipment so that, in the space of one week, they won for themselves an armoury which enabled them to resist and finally defeat the onslaughts which the Germans then launched against them. This absorption of thousands of items of military equipment proved in itself a gargantuan task of assimilation and reorganization, but it was carried through with incredible speed.

Moreoever, when the Germans were finally driven out of Yugoslavia by the efforts of 300,000 partisans, and by the pressure of allied armies advancing from both south and east, the Yugoslav Communist party had to hand a fully-equipped and organised regular army by which to seize and maintain power in the country.

The Communists had spared no pains in preparing themselves politically for this situation; indeed, this necessity had been foremost in their thoughts throughout the years of struggle. As early as November 1942, the first session of the provisional parliament of Yugoslavia was held at Bihac in Croatia; a second session was held on November 29th, 1943, at Jajce. At this second meeting the Anti-Fascist Council of the National Liberation of Yugoslavia took over all legislative and executive power for the duration of the war. The Council passed a motion that 'King Peter II, Kara Georgevic, is forbidden to return to the country until after the liberation of the entire country. Then the problem of the king, as well as the question of the monarchy, can be decided.'

Appointed as Chairman of the Council and Commissioner for National Defence was Josip Broz Tito; born in the district of Klanjec; Croat, aged 55; metal worker in Zagreb; Marshal of Yugoslavia; Communist.

After the defeat of the Germans in 1945, Marshal Tito was established as Yugoslavia's first Communist Prime Minister.

Chapter 7

Introduction to Greece

Marshal Tito led the Communists to power in Yugoslavia in the face of immense difficulties, any one of which might have deterred a lesser man. He succeeded by dint of magnificent personal leadership and by identifying the people with his own aims through the medium of excellent and incessant propaganda and without recourse to the methods of terror advocated by many of his mentors. He brought the struggle to a successful conclusion by brilliant organization and with a determination which was blind to every obstacle or set-back.

During the same period the Communists were making a similar attempt to take hold of the reins of power in Greece, in circumstances which appeared very much more favourable to their cause than any enjoyed by Marshal Tito. Yet in Greece the Communists failed.

YUGOSLAVIA

BULGARIA

MACEDONIA

THRACE

ALBANIA

2,800

3,500

Vitsi

100

1,200

Grammos
Mts.

100

500

Salonika

150

400

850

350

150

1450

300

1,000

200

140

150

200

EPIRUS

650

350

250

350

P
I
N
D
U
S

M
T
S.

THESSALY

AEGEAN SEA

4600

280

150

30

160

Patras

Athens

3000

PELOPONNESE

IONIAN

SEA

TURKEY

SEA OF CRETE

CRETE

GREECE – SHOWING AREAS CONTROLLED BY ELAS
IN JANUARY, 1949.

ELAS-Controlled areas with approximate strengths.

Total ELAS strength - 23,210.

0   50   100

Narrative 6

Greece — 1941 to 1949

'What boots the oft-repeated tale of strife,
The feast of vultures and the waste of life?
The varying fortune of each separate field,
The fierce that vanquish and the faint that yield?
The smoking ruin and the crumbled wall?
In this struggle was the same with all.'

BYRON

The Italians swooped down from the mountains of Albania. General Metaxas, dictator of Greece, met them with the one word *'Okki'* ('No'), a refusal which has an honoured place in the long history of Greek heroics. He opposed them with an army, recently reorganized though poorly equipped, composed of soldiers whose fighting prowess and daring tactics forced the Italians back thirty miles beyond the border. In May 1941, the efficient military machine which the Germans had perfected took over from the Italians and subjected the Greek people to a violent and impetuous onslaught to which they quickly succumbed. The Greeks as quickly rallied; inspired by that passionate love of freedom which has been their known heritage for over two thousand years, they began to devise means of aggressive resistance.

At this time the Communist Party of Greece (*Kommunistikon Komma Ellados* – KKE) had little following among the people, but its leaders were quick to take advantage of the prevailing climate. Under the name of the 'National Liberation Front' (*Ethnikon Apeleftherotikon Metopon* – EAM), a label deliberately designed to give the movement a national and non-political appearance, they raised an armed force of thousands of patriotic citizens who had no other desire than to fight the Italians and Germans. To this force they gave the name of *Ethnikos Laikos Apeleftherotikon Stratos* – ELAS.

Throughout the war years EAM and ELAS resorted to typically

Communist methods by which to increase and maintain their numbers. The occupying armies provided them with the first essential, a suitable psychological undercurrent. The very presence of the invaders created resentment in the Greek people; their barbarous behaviour turned resentment to hatred. EAM, raising the banner of resistance, persuaded the citizens to flock to the colours; those who refused were either dubbed traitors and collaborators, their houses burned and their families slaughtered, or were compulsorily enlisted.

ELAS also needed arms and trained leaders. The former were provided by disbanding Greek soldiers, by air delivery from Greece's allies, the British, and in 1943, after the capitulation of their armies in Italy, by Italian soldiers. For leaders also ELAS looked to the disbanded Greek regular army, drawing into their ranks experienced officers and NCOs whose political views were watched and influenced by commissars. Once the citizens had been recruited they were subjected to intense propaganda and political instruction so that many were converted who started the war with no allegiance to Communism. Propaganda was also directed at the world at large and succeeded in giving the impression abroad that the movement was solely devoted to resistance.

Although in the main adopting guerilla tactics ELAS was given the semblance of a regular army, but its fighting ability fell far short of Communist claims. Manpower and equipment were conserved by deploying against Germans and Italians only with sufficient frequency and in sufficient strength to justify the army's existence in the eyes of the people. The majority of ELAS' operations were devoted to eliminating or absorbing guerilla bands established by other political organisations. The British military officers who fought with the Greek guerillas – and there were many – made every effort to bring together the various bands and to concentrate their efforts against the common enemy, but the leaders of EAM and ELAS would only prevaricate and would find every conceivable excuse for refusing battle, except only against their fellow countrymen. By these means EAM succeeded in eliminating all other guerilla forces, except that of General 'Papa' Zervas' National Democratic League which firmly established itself in Western Greece, at the same time gaining control over large areas of the countryside, particularly in the mountainous regions. They established a major stronghold in the Pindus mountains in central and northern Thessaly, and there they sheltered, unmolested by the armies of occupation whose interests lay in the main lines of communication.

At the end of September 1944, the Germans beat a hasty retreat from Greece. A British parachute brigade, landing first at Patras, followed hard on their heels. General Zervas harried the enemy as they passed through Epirus, while ELAS descended upon the remnants of Greek security battalions which had served the axis powers.

On October the 18th the Greek government returned to Athens from exile, under Prime Minister Papandreou. His cabinet, composed of a number of leaders of varying political hues, including Communists, faced the enormous task of restoring to peace and prosperity a country on the verge of economic collapse, and one in which the morals of the people had been seriously undermined by years of war-time occupation, a condition in which sabotage, theft, idleness and violence had been advocated as patriotic duties. The tradition of close-knit family life which had existed in the provinces had been deliberately broken down by EAM officials.

The government also faced a Communist political organisation with a broad base of 2,000,000 people, out of a total population of 11,000,000, with an army firmly entrenched and with strong cells in every town and village. The machine which the KKE had brought into being during the occupation continued to function after the liberation.

With the Greek government there arrived in Athens a senior British General – Scobie – and by the end of October the British force under his command amounted to a complete division in strength. After weeks of fruitless negotiation, General Scobie, whose appointment was Commander-in-Chief of all Allied Forces in Greece, ordered the disbandment of guerilla units. ELAS refused to disarm and the officials of the KKE promptly resigned from the government, thus creating a critical situation in Athens. The issue between left and right had been clearly joined; the government would have to take action one way or another.

On the 3rd of December, the KKE staged a demonstration in the capital. Columns of marchers, mostly women and children and many at first in holiday mood, burst through police cordons and barricades into Constitution Square, converging on police headquarters.

A handful of fifteen to twenty policemen protected the head-quarters building. Instilled by a spirit of fear at the sight of wounded comrades being brought in from the suburbs, they took cover behind a low wall facing into the Square. The crowd, six hundred in number, close-packed and by now both angered and disrespectful, advanced to within a hundred yards of the fearful few. Suddenly a man rushed out of the building, shouting, 'Shoot them down! Shoot them down!' Hurling himself behind cover, he opened fire. The police, now panic-stricken, added a fusillade to his opening shots.

The crowd, utterly stupefied, were silent for a moment then rushed for refuge. The Square was soon emptied, but for banners and placards strewn over the ground and the distorted bodies of the killed and maimed. But the respite was brief. Other demon-strators soon streamed into the Square and when they saw what treatment had been meted out to those who had gone before them, their anger and excitement rose to a paroxysm. In the greatest demonstration that Athens had ever seen, sixty thousand persons jammed the Square waving handkerchiefs dipped in the blood of the victims, while other thousands stood outside. At 2 o'clock in the afternoon a company of British paratroopers arrived on the scene. Dismounting from trucks they formed a cordon and, with remarkable good humour being displayed by both soldiers and the immense crowd, they moved slowly forward, herding the demon-strators in front of them. Within twenty minutes the Square was empty and a strange silence pervaded the city.

This violent event was made the excuse by ELAS for a full-scale armed attack upon Athens. For two weeks the battle ebbed and flowed until the arrival of two divisions of British reinforcements temporarily put paid to Communist military ambitions.

In assaulting Athens the KKE leaders made four disastrous mistakes; they depended on a 'reserve' of 15,000 Athenians, poorly equipped and ill-trained, who in the event proved ready to snipe at both Greek and British soldiers from their own homes, but would go no further; they relied upon reinforcements which were located in Thessaly, eleven days' march away, and whose movement was restricted to the hours of darkness by the Royal Air Force operating Spitfires out of Hassini airfield; they launched the attack, persuaded by a fanatical Communist element, while their councils were still divided, so that many soldiers went into action with but faint hearts. Finally, angered by unfounded rumours of the perpetration of atrocities by Greek and British troops on ELAS prisoners, they marched hostages into the mountains through the bitter winter weather; of the 15,000 ill-clad and under-fed men, women and children who started out on this terrible march, only 4,000 survived. The people of Greece neither forgave nor forgot.

In defending Athens the British and Greek government forces, conditioned by two years of victorious fighting in Africa and Italy, made one mistake which brought them to the verge of defeat: they grossly underestimated the strength and fighting prowess of their opponents. Only the timely arrival of reinforcements rescued them from a desperate situation when they were hemmed into a space in the centre of the city, only two miles long and six blocks wide, with no means of re-supply.

After their failure at Athens, the Communist leaders, by signing the Varzika Agreement on February 15th, 1945, deferred but by no means surrendered their long-term aims. They withdrew their army into the mountains, handing over to authority those weapons which might be of no further use, while hiding the remainder. There followed a year of peace.

Early in 1946, encouraged by their neighbours in Bulgaria, Albania and Yugoslavia (Marshal Tito's support to the KKE was withdrawn and his borders closed when he broke with the *Comintern* in 1949), the Communist guerillas again took up arms. Their targets were isolated police and military posts and lonely villages which they would systematically destroy before returning to the hills. They struck also at the main lines of communication.

For three years the Greek government waged a ceaseless but fruitless war against this new threat, the bases in Athens and Salonika still secured by British troops, Greek military formations guided by British advisers and the country's economy bolstered by generous aid from both British and American sources.

During these years the guerillas based their tactics on the following principle: a superiority of armed strength at the point of attack, maintaining this superiority throughout the course of the fight by cutting off all routes by which reinforcements might arrive. In all cases they made a swift strike, then an equally swift retreat to a prepared redoubt either within the country or on foreign soil.

More lightly equipped, and with a thorough knowledge of the ground, they were able easily to outdistance pursuing units of the Greek National Army.

Parallel to military action the Communists engineered intense underground activity. They organised networks of recruiters, suppliers, spies and informers over large areas. In this way, and under the misleading heading of 'self-defence', they established control over many regions, particularly in the mountains. The *Ipefthinos* (lit: the Responsible), planted as an EAM agent in each village, exacted obedience to Communist principles and demanded the services required by the guerillas; those who refused to conform were either shot or driven out. By a mixture of terrorism and propaganda this civilian hierarchy obtained the people's support for EAM and ELAS.

The Greek National Army (GNA) was ill-prepared for this form of warfare. Although stronger in numbers than the guerillas the army had been raised anew in 1945 and, with practically no training and with very few experienced leaders, were at once involved in operations against the guerillas. The Communists had penetrated the lower echelons and there were cases of soldiers turning against their comrades in the course of battle and killing their officers. Government troops were forced back on the defensive by the need to deploy units in static positions in the towns and at centres of communication, while the movement of supply convoys demanded increasingly larger escorts. Politics dogged the footsteps of the soldiers who were too often positioned at the behest of ministers whose sole interest was the security of their own constituencies.

Through the years 1947–8 the police and army made slight progress. Communist elements were removed and sent to rehabilitation camps; they were later allowed to rejoin their units if they sincerely disowned Communism. A number of large-scale pincer-type operations were mounted in the hope of encircling guerilla hideouts, but these attempts broke down on the efficiency of the enemy's intelligence system and due to the need to retain large numbers of fighting men in those areas which had been cleared. The population would support the army only when they were sure that the army could guarantee continued security; but there were never enough soldiers to go round, and the few armed peasant units had so far proved ineffective.

In one important respect the Greek government succeeded in

containing the Communists by frustrating all attempts to form a 'Free Greek Government' in a town near the border which they could then name their 'capital'. The KKE was thus deprived of official recognition by other Communist governments, which in turn might well have led to open military aid as opposed to the facilities for sanctuary and limited re-equipping which they already enjoyed.

After three years of civil war the military situation was far from satisfactory. The guerillas held the initiative. They replaced battle losses by abducting peasants from the villages (during 1948 they kidnapped no fewer than 24,870 men and women for ELAS) and so were able to maintain their strength and fighting spirit, and they were further reinforced by cadres of officers and soldiers trained in neighbouring satellite countries. Increasing supplies of arms and ammunition flowed in over the borders. Through the 'self defence' system they possessed an intelligence service which ensured that no movement could be made by units of the Greek National Army which was not made known to the guerillas. Furthermore, the people, for fear of ELAS reprisals, were unwilling to give information to their own army. The guerillas held sway over large areas, from the Peloponnese to Thrace.

In 1948 the organisation of ELAS changed. The small bands were collected into divisions and brigades (a brigade numbering 600–800 men and women) and were equipped with mortars, machine-guns and light artillery in addition to rifles. They fortified with mines, wire and military works a firm base in the mountainous regions of Grammos-Vitsi, near the Greek-Albanian-Yugoslav border.

From this base, and from regional strongholds, an army of 23,000 were able to terrorise a whole nation whose people lived in constant fear, not knowing where the Communists might strike next. Both villages and towns suffered from their depredations, and each attack added to the 700,000 refugees whom the government was already compelled to shelter and feed.

Propaganda had convinced many people that their troubles were due to the excesses of the 'right', and that only appeasement could put an end to banditry. This belief received wide credence abroad so that the government and its British and American friends suffered endless harangues on the advantage of appeasement over continuing the fight. But the Greek government rightly concluded that the only terms acceptable to the Communists would involve complete submission.

In January 1949, a dramatic change came over the situation when Field Marshal Papagos was appointed to command the armed forces, with wide new powers and with considerable freedom from political control. The plan which he then drew up, in agreement with the American and British missions, evolved from a logical mind and from a man fully aware of the facilities needed to carry it through to complete success.

He first developed the armed peasant units unto a National Defence Corps of 50,000 men, posting in regular army officers to give professional advice and training. This corps was to be responsible for the security of towns and villages once freed of the Communist threat, thus leaving the Greek National Army of 147,000 free to conduct mobile operations.

The Field Marshal appreciated that this army, although seven times stronger than its opponents, was still not numerous enough successfully to fight the bands in the country and reduce the Grammos-Vitsi bastion at the same time. He planned to hold the Grammos-Vitsi area on the northern border with a minimum force, while clearing the rest of the country of the guerilla threat.

He launched these new operations at the beginning of 1949. Before starting in any one area the security forces arrested and interned all known Communist sympathisers and suspected informers. Army units then advanced on a broad front, in considerable depth and from many directions, vigorously and boldly seeking out and attacking guerilla bands. The troops maintained pursuit of the enemy by day and night. The guerillas, their intelligence system destroyed, their footsteps dogged, their every move forestalled by the GNA, were unable to avoid battle against superior odds; nor could they maintain themselves from their hidden supply bases. In the short space of two months the guerillas in the Peloponnese had lost most of their leaders and, with this loss, their morale and fighting capability collapsed.

By similar means the Greek National Army cleared the whole of central Greece during the spring and early summer of 1949, and by late July was ready to undertake 'Operation Torch' which, in two swift strokes, reduced the guerilla redoubts in both Vitsi and Grammos. By the end of the year a few starving and desperate bands were left in the mountains, intent only on survival, while the 'Free Greek Government' had announced that it would cease further operations 'in order to save the Greeks from destruction!'

Given limited support by British soldiers and generous economic and military aid by their British and American friends, the Greek National Army, together with the Greek people defeated the Communists in their midst. Throughout these years of conflict, the Greeks learnt many lessons from their bitter experience.

They learnt that Communist guerilla warfare is based on a two-fold attack, by arms and propaganda. Propaganda precedes armed conflict and is carried on during and after it – its aim, to disintegrate the morale of a nation while gaining sympathy abroad. By any sort of armed or criminal action they seek to reduce the population to a state of fear and destitution, thus creating conditions for the acceptance of Communist ideals. The best antidote to this form of aggression is early diagnosis and ruthless suppression; any leniency shown to the hard-core Communists will be paid for later in blood and money. While suppressing the incorrigibles, the government must institute an exhaustive programme of public education.

They learnt that when a nation reaches the point where it has to engage in military operations against guerillas, the latter have won the first round. The subsequent process is bound to be both painful and expensive. Once battle is joined, governmental action must be directed at one and the same time against the armed guerillas, against the subversive organisation which supports them, and against the impact which they may have made, either by persuasion or terror, upon the minds of the people. The particular form which these counter-measures should take must be decided in the light of the situation prevailing in the country at the time, but in general they should take the form of unremitting pursuit by day and night of the hard-core Communists and armed guerillas, a constant watch for subversion in towns and villages, and a continuing programme of public education.

In Greece the final outcome rested upon the attitude of the Greek people. They were never in sympathy with Communist preachings or ideals and, as a result, the KKE were compelled to resort to methods of deception, force and terror to enlist their aid. By clever propaganda they attempted to lay the blame for hardship and privation upon the shoulders of the government, but no amount of propaganda will gainsay a house destroyed, a family brutally murdered or a way of life turned upside down. The Greek people looked to their own government for succour and when it came, in sufficient strength and under the leadership of Field Marshal Papagos, they gave its champions their united support.

Chapter 8

Introduction to Asia—World War II and after

While the Communists were extending their sway over Europe, with the Russian army swallowing up country after country in its victorious march westward, while Marshal Tito was successfully fighting for power in Yugoslavia and while the Greek people were engaged in bloody civil war, international Communism was attempting to fill the power vacuums left in so many countries in Asia as a legacy of Japanese occupation and defeat.

In China, the struggle between the Communists under Mao Tse-tung and the ruling party, the Kuomintang, under Generalissimo Chiang Kai-shek, had flared into the open as early as 1927. The Japanese invasion of China in 1936 strengthened the arm of the Communist leader while depleting the strength of Chiang Kai-shek's fighting forces. This long drawn out struggle for power in the largest and most populous country in the world will be examined in a later chapter.

During 1941 and 1942 the Japanese attacked and occupied all the colonial territories in south-east Asia – the Philippines, Malaya, French Indo-China and the Dutch East Indies. At the collapse of the colonial administrations, the best-organised political bodies remaining in these territories were the local Communist parties, and sooner or later during the war years each in turn rallied people to arms under the twin banners of resistance to the invaders and freedom from colonial rule. In each country, adopting guerilla strategy and tactics, the Communist parties aimed at taking over the reins of government as soon as possible after the defeat of the Japanese.

In the Philippines and in Malaya, after long and bitter struggles, their efforts were frustrated; in French Indo-China they came so near to success that even today, twenty-two years after the end of World War II, the world is anxiously awaiting the outcome of a guerilla war which seems to promise no ending; in the Dutch East Indies the Communist party, which throughout its short history has shown itself to be peculiarly inept, made its presence felt more in the political than in the military field until, in October, 1965, after an abortive coup, the Indonesian people slaughtered more than half a million of its members.

In the Philippines and Malaya we shall see how comparatively small and isolated Communist guerilla forces held to ransom for many years the representatives of law and order; in French Indo-China we shall see the techniques of Communist guerilla warfare developed to the highest degree of efficiency.

Narrative 7

The Huk Campaign in the Philippines — 1942 to 1957

'The surest way to prevent seditions, if the times do bear it, is to take away the matter of them.'

FRANCIS BACON: *Essays*

The winter of the year 1941, the spring of 1942; Japanese navies, armies and air forces on the rampage throughout Asia; Pearl Harbour, Hong Kong, Singapore, the Dutch East Indies, and Bataan in the Philippines. The peoples of Asia take up arms against the conquerors, rallying to the colours of those who appear best able to direct resistance. In the Philippines it is to the Communist Party (CPP), which formally established an army on March 29th, 1942, at Cabiao on the Pampanga border. They called this army Hukbalahap, a name to be conjured with – *Hukbo ng Bayan Laban sa Hapon*: 'People's Army against the Japanese'; for short, 'Huk'.

The title was self-explanatory, but the guerillas' performance belied the banner under which they fought. Although they claimed to have killed some 25,000 spies and collaborators during the years of occupation, and to have made many attacks on Japanese shipments, garrisons and convoys, they turned their energy and armoury also against their own people.

The long-term aims of the Huks soon became clear. Initially there were two groups competing for power within the Party, Socialist and Communist, but the problem of leadership was firmly settled by the Chinese Communist 'General' Ong Kiet, sent to the Philippines for the purpose. By 1943 the Hukbalahap, under the leadership of Luis Taruc, a Filipino born of peasant stock, were firmly entrenched in the Communist camp and under militant Communist control – their aim, to advance into the political and economic vacuum which would inevitably follow upon the with-

124

drawal of the Japanese at the end of the war, and seize control of the government by force.

They based themselves on the rice- and coconut-producing region of central Luzon, dividing the area into military districts. From there they proceeded to identify themselves with the causes of both nationalism and the patriotic war against the invaders. Thus they never lacked for recruits from among a volatile people ever given to little wars, and susceptible to the cries of independence and freedom.

The Huks, first in the field as a responsible organisation, gained quickly in strength, an advantage which they dissipated, together with much of the goodwill of the people, by attacking not only the Japanese but also those other native guerilla forces which had the backing of the American High Command in the Far East. So frequent were these small internecine struggles that General MacArthur, early in the campaign, refused either moral or material aid to the Huks, denying them a source of psychological and military assistance which they might have done well to have courted There was no alternative source for them; the Communists in China were too much taken up with their own affairs to take more than a remote interest. Yet all attempts by American officers fighting with the guerillas in the Philippines to bring the opposing armies together were frustrated by Huk obduracy.

The war ended and the Japanese, driven out by the massive war-machine carried in America's Pacific Fleet, returned to their own country. In the full flush of victory the new Philippine republic was born.

At this critical moment the Huks lost face in many fields. The Americans, by refusing to recognise or pay any Huk ex-guerilla, except only the members of one deserving unit, deprived the CPP of the prestige and funds they needed to carry on a 'legal' struggle for power. Filipino and American troops and police took stern measures against the guerillas, killing or imprisoning many leaders, including Luis Taruc and his fanatical, energetic and brutal assistant, Casto Alejandrino. Beset from all sides the Huks took to the swamps, the jungles and the hills.

With the departure of the Japanese and with the Filipinos' attainment of independence, the Huks had to find a new cause round which to rally the people. They had not far to look. As late as 1940 the majority of the people lived under an agricultural system based on the worst of feudal practices. Millions of peasants were bound to the land in a state of semi-slavery, drawing wages which barely enabled them to subsist. In 1938, the late Manuel Quezon said of the Filipino worker: 'As he works from sunrise to sundown, his employer gets richer while he remains poor. He has to drink the same polluted water his ancestors drank for ages. Malaria, dysentry and tuberculosis still threaten him and his family at every turn. His children cannot go to school or, if they do, they cannot finish the whole primary instruction'.

The Huks took up the cry of land reform and directed their political and economic propaganda against the landlords, police and army, and against 'American imperialism'. They set themselves up as champions of a broader democracy which was to include the peasants and the workers.

Some semblance of order and co-ordination was restored to their efforts when Taruc and Alejandrino were released from prison by the Philippine government in the spring of 1946, but even these two were either unwilling or unable to prevent the orgy of sense-less revenge killings in which the Huks indulged at this time, nor to check the flow into their ranks of outlaws and bandits, many non-Communists, who fell into their embrace for lack of anywhere else to turn. It was fortunate for the CPP that this upsurge of lawlessness was looked upon by a simple people as a natural consequence of war in a country where banditry and outlawry had always been a part of life.

The strategy of the Communist Party, using the Huks as its military arm, was set out in a memorandum issued by the Party Secretariat. In part, this memorandum read:

'Aim: To establish a new democracy by overthrowing American imperialism.

Direction of the main blow: Isolation of national bourgeoisie and other elements who compromise with imperialism, and the winning over of the masses.

Main forces: The proletarians and land-less peasants.

Reserves: The middle-class and rice peasants, the Soviet Union and the new democracies (other Communist states).

Disposition of the main forces and reserves: An alliance of the working class and peasantry.

Revolution:

1 Period of preparation – battle for reserves or strategic defence.
2 Seizure of national power – military offensive or strategic offence'

The statement of aim is interesting. International Communism's line for Asia at this time stressed the liberation of the masses from colonialism, but the Philippines was not a colony; as a substitute the CPP evolved a definition of 'American imperialism'.

From 1946 until 1951 the Communists prepared themselves for the drive to power. Preparations included intensive propaganda aimed at winning the support of the people for their professed aims of social and economic reform and the riddance of those who sided with American imperialism. The struggle for the hearts and minds of the people was not confined to propaganda; wherever and whenever the people resisted blandishment, terror methods were adopted – pillage, murder, arson, threats. Both processes were continuous and achieved a large measure of success.

In the military field the Huks were engaged, between 1946 and 1948, in fending off punitive drives conducted by the Philippine constabulary, but while the armed element were so occupied the organisation and education departments of the CPP actively carried on with the conversion of the masses.

In 1949 the Party was invigorated by the successes of Mao Tse-tung in China and Ho Chi-minh in Indo-China. They saw in these victories of the peasants and proletariat promise of the fulfilment of the plans of international Communism for the domination of the whole of Asia.

The CPP now changed the name of Hukbalahap to the more revolutionary title of 'People's Liberation Army – *Hukbong Mapagpalaya ng Bayan* (HMB). In name, as well as in form, the Huks were now displayed as the armed forces of the CPP, with Major-General Luis Taruc as Chief of Staff. Above this military arm was a highly organised revolutionary civil government, its Secretary-General Dr. Jesus Lava, who subjected the HMB to strict Party control. On his instructions the newly-named army stepped up its reign of terror.

By 1950 the HMB, with a minimum of 19,000 men active in the field and backed by 54,000 Communist sympathisers (the figures are approximate; the estimates made at the time varied enormously), were successfully staging large-scale raids and ambushes near the major city of Manila and penetrating other important towns on the island of Luzon. Large areas of the countryside fell into their hands where they imposed their own formal government in the towns and *barrios* (villages), collecting taxes, occupying farms and running schools. One half of the politbureau worked in Manila, the other half with the troops in the field.

The CPP Finance Department levied contributions to support the military drive. Large estates were harvested by HMB units. Destruction of rice, sugar and coconut crops produced desperate economic problems in a young nation which had not yet recovered from the effects of Japanese exploitation. The Communist organisation prospered on the hostility engendered by the tenant-landlord relationship and by the behaviour of the constabulary.

From the beginning the authorities had looked upon the Huks' activities as a matter for police action and had initiated a campaign of trial and error to combat the threat. One remedy was applied by the police and, when this failed, another was set in train, but none succeeded.

In 1946 Manuel Roxas became President of the Republic. He first tried to persuade the CPP to disband their military units and surrender their arms, but acts of terror continued. He then launched the whole of the national police force against the enemy with the task of reducing them by military action alone. However, the constabulary were not trained for such a delicate and difficult mission. During the years of occupation selection of officers had been haphazard and their training skimpy. They were deployed on a battle-field where military action alone was unlikely to succeed and they were given no other guidance than to use force. Application of force became less and less discriminating until the Filipino farmers and workers, and the people of the *barrios*, came to look upon their own policemen as the enemy, the Huks as friends. It was not long before disrespect for the police was extended to the armed forces and the central government.

After a year of fruitless campaigning a new President – Quirino – reacted against force and attempted to bring about an amnesty, but after months of negotiations, in which the Communists displayed all their flair for double-dealing, President Quirino again resumed police action. The respite had given the Huks an opportunity to reorganise and replenish their supplies and the resumption of police action led to no more success than it had enjoyed in previous years.

Meanwhile the country was approaching economic chaos. Graft and corruption were rampant in government circles. With a vacillating policy to guide them, with certain innate weaknesses in leadership, organisation and training, the police and the armed forces became less and less effective. The Philippine government was in grave danger of losing the war.

In this situation there were only two redeeming features; the first a realisation in certain officials that the solution to the problem lay beyond the reach of normal police action and that an integrated national policy had to be evolved and implemented; the second a man who was to evolve such a policy and put it into effect.

Ramon Magsaysay had fought against the Japanese as a young guerilla in his home province of Zambales. After the war he had been elected to Congress where he was appointed chairman of the Committee on National Defence. On 1 September 1950, President Quirino appointed him Secretary of National Defence, his first task to defeat the HMB and to prescribe a cure for the country's parlous state of internal military instability.

Magsaysay made an immediate appreciation of the problems affecting his country. Why were the Communists supported by the people? Where had his government failed in the past? His terms of reference covered the military field only, but his appreciation incorporated the whole field of national internal policy. He concluded that the government in power would not be accepted by the populace as better than a Communist government unless and until it had proved itself to be so. The situation which had given rise to Communism in the years immediately following the war still existed, and until the government radically changed that situation Communism would not be eliminated.

The Communists had gained popular support because, in the top echelons, the Philippine government had allowed itself to drift into inefficient and corrupt practices; because the people had received harsh treatment from the police; because of a lack of social and economic reforms so much needed to lift the burden of poverty from the shoulders of the peasants; and because past policies had allowed the masses to feel that the government was not interested in them while the Communists were.

Although the most dangerous short-term threat came from the

HMB's military campaign, Magsaysay realised that in order to achieve final and lasting victory, new military techniques must be supported by a fresh and dynamic political, psychological, social and economic policy which would appeal to the people. He decided that the answer lay in combining persistent and ruthless blows against the Communist Party and its guerilla army with a firm offer to the people of friendship and reform.

Company-size police units had so far borne the brunt of the fighting, and had proved ineffective. The armed forces on the other hand consisted mostly of administrative units with only two infantry battalions available for fighting. It was obvious to Magsaysay that re-organisation and re-training were needed before the two services would be fit to counter the hit-and-run type of HMB guerilla war. It appeared to him, however, that the conventional organisation into divisions, regiments and battalions was quite inappropriate.

Instead he activated twenty-six independent and self-sufficient battalion combat teams (BCTs), each of three rifle companies, a heavy weapons company, a field artillery battery (the gunners were also trained as infantrymen), a reconnaissance company and an administrative company. Each BCT had its own intelligence, psychological warfare, medical and dental detachments. The total strength of the BCTs varied according to the tactical task allotted to them, but on average numbered 1,000 men each. The efforts of the BCTs and police units were to be co-ordinated by sector commanders whose small tactical headquarters were capable of controlling the operations of any number of combat teams.

Magsaysay aimed at a total strength for the newly-organised forces of 30,000 officers and men.

These major units would not in themselves be able to destroy the fighting potential of the HMB. The army needed scouts and long-range patrollers who would carry the war into the enemy's deeper strongholds in the dense jungles of the Sierra Madre mountains, and in the wildernesses of the Candaba Swamp. In addition, and in order to leave the BCTs free for mobile warfare, other units were needed to hold secure those areas which had been cleared of Communist bands and cells.

For the first purpose Magsaysay raised a number of Scout Ranger teams which he counted as the army's strategic reserve. These section-size teams consisted of highly-trained, physically fit men who were capable of sustained patrolling for several days without re-supply. They could be deployed into critical areas either by air or by road.

For the second purpose civilian commandos were brought into being, the men and women fully armed and led by regular officers and NCOs. Their role was to defend and to keep secure any community already freed by the BCTs.

To co-ordinate the activities of the BCTs and the civilian commandos, and to iron out the inevitable difficulties which must arise when military and civilian interests clashed, Magsaysay established a number of civilian advisory committees.

Once trained, and not before, these new forces were launched against the HMB, mixing conventional with unorthodox tactics. Before hunting down guerilla units they mounted intensive drives to cut out the enemy's sources of intelligence, food and supply; they engaged in sniping and ambushes and in raids on HMB installations and camps; they infiltrated enemy areas with agents in disguise; they screened whole *barrios* when it was thought that the armed enemy were mixing with the civilian population. Having first thrown the guerillas into disarray by physically denying them access to towns, villages and farms, the BCTs and the tough Ranger groups set forth on a remorseless hunt for the armed bands. They hunted until they found; when they found they killed.

Within months large concentrations of guerillas had been broken up into small groups of only thirty to forty, intent on avoiding rather than courting battle. By 1954 the Communist army had suffered 31,465 casualties in killed, wounded, captured or surrendered, of which more than half had surrendered; they had lost 43,000 weapons and 15,000,000 rounds of ammunition; and this at a total cost to the Philippine armed forces of 1,578 dead. By 1957 the HMB had been reduced to a number of small bands roaming the swamps and jungles, intent only on avoiding death or capture, a handful of hunted but still dangerous men.

Magsaysay and the forces of law and order had now reached an extraordinarily difficult stage in counter-guerilla fighting. The enemy were becoming more and more difficult to find, yet they still existed, and those that remained were the fanatical, hard-core Communists. The people and the government had assimilated a sense of security from the fact that overt actions by the HMB had virtually ceased. Magsaysay found it increasingly difficult to justify the maintenance in the field of large military formations and, indeed, the results now achieved by the combat teams were so small in comparison with the efforts involved that the expense in both dollars and military potential seemed to be quite unwarranted. But the battle was still on, and Magsaysay fully realised that entirely to withdraw at this stage would leave the hard-core Communists in the field and give them an opportunity for resuscitating the movement.

He solved the problem by withdrawing the BCTs from their under-productive missions and merging them into regular formations for the external defence of the Philippines, while retaining for internal security the Scout Ranger detachments which remained ready at all times for emergency missions against the guerillas.

Magsaysay, while Secretary of National Defence, was limited by the charter of his own department in the extent to which he was able to carry through the psychological, social and economic war against the Communists in concert with his military campaign. He none the less succeeded in assuming powers for the Philippine Defence Department which were probably unique among defence departments throughout the world. But by 1953 he had so gained the confidence of the people that he was appointed President of the Republic and was then able to bring to bear upon the problem the resources of every government department.

While raising and training the armed forces he spared no pains to make them acceptable to the people, without whose support he saw no hope of final victory. He dismissed or demoted all officers who were either inefficient or were liable to adopt the wrong attitude towards the people. He insisted on the highest standards of military skill and human behaviour. He ordered the armed forces, when they were not fighting, to engage in public works particularly in the village areas; the army built bridges, roads and school-houses, and dug wells. When he became President he extended these principles to all government departments, ruthlessly weeding out the inefficient and the corrupt. He then sent civil officers out to the demoralised people in Communist-controlled territory to explain the new army and the modern government and to gain their support. Thus he instilled a positive attitude in both the government and the armed forces, and saw to it that the people understood this novel approach.

As a further means of gaining popular support he offered

rewards for information leading to the capture or killing of Communist leaders and members of the HMB. The rewards were adequate, representing many months of toil – in some cases many years – to the peasant, but the red tape surrounding payments and the difficulties in the way of establishing claims frustrated any chance of success for the scheme. If rewards are to induce they must be paid on the spot.

In the psychological, social and economic field, Magsaysay, both as Secretary of Defence and later as President, exerted even more influence for reform than he had over the armed services.

He let it be known that all guerillas who surrendered would be spared and re-settled on fertile land, each with 10 hectares (25 acres) to farm and a government-built house. In his own words: 'They are fighting the government because they want a house and land of their own. All right, they can stop fighting because I will give it to them.' The offer led directly to the surrender of thousands.

As President he continued far-reaching social and economic improvements which he had initiated while still in the Defence Department, countering each Communist slogan – 'Land for the landless'; 'Equality for all' – by a tangible and immediate answer. He ensured that landless peasants obtained land, together with a government loan to help them over the first harvest; he appointed a commission to eliminate the abuses of the tenant-landlord system; he established large settlements in the jungles which absorbed both the ex-Communists and peasants from crowded areas; he made loans to small businesses and new farms. Finally, he outlawed the Communist Party.

Throughout these twelve years of struggle the government of the United States of America adopted a wise attitude towards the problems of a country for which they had inherited a special responsibility.

An early insight into the long-term aims of the Huks dictated the decision, implemented by General MacArthur, to refuse them moral support or material aid during the days of Japanese occupation. At the end of the war the American liberating forces continued this same policy by refusing recognition to the Huks, and by capturing many of their leaders and handing them over to the Philippine government.

Even in the darkest days of 1950, when a demoralised constabulary and a mere handful of regular soldiers confronted the full might of the HMB, when the question must have arisen in the mind of Magsaysay and his well-wishers as to who should do the fighting, the USA resisted the temptation to deploy American soldiers against the guerillas, nor did Magsaysay invite such deployment. Lt. Col. Villa-Rial, in his article 'Huk Hunting' writes: 'Foreign troops are certain to be less welcome among the people than are the regular armed forces of their own government. Local populations will shelter their own people against operations of foreign troops, even though those they shelter may be outlaws. For this reason native troops would be more effective than foreign forces in operations against native Communist conspirators. It would be rare indeed if the use of foreign troops would not in itself doom to failure an anti-guerilla campaign.'

Events in Greece, Malaya, Kenya and South Vietnam show that Villa-Rial carries his argument too far, but its application to the guerilla war in the Philippines is relevant. Further, the use of American troops would have lent some semblance of truth to the CPP's accusations of 'American imperialism'. While steering clear of direct involvement the Americans made available advice when it was sought, and generous military and economic aid.

The decisive defeat of the Communists in the Philippines was brought about by the Filipino people themselves.

On March 17th, 1957, a C.47 aeroplane took off in the moonlight from an airstrip somewhere in the Philippines. A few minutes later an orange flame flickered across the mountainside, three thousand feet up. The aeroplane with all its passengers had plunged into the deep jungle, and there died, in the depths of one of those guerilla strongholds which he had so successfully penetrated, one of the most humane, perceptive and skilful of the anti-guerilla fighters of the post-war era – President Ramon Magsaysay.

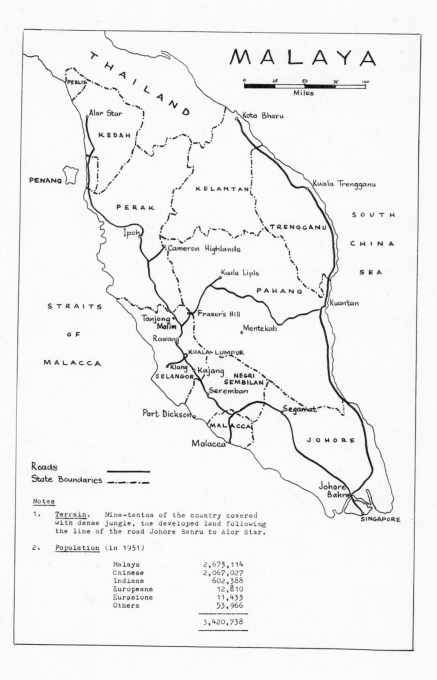

MALAYA

Miles
0   25   50   75   100

THAILAND

PERLIS

Alor Star

KEDAH

PENANG

PERAK

Ipoh

Cameron Highlands

Kota Bharu

KELANTAN

Kuala Trengganu

TRENGGANU

SOUTH

CHINA

SEA

Kuala Lipis

PAHANG

Kuantan

STRAITS

OF

MALACCA

Tanjong Malim

Fraser's Hill

Mentekab

Rawang

KUALA LUMPUR

Klang

Kajang

SELANGOR

NEGRI SEMBILAN

Seremban

Port Dickson

Segamat

MALACCA

Malacca

JOHORE

Johore Bahru

SINGAPORE

Roads ──────
State Boundaries ─·─·─·─

Notes

1. Terrain. Nine-tenths of the country covered
    with dense jungle, the developed land following
    the line of the road Johore Bahru to Alor Star.

2. Population (in 1951)

Malays	2,673,114
Chinese	2,067,027
Indians	602,388
Europeans	12,810
Eurasions	11,433
Others	53,966
	5,420,738

Chapter 9

The Campaign in Malaya against the Communist Insurgents—1948 to 1952

Although the Communists had been active in Singapore and Malaya since 1922, the Malayan Communist Party (MCP) did not come into being until April, 1930. Its membership, almost exclusively Chinese, numbered 15,000 by June, 1931, with a further 10,000 active sympathisers.

The MCP, outlawed by the government, then passed through a number of vicissitudes until, in April 1939, Lai Teck became Secretary-General. An able man, with all the Communist's flair for turning political somersaults, Lai Teck strengthened the Party's organisation and content while riding out the various contradictory instructions issued to him by the Comintern. The struggle in China between the Nationalists and Mao Tse-tung's Communists produced one set of instructions; the 1939 non-aggression pact between Stalin and Hitler another; and he received yet another when the Wehrmacht invaded Russia in 1941, while the threat of Japanese conquest in Asia turned the tables yet again. By July 1941, Lai Teck, on instructions from his Russian mentors, put an end to subversive activity and incitement to industrial unrest and ranged his party alongside the British and Malayan authorities in anticipation of a Japanese invasion. This compliance with authority was to be a temporary expedient only; the MCP never once lost sight of its primary aim – to establish a Soviet Republic in Malaya as soon as possible after the end of the war.

The fortunes of the MCP during the war followed a familiar pattern. British instructors trained one hundred and sixty-five potential Chinese Communist leaders in sabotage and guerilla techniques. This training was conducted at 101 Special Training School, an establishment which was hastily brought into being on December 20th, 1941, twelve days after the Japanese had landed at Kota Bharu in the north-east corner of Malaya. Lai Teck chose his men carefully; the British instructors were duly impressed with the material which he sent them.

As the Japanese armies advanced through the country, carrying all before them, these men disappeared into the jungle to raise a guerilla army which in March, 1942, was given the title of the Malayan People's Anti-Japanese Army (MPAJA). Initially the guerillas, although under strength, poorly led and badly equipped, struck out at the Japanese, but the latter took immediate and energetic counter measures, hunting down the guerillas in their lairs and ruthlessly torturing and executing thousands of Chinese who were thought to be supporting them. Lai Teck foresaw the destruction of his army and issued instructions that there was to be no more fighting against the Japanese.

Concealed in hiding-places on the mountains and in the swamps, protected by the interminable forests, unmolested by the invaders who were content with a policy of live and let live provided the highly-developed western coastline was left free for plunder, the MPAJA gathered strength. In the jungle camps recruits were subjected by political commissars to lectures, discussions and self-criticism meetings and to all the crude techniques of Communist brain-washing.

Later in the war British officers of Force 136 landed secretly on the coast and made contact with the guerillas, but were unable to stir them to action. The British also delivered to the MPAJA, during the summer of 1945, 3,500 small arms and 500 trained fighters, many of them natives of the country, but even this support failed to bring about any worth-while results. During the planning for the re-conquest of Malaya by the British, under the code-name 'Operation Zipper', the MCP appeared to give full co-operation, but Lai Teck neither revealed his political aims nor committed his troops to action.

From the Allies' point of view, the MPAJA achieved nothing during the war. Japanese reports show that it was never a strategic threat and seldom even a military annoyance.

The abrupt ending of the war against Japan in 1945 surprised both the Allied authorities in south-east Asia and the Malayan

Communist Party, but the latter recovered first. With an army of over 10,000 strong (organised into eight regiments and a number of 'Traitor Killing Squads'), with a well-organised political movement regulated by Lai Teck, the Communists took over effective control of most of Malaya. The erstwhile guerillas, parading among the people in British-made jungle green uniforms, set up People's Committees in towns and villages and generally infused a new spirit into the Chinese community, persuading its members that the British were discredited and would never return. This was the moment when Lai Teck might have seized power by a coup d'etat, but the members of his Central Executive and Military Committees were divided; he himself weakened and allowed the opportunity to slip from his grasp.

In August large numbers of British and Indian troops hurried to the mainland. In September a British military administration arrived in the capital town of Kuala Lumpur, a governing body which stood no nonsense. Refusing to recognise the People's Committees, clamping down on left-wing propaganda, disregarding the MCP's demands for political concessions, the administration finally forced the surrender of the MPAJA. Out of a total of 10,000 mobilised Communist soldiers, 6,800 were officially disbanded at a number of ceremonies at which British officers expressed full appreciation of the activities of the wartime resistance. Each demobilised man and woman received 350 dollars (£45), a sack of rice and a job. The balance of the MPAJA, a hard core of 4,000 of the most experienced men and leaders remained in being. As a further safeguard the MPAJA, while surrendering 5,497 weapons to the authorities, concealed a large balance which they had obtained, unknown to the British, from departing Japanese soldiers.

During 1946 and 1947, keeping the militant arm out of sight, the MCP concentrated their efforts on making political progress and on infiltrating the trades unions. They eventually gained control of 200 of the 277 registered trade unions, and the resulting organised labour unrest seriously affected an economy which was struggling out of a depression resulting from years of Japanese occupation and plunder.

In March, 1947, the MCP received the most severe blow of its brief and inglorious career – Lai Teck absconded, taking the Party's funds with him.

Chen Ping (awarded the Order of the British Empire in 1945) was elected Secretary-General in Lai Teck's place. Since his predecessor and all his policies had been thoroughly discredited, Chen Ping had little difficulty in forcing his own ideas upon his colleagues. The 'moderate' policies of the past were to be discarded; general insurrection was to take their place.

The new Secretary-General and his military commander, Lau Yew, began to organise a Malayan People's Anti-British Army (MPABA), with a view to establishing a Communist republic in Malaya in four stages. During the first stage Europeans were to be expelled from lonely rubber estates and tin mines, and police and officials ousted from isolated villages; during the second stage 'liberated areas' were to be established in the regions denuded of government authority; the Communists were then to expand outwards from these areas into the larger towns and villages. At the fourth and final stage the guerilla army was to launch a concentrated attack against British forces which they assumed would by then be concentrated in the major centres of administration. Lau Yew, a keen student of Mao Tse-tung's works, saw in this plan an application of Mao's ideas which were well on their way to fulfilment in China.

In late February 1948, Chen Ping and Lau Yew launched upon the peoples of Malaya a campaign of violence and intimidation directed at all sections of the community. Chinese, Malays, Indians and Europeans were terrorised and killed, police posts attacked, roads ambushed, communications cut; rubber trees were slashed and tin-mining machinery blown up.[1] But it soon became apparent that the guerillas were failing to achieve results commensurate with the sacrifices made. The 'liberated areas' did not materialise; police posts, when overrun, were quickly replaced; guerilla fighters of the MPABA and their helpers were being consigned to death or to detention camps in ever-increasing numbers. The people had not risen as expected against their British overlords.

Chen Ping and Lau Yew had overlooked the need to train their soldiers before committing them to action. They had under-

[1] *Note:* The prosperity of Malaya depended on the production of natural rubber and tin. A rubber tree begins to yield after seven years of growth; slashing the tree, the work of a few seconds, stops the yield and kills the tree. Tin is extracted by dredgers floating on flooded ground.

estimated the bravery and obstinacy of the British planter and the trust and devotion of his Chinese and Indian employees. They had underrated the efficiency of the Malayan police intelligence service and the courage of the constabulary. If they considered it at all, they had set too low a value on the talents of the British civilian and military authorities. They had also overestimated the potential value attributed to them by Communist parties overseas; efforts to gain support abroad met with little response.

The government was quick to react – politically, administratively and militarily.

On 1st of February, aware of impending danger, the British government brought into being the Malayan Federation, a formula which restored sovereign rights to the Malay Sultans and improved conditions of citizenship. By encouraging the formation of the Malayan Chinese Association (MCA), they provided the Chinese with a means of political expression which had previously been available only through the MCP.

A system of national registration was introduced which compelled all citizens over twelve years of age to carry identity cards. A Special Constabulary, 24,000 strong, was raised and armed within three months to take over guard duties in static posts on the plantations and in the tin-mines. The police, 10,223 strong, were re-equipped under the energetic direction of a new Police Commissioner, Colonel W. N. Gray.

Major-General Boucher, the Army Commander, flung his thirteen battalions against the guerillas, relying on the principles of mobility, surprise and offensive action. 'Ferret Force' units, specially trained and guided by expert trackers found from among the famous head-hunting Dyaks of Borneo, were sent into the jungles to live there and to hunt down and kill the insurgents. The army was ably supported by one hundred aircraft of the Royal Air Force.

On July 16th, 1948, the security forces dealt the MPABA a shattering blow by killing in battle its leader, Lau Yew.

The MCP needed time to recover from the effects of these near-mortal blows and an accident far removed from the seat of war was to give them the opportunity they needed. On the 2nd of July Sir Edward Gent, the High Commissioner of Malaya, died in an air accident in the United Kingdom. There was delay in appointing his successor; there was delay also in sending much-needed

British reinforcements. During the pause the guerillas, capitalising on the fear which they had already instilled into people in out-lying areas, recouped their strength; by the spring of 1949 the MPABA numbered 4,000 men and women.

The Big Three of the Malayan Communist Party's politbureau, Chen Ping, Yeung Kwoo and Lau Lee, reorganised this army into ten regiments each responsible to a general headquarters, and re-named it the Malayan Races Liberation Army (MRLA). They also put the *Min Yuen* on to a formal footing. The name '*Min Yuen*' is a contraction of *Min Chung Yuen Thong*, or 'People's Revolutionary Army'. Thirty to forty thousand in number, its tasks were to produce recruits for the armed guerillas when required and to provide the army with intelligence, transport and supplies. The *Min Yuen* was composed mainly of Chinese 'squatters' who lived scattered throughout the country in small settlements at the edge of the jungle. The squatters had no legal rights whatsoever; they had just moved on to the land during the time of Japanese occupation. Nature provided them with a fertile soil, with materials wherewith to build and a warm climate; the government provided them with nothing.

Meanwhile the security forces had not been idle. Soldiers in-fested the jungles and stayed there. The police arrested thousands of known sympathisers and deported them to Nationalist China (in 1949, 10,300 Chinese were deported). The three-hundred mile-long frontier between Malaya and Thailand, although never completely closed, had become by agreement with the Thais a place of danger for guerilla units. The Royal Air Force dropped into the jungle one million leaflets offering surrender terms.

The years 1950-52 saw important changes in the policies and techniques adopted both by the insurgents and by the counter-insurgents.

The latter were initiated, and in part carried through, by General Briggs, then Director of Operations. His plan aimed at a methodical clearing of the country from south to north, first isolating the MRLA from the people who supported it. Once cleared, each succeeding area was to be handed over for security to the police, thus leaving the Army free for further mobile operations. The main features of his plan were close co-ordination of civil administration, police and military at all levels, and re-settlement of the Chinese squatters. This brief account does no justice to a brilliant plan, nor does it give even a first impression of the immense physical and political difficulties which stood in the way of its implementation. But General Briggs while he remained in office, and Sir Henry Gurney the new High Commissioner, were to put it into effect. Later, General Templer was to improve upon it and carry it through to a successful conclusion.

Changes in the policies of the MCP were initiated at a full meeting of the Central Executive Committee held in the Pahang jungles in September 1951, a meeting attended by visiting members of the Chinese Red Army. The Party admitted that resort to terrorism had been a mistake, and one of which their opponents' propaganda had made full play. In future there was to be no more murder, abduction or arson, no more slashing of rubber trees or other industrial damage, no more burning or blasting of civilian installations. The people were to be wooed, not bullied. In the military field the MRLA, which to date had been courting disaster by operating in large units, were in future to change their methods. The Executive sent out instructions in a document dated the 1st of October, telling all commanders to reduce to units of only twenty to thirty strong, and to adopt true guerilla tactics – the lightning raid against a weak target, the swift withdrawal. But due to the slowness of jungle communications many months were to elapse before all units received these new orders.

The year 1951 ended sadly for the security forces. On October 6th the High Commissioner, Sir Henry Gurney, was killed in ambush on the mountainous road to Fraser's Hill by a platoon of thirty-eight guerillas, led by one Siu Mah. In November, General Briggs, who had shown a true understanding of Communist guerilla warfare, was compelled to resign by ill-health. In the New Year, Colonel Gray, the dynamic Police Commissioner, also resigned. With the leadership gone civilian morale sank rapidly and depression settled over the country.

Four months after Sir Henry Gurney's death, in February, 1952, General Sir Gerald Templer was appointed High Commissioner and Director of Operations, thus combining in one person the highest civilian and military positions. The Briggs plan, improved upon in certain details by the new leader, went into full swing.

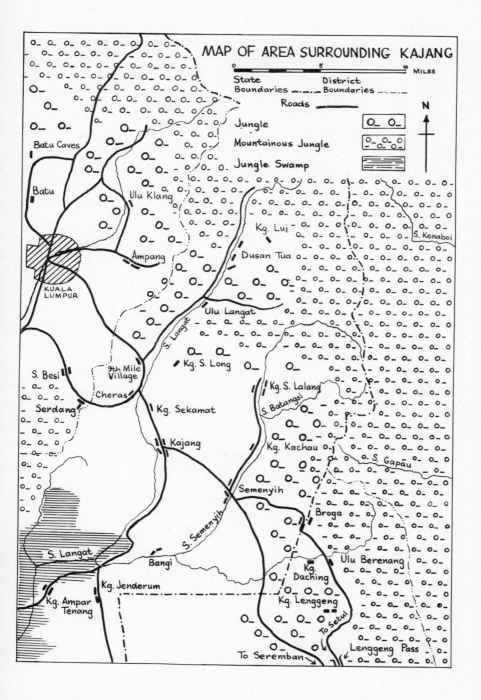

MAP OF AREA SURROUNDING KAJANG

State Boundaries _ . _ . _   District Boundaries _ . . _ . . _

Roads _____

Jungle

Mountainous Jungle

Jungle Swamp

N

Batu Caves

Batu

Ulu Klang

KUALA LUMPUR

Ampang

Kg. Lui

Dusan Tua

S. Kenaboi

Ulu Langat

S. Langat

Kg. S. Long

Kg. S. Lalang

S. Besi

9th Mile Village

Cheras

Serdang

Kg. Sekamat

S. Batangsi

Kajang

Kg. Kachau

S. Gapau

Semenyih

Broga

S. Semenyih

S. Langat

Bangi

Ulu Berenang

Kg. Jenderum

Kg. Daching

Kg. Ampar Tenang

Kg. Lenggeng

To Setul

To Seremban

Lenggeng Pass

Narrative 8

The Campaign in Malaya against the Communist Insurgents — 1952 to 1960

'The perplex'd paths of this drear wood
The nodding horror of whose shady brows
Threats the forlorn and wand'ring passenger.'

MILTON : *Comus*

On a hot and humid day in 1952 Lieutenant-Colonel Robson strolled into the Joint Operations Centre in Kajang. In a wooden hut built on concrete piles, the Centre was divided into one main office with three smaller rooms leading off it. Army and police operations maps covered the walls of the main office from floor to ceiling. The furnishings within this map-lined cell were sparse; at one end two tables, six-foot, GS – one for the battalion the other for the police intelligence officer, two men who sat side by side and worked together; at the other end three utility desks, one for Lieutenant-Colonel Robson, the Commanding Officer (CO) of the British battalion stationed in Kajang, the second for the Police Officer in charge of the district (OCPD), and the third for the District Officer (DO), the British civilian who administered the district which centred on Kajang. In the three smaller rooms were the radio centre containing both military and police wireless stations, the clerks' office where soldiers and policemen worked together, and a conference room.

Robson threw his hat on to his desk; 'Good morning, Peter,' he said.

'Good morning, Charles,' said the police officer. 'I hear you had a successful ambush last night.'

'Yes, we did. We killed a couple and captured a third. Thanks very much for the information.'

'Oh, that wasn't very hard to come by. Analysis of a number of incidents pointed to there being a bandit unit operating somewhere in that area, and then we had one of those strokes of luck we so often need when we picked up a woman courier. She turned out to be a long-standing member of the *Min Yuen*, but she was obviously fed-up with the whole business because under interrogation she sang like a bird. The only pity was that she did not know where the guerilla camp was, but these couriers seldom do; they only know the way to and from the letter boxes.'

'I have two platoons looking for the camp now,' said Robson. 'There was some sort of track leading out from the site we ambushed and the Dyaks should be able to follow it. The trouble is that there appears to be a confusion of footmarks and my men were in doubt as to which direction to take.'

'It sounds a difficult problem. Do you think your men will be able to pull it off?'

'Oh, yes, I think so. They had six weeks of excellent training in Singapore before coming up here, and they have now been on the job for three months. I agree that they still have a lot to learn, but they have assimilated the basic essentials of jungle work. Where is the District Officer?'

'Jimmy Potter? Why so formal? You don't like that man, do you?' said the OCPD.

'I do not dislike him, but he gets in my hair,' replied Robson. 'I only have to send off a small patrol and he wants to know all about it. My men cannot even drive through a village without him enquiring into every detail. I have enough difficulty in maintaining secrecy without explaining my every move to a whole lot of civilians.'

'Look, Charles,' said the OCPD, 'you are new to the job, I know, but you will just have to learn to operate that way. Jimmy can do more for these people than the whole of your battalion and my police force put together. We are a team, and information has to be shared and decisions taken jointly.'

'Expound, Peter,' said Robson, 'you have my ears.'

'All right. Now take that squalid little township, Broga. Jimmy is running a new drain through there. Every time you and I put it under curfew he gets no labour; it takes days after a curfew to persuade them to show their faces again. The people have to bring their produce down to the road to load it on to lorries for market; they will be scared to do this if every time they move a soldier or copper jumps out on them demanding to see identity cards, asking where they are going and so on. A number of the townspeople work on the rubber estates near Semenyih; they have to start tapping at first light and a road block can make them anything up to five hours late, and that means a ton or two of latex lost. Only Jimmy can advise on all this, and we must listen. One other thing, apart from it being the right method we simply have to make the system work. If there is any rift between us you can be sure that Templer will be on our tails and someone will get the boot; well, it's not going to be me. Believe me, Charles, I had my problems when this joint system of operating started. You can imagine how I felt towards the army, barging in as they did on my territory and taking over the whole show after the police had failed to maintain law and order. We had problems of morale which you just cannot imagine.'

'Right! Anyway, where is the District Officer?'

'He has gone up to the squatter area beyond Ulu Langat to watch the evacuation.'

'Oh, yes! I received a report from my men that they had successfully surrounded the place by dawn. The loud hailer entered the area almost immediately afterwards to explain what was to happen. I am going up there myself to watch progress.'

Lieutenant-Colonel Robson walked out on to the dusty parade ground where an armoured scout car waited. The CO climbed in and took a firm grip on the guide handles of the twin Vickers mounted on the body of the vehicle. The driver drove the car away at as fast a speed as the road allowed.

Everyone drove fast along the roads of Malaya. The jungle or rubber trees grew right up to the road-side, providing ideal ambush sites, and the enemy were now operating in small parties so that no extensive ambush was expected. The best method of avoiding an ambush was to drive through it fast before the enemy had time to bring effective fire to bear. If there was a block across the road, then you reversed out at top speed. On the slow stretches in the mountains an escort was necessary, travelling in a separate vehicle at least one hundred yards behind or in front. Then either you or the escort took the brunt of the opening volley of fire. Whichever party remained outside the ambush dismounted and attacked the ambushers. But whatever the system, safe travel on the roads required ceaseless vigilance, eyes and ears alert, weapons at the ready at all times.

At Ulu Langat the armoured car swung off the main road and bumped down a dirt track until it ended at the jungle's edge. There, a group of three-ton trucks was assembled, guarded by a platoon of soldiers. The CO detached a section to escort him over the two miles of primitive track leading into the squatter area.

The evacuation was well under way. The squatters, a dirty, ragged lot, had collected into two impassive groups, the men squatting on the ground, seeing nothing, saying nothing, the women and children in a frightened huddle nearby, their possessions wrapped in cloth bundles, piled high. One ancient crone clasped to her bosom a Singer sewing machine.

The makeshift bamboo and *atap* huts were still spewing out their human and animal contents; the soldiers were bustling here and there, hastening the process. The CO called to the Company Commander:

'Who is that bloody man over there knocking those two people about?' he asked.

'Corporal Smithson,' replied the Company Commander. 'He is a bit tough, but he is marvellous in the jungle.'

'He may be good in the jungle, but he is no damn good here,' said the CO. 'Send him to me.'

The Company Commander moved away. The Corporal doubled over and stood smartly to attention in front of his Commanding Officer.

'What's your name?' said Robson.

'Corporal Smithson, sir.'

'What the hell are you doing roughing those two people up?'

'Well, they're bolshie, sir. They won't do a thing what I tell them, sir.'

'Wouldn't you feel bolshie,' asked the CO, 'if you were being forcibly removed from your home?'

'Suppose I would, sir,' replied Corporal Smithson. 'Yes, sir.'

'Well, then, get hold of the Chinese interpreter. Take him across and explain to those two people just why it is that we are moving them. Make it clear that they have to go like everybody else, whether they like it or not, and then give them all the help you can.'

The Corporal saluted and doubled away. The CO turned to the Company Commander.

'I don't want to see this sort of thing ever again. Make quite certain that your men understand what is going on. The idea is to divorce the squatters from the bandits to whom they provide both food and intelligence. We are also removing these people from the dangers of intimidation and taking them to a place where the government can give them some decent facilities. But no crimes have been proven against them and they must therefore be treated like innocent people. Obviously they cannot now see the benefits that will accrue from the move, but they will. We have to win the hearts and minds of these people and we will not do it by knocking them about. Make it clear to your men that this is the policy and they are to carry it through, no matter how much provocation they have to put up with, and you can assure them that they will have to face up to plenty of provocation during the next three years. If I see another example of behaviour like this in your Company, you'll be on your way out.'

'Sorry, sir,' said the Company Commander, 'I'll see to it.'

'Good! I am sure that you will put it right. I should say that I have had a lecture on the same subject myself this morning.'

The squatters moved off, straggling along the narrow track, the escorting soldiers weighed down with children, cooking pots, water jars, cloth bundles, with everything that the squatters could not themselves carry. As the last one left other soldiers filled the area, appearing from the surrounding jungle. They methodically destroyed every growing crop, fired the dwelling places and marched away.

Lieutenant-Colonel Robson walked back to his armoured car, saw the squatters loaded on to the trucks and drove away to the New Village which had been laid out beside the main road between Kampong Sekamat and Kajang. A high fence of barbed wire surrounded the place with watch towers, manned by Malays of the Special Constabulary, built at intervals of a hundred yards. Inside were neat rows of recently-built *bashas* – wood and *atap* huts, and behind these were a few shops, a medical centre and a school. Water supply had already been run into the village; electricity would follow.

The newcomers were met by the village council, the District Officer and Robson. They clambered out of the trucks and stood around, staring out, lost and bewildered, while the headman harangued them in a language of gulps and swallows, quite incomprehensible to the Englishmen. The DO turned to Robson:

'What do you think of it?' he asked.

'It looks pretty good to me.'

'It is good. Here we can give them protection and amenities which they have never enjoyed, nor were ever likely to enjoy in the jungle squatter areas. Before they settle each one will have a medical inspection and I expect that it will be their first sight of a doctor. And that school, that's a winner!'

The CO turned to go. For him the evacuation had removed a source of supply for the armed guerillas; for the policeman sitting in his office in Kajang it meant one less distant place to patrol and guard, and one hundred and fifty fewer people forcibly engaged in crime. On his return to the office the CO asked his police colleague:

'Peter, how many of these people have we re-settled over the whole country?'

'The last figures I have are for March this year. By then we had settled 423,000 Chinese, mostly squatters, but the figures include some rubber estate workers and tin miners. We have accommodated them in 412 new villages. The next task, of course, is to improve conditions in the Malay *kampongs* or the Malays will think that we are favouring the Chinese – but Jimmy will be able to tell you more about that.'

Two days later Robson answered an urgent call to the Operations Room; the OCPD was already there.

'Ah, Charles,' he said. 'We have some information that you may be able to use. One of the squatters whom we moved a couple of days ago has come up with the news that there was a bandit camp feeding from his area. He is prepared to show you the track they use when they come in for supplies. The squatters were expecting the bandits to call tomorrow evening. Looking at the map I would say that the camp is probably located on the Sungei Kenaboi.'

'Thank you, Peter, I will deal with this. I will have to send off a platoon tonight to make sure. If they have to wait an extra twenty-four hours, then the wait will probably be worth while. Can you let me have a Chinese interpreter?'

Robson returned to his battalion and went through the plan with the company and platoon commanders concerned. They were to wait in ambush on the track and to capture any bandit who came into it. The ambush was to be silent – no shooting, no noise. They were then to interrogate the captured men and persuade them to lead the soldiers back to the guerillas' camp. If persuasion failed, the platoon commander was to find the camp and attack it.

The platoon officer inspected his men. The soldiers paraded with every item laid out on the ground; the officer and his sergeant checked each item with minute attention to detail. Every item was an essential; if anything was missing or in bad condition, it could mean disaster.

The platoon filed off into waiting trucks. As they climbed in the rain came, a heavy tropical downpour which was to continue for the next three days. The trucks, left open to give full vision and allow of speedy action in case of ambush, drove off.

The men marched steadily through the dense forest, making a great circuit round Ulu Langat village. If the villagers should see them the news of their coming would be carried into the jungle. Just before dark the squatter led them up to the track. The platoon commander withdrew his men to a distance and there set up camp for the night beside a small stream.

At dawn he selected the ambush site and brought the men into it from behind, so that they would make no mark on the track itself. The soldiers made hides by pulling down the undergrowth; in each hide were two men, one yard away from the track yet invisible from it. They lay down to wait.

The officer lay beside the Bren gunner, the muzzles of their two weapons resting on the edge of the track. They waited all day. As night fell the damp cold ate its way into their bodies; insects found them and came crawling into their clothes, setting up a maddening irritation; ants swarmed from all directions; mosquitoes descended in clouds, stinging hands and faces; the rain dripped incessantly from the leafy canopy overhead. There was nothing to see and only the monotonous chorus of the insects to hear. By 10 p.m. even this noise was hushed, only an occasional clack or screech or distant wail coming to the men through the darkness.

At four o'clock in the morning the men heard slight noises which did not belong to the jungle. Someone was approaching. They became alert. Suddenly a group of bandits stood before them, hesitantly feeling their way forward. Without a sound the officer leapt upon the nearest man and chopped him down. The soldiers jumped out of hiding and within seconds had captured the others. In complete silence they gagged and bound the prisoners and carried them off into the darkness. The whole incident had lasted only twenty seconds.

Back at the camp which they had occupied on the previous night the interrogation started, the Chinese interpreter questioning each guerilla in turn. By dawn one of the prisoners had agreed to take the soldiers to the place where his comrades were in camp. An NCO and two men marched the others away, taking the short route out of the jungle, through the old squatter area and into Ulu Langat. There they would telephone for transport from the police station.

The platoon set out in single file along the jungle trail leading to the bandits' camp. Towards evening the prisoner told them that they were coming near to the place. The platoon commander decided that it would be futile to attempt an attack in the darkness, so he drew the men back into the jungle to sleep where they lay. There could be no building of shelters, no fires, no cooking, no word or sound which might betray their presence.

At dawn they were on the move again, travelling very slowly, step by step. The prisoner held up his hand and the signal went silently back down the line for everyone to halt. A whispered consultation was held in which the bandit described the layout of the camp and the positions of the sentries.

There followed six hours of infinitely slow and careful movement through the jungle, as the platoon surrounded the camp. No single word was spoken, every order and instruction being given by hand signal. The Platoon Commander, once he had made his plan, had no control over his men until he gave the signal for attack. Every man had to do the right thing; one small mistake, one warning sound, and the bandits would be away into the shelter of the dense undergrowth. At the appointed time the soldiers started closing in, leaving two small ambushes on the track leading into and out of the camp.

The young officer, belly-crawling through the undergrowth with the prisoner beside him, suddenly looked down upon the guerillas. They appeared to be about twenty in number and were going about their daily chores, unaware that danger threatened. The officer waited for yet one more hour to allow time for other men to crawl up to the edge of the clearing where they in turn waited in silence. Meanwhile he watched the khaki-clad cloth-capped figures below.

Taking aim at one whom he thought to be the leader from the fact that there was a red star on his cap, he fired. The silence of the forest was immediately shattered by a fusillade of small arms as the covering section fired round after round into whatever target presented itself. Bren guns and rifles spat out bullets, grenades exploded. This opening volley lasted for thirty seconds, then the assault section charged in.

The guerillas, leaving only a few men to hold off their attackers, rushed for the shelter of the jungle, leaving five dead and two wounded on the ground. The men in ambush on the track killed two more. When the assault party had passed through the platoon commander called for cease fire, and a strange silence fell. The whole engagement had lasted for exactly sixty-five seconds.

The young officer surveyed the scene. The camp, sited above the Sungei Kenaboi, was laid out round a parade ground with a red flag with the Communist star drooping from a central flag pole. Around this central area were the sleeping huts, built of bamboo and *atap*, each with a split bamboo sleeping platform twelve inches above the ground. There was an office hut, a kitchen, and two or three shacks in which food and ammunition were stored. The whole was perfectly camouflaged from the air; the bandits had in no way disturbed the canopy formed by the tree tops, nor the taller undergrowth which provided a second screen below. The sentry posts, sited three hundred yards away, were connected to the camp itself by jungle twine.

The prisoner explained the camp routine. Roll-call at 5.30 a.m., followed by drill and weapon training; breakfast at 9 a.m.; at 10 a.m. political indoctrination and lectures until mid-day; in the afternoon, camp fatigues and tactical training; in the evening two more hours of political instruction before going early to bed. The camp was spotlessly clean.

The soldiers searched, collecting documents and ammunition to be taken away, puncturing food containers so that the scavengers of the jungle should destroy the contents. The platoon commander was then faced with the problem of evacuating the wounded, three of his own men and two guerillas. To carry them out would sub-ject the carriers to the danger of counter-attack during the forty-eight hours' march out of the jungle, and would subject the wounded to a terrible journey. He began the laborious process of hacking down the giant trees to clear the way for a helicopter.

After twenty-four hours of continuous labour the clearing was ready and the officer called in the Sikorsky S-55 by radio. The helicopter carefully and delicately dropped down into the tiny clearing and a doctor scrambled out. One by one the wounded were taken out, the Sikorsky returning for a final load of ammunition and documents.

After yet one more night in the camp the platoon marched out, carrying with them the guerilla dead whom the police would need for identification. The dead must be deleted from the lists of wanted men; the police must assess the reward to be paid to the informer. He was in the event paid ten thousand dollars, a sum which he would not have earned in a life-time of labour.

Back in the operations centre, Robson and his two colleagues received morning and evening reports of the progress of the operation. The other prisoners, although unwilling to lead their captors to the bandit camp, spoke of demoralisation among the guerillas. The officers decided that an appeal to those who had escaped the platoon's attack might bring them out of the jungles to surrender. The Royal Air Force flew Dakotas over the wilderness, dropping thousands of leaflets setting out surrender terms, while 'voice' aircraft broadcast over the forests. The men of the platoon, while still in the bandit camp, heard the loud voice from the sky. The prisoner with them looked up, turned to the interpreter and said, 'Such appeals will not help. We are too frightened to leave our comrades in the day-time and at night it is too difficult to find a way out.'

This conversation was reported to the operations room and the Commanding Officer devised a plan to place searchlights and sound trucks at the jungle's edge to guide the guerillas out at night. Details of the plan were broadcast over the jungles on the following day, but still the guerillas were slow to surrender.

Three weeks after the attack at the Sungei Kenaboi, Lieutenant-Colonel Robson reported to the OCPD that one of his patrols had come across fresh footmarks in the jungles near Ulu Beranang. The two men stood in front of the operations map. The police officer said:

'Now that is very interesting. I received a report this morning that Chen Yun had been seen in the village two nights ago. Of course, we receive these reports of bandits sighted every day, but this does seem to link in with what your patrol have found. Did they find anything else?'

'No. The tracks disappeared and they were unable to follow them. However, they did pick up a cigarette packet which had been thrown down only twenty-four hours or so before.'

'Well, it is not much to go on, but my informant in Ulu Beranang is insistent that there is an air of tension in the place. If you agree, I suggest some form of operation there. What do you think, Jimmy?'

The District Officer said, 'I have no objection, provided that you keep it to the east of the Semenyih-Setul road. I do not want any disturbance to the west of the road where it has been very quiet for the last six months and where we have been making considerable progress in the *kampongs*.'

Lieutenant-Colonel Robson said, 'I have insufficient troops available thoroughly to comb the area. I think we should bring in the RAF.'

The three officers agreed and a plan was made to lay ambushes in a wide arc round Ulu Beranang; the RAF were then to bomb and rocket inside the arc to drive into the ambushes any guerillas who might be lurking there.

Three days later the ambushes were in position and the aircraft overhead, spraying the forests with bombs, rockets and cannon-fire. Almost at once the army officer in charge of the operation received reports from his soldiers that they themselves were on the receiving end of this hail of fire from the sky. He called up the Squadron Leader on the radio:

'You are bombing my men,' he said. 'Move off to the west.'

'I can't do that,' replied the Squadron Leader. 'We have strict instructions to take no action within one mile of the road. Hearts and minds, you know; we cannot risk hitting a civilian. Are you sure you have your map reading right?'

'Certainly! You can see that the country is hilly and this makes it easy for us. We have the inter-state boundary line to check on. For God's sake move off to the west.'

'Wilco,' said the Squadron Leader, 'I will reduce the target area. It's bloody difficult to discriminate from up here; I can't see a thing but tree-tops.'

'Much obliged,' said the army officer. 'Good luck!'

The operation continued for three days and nights, during which six guerillas were killed in ambush. Lieutenant-Colonel Robson reported the results to his two colleagues. The police officer commented to the District Officer:

'Look, Jimmy, the people of Broga must have known about this lot. They would have depended on Broga for an alternative source of supply to Ulu Beranang, but we have had no word of information from there. If that community does not improve its behaviour, it will suffer the same fate as Tanjong Malim.'

'What happened there?' asked Robson.

The policeman replied, 'There had been no fewer than forty incidents round that place in the first twelve weeks of the year including a dozen murders, five cases of arson and attacks on three police posts. Last month twelve men were killed by bandits on the outskirts of the town. When no information was forthcoming about the killers, General Templer went there and dealt with the matter himself. He imposed a twenty-two hour curfew, withdrew all bus services and cut the rice ration. The troops distributed a questionnaire to each house in turn, inviting the householders to say what they knew about the Communists. The questionnaire papers had to be returned to a sealed box which General Templer then opened in the presence of a number of the town leaders. You see the point. Since all papers had to be returned, the Communists could not tell which included information and which did not, so there were no reprisals. Instead, after nine days we arrested thirty of the citizens and relaxed the restrictions. We might try this out in Broga if we have another incident there. What do you think, Jimmy?'

The DO answered, 'The questionnaires sound a very good idea, but collective punishment, no! – only as a very last resort. You do not win the hearts and minds of innocent people by inflicting punishment indiscriminately.'

'All right, Jimmy. You get your drain through and see if that helps,' said the OCPD. 'Meanwhile, we will keep an eye on the place.'

Jimmy said, 'Why not make another effort to raise a Home Guard unit in the town?'

'Not a hope; the citizens are Chinese to a man. There are 60,000 members in the Home Guard up and down the country and all but a mere handful are Malays; the Chinese are most reluctant to join.'

September, 1952, was a particularly good month for the security forces in Malaya.

A big step forward was taken in the attempt to convince the people that a united Malayan nation would emerge from the struggle, when all aliens born in Malaya were granted full citizenship. At one stroke of the pen, 1,200,000 Chinese and 180,000 Indians assumed full rights previously enjoyed only by their Malay compatriots. Regulations were relaxed to make it easier for other resident aliens to qualify for citizenship. The people began to assimilate the fact that independence and self-rule were on the way, that it was not going to be brought about by Communist agitation and armed insurrection, but by constitutional means, and that all would have an equal share of the fruits of victory.

Difficulties still stood in the way of more rapid political progress. There were only two major, legally established political parties, the United Malays National Organisation (UMNO) and the Malayan Chinese Association (MCA). Each mistrusted the other and both were uncertain of British intentions. Only time and patience would bring the parties together.

Administrative steps taken to improve the situation included the imposition of strict control over food distribution, a control which the police were now strong enough to enforce, and an increase in the rewards offered for information leading to the killing or capture of insurgents. (Chen Ping was worth £30,000 to an informant if taken alive, £15,000 dead).

By the end of 1952 the jungle fighting had turned against the MRLA. During the year, 1,097 Communist guerillas had been killed; more had been captured or had surrendered. In some parts of the country, particularly in Johore and Pahang, the MRLA was still strong and aggressive; in other parts weak and defensive. Differences of opinion, promoted by lack of success, rent the leadership both in the Politbureau and in units. But the dense jungle concealed the deficiencies and enabled the fanatical hardcore, perhaps five hundred strong, to replace losses with new recruits – some lured by the Communists' promises, some forcibly abducted from their homes – and so keep the movement alive.

In March, 1953, Lieutenant-Colonel Robson withdrew his battalion to Penang for rest and re-training. The unit was losing efficiency; skills, drills and general alertness were failing after sixteen months of continuous operations. Officers and NCOs needed time and facilities to repair the machine; neither was available while the battalion remained face to face with the enemy. Two months later Robson returned to his old operations centre. Peter Harrington and Jimmy Potter were still in office; he asked the former to bring him up to date:

'Things are going pretty well,' said the police officer. 'You will recall "Operation Service". The constables have at last got the message and are bending over backwards to help the people. Their faces split from ear to ear whenever they see a citizen in trouble, and they leap to his aid. As a result, the attitude of the people towards the police is rapidly changing.

'The new villages are flourishing, thanks to Jimmy's efforts. Councils have now taken over responsibility in all the villages and are even becoming somewhat of a nuisance for the inordinate demands they make for various amenities – but that is local government anywhere in the world. Every new village in the district now has its own Home Guard, Chinese-manned; that represents real progress.

'The news from Kuala Lumpur is also good. UMNO and the MCA are less suspicious and both are impressed by the steps the High Commissioner is taking to prepare the country for self-government. The Communist cries against colonialism are beginning to sound very thin indeed.

'So much for the "hearts and minds" front. It is all General Templer's doing, of course. At every meeting he attends, in every speech and broadcast he makes and even in private conversation his unchanging theme is "win the hearts and minds of the people". Compared with Templer, our friend Mao Tse-tung, with all his brilliant allegories, is a mere amateur in this field.

'We have changed the system of rewards, offering payment for capturing bandits alive rather than for information leading to their death. The leaflet campaign is in full swing; the RAF have dropped forty million over the jungles this year, and with the leaflets go a safe conduct pass which any guerilla can use when he leaves the jungle. It guarantees good treatment, food, cigarettes and medical attention as initial inducements. The propaganda campaign by radio and voice aircraft continues.

'We have made some alterations in the Police Force. We now have a complete unit called the Special Operational Volunteer Force, about one hundred and eighty strong, all former guerillas.

I do not like it myself; I would prefer to see them divided among districts in areas which they know, using soldiers or police as fighters while they inform and guide. I rather suspect that is how they will be used later on.

'We are making a move to get the Special Constables into the jungle; we have seventy thousand in the force and they will be of value once their training is completed. My lists of MRLA and MCP members is now very thorough and detailed; if you want information, we have it.

'But I can tell you that the bandits are becoming very difficult to find; you have to go deeper into the jungles and stay there longer. The chaps who have been here while you have been poodle-faking in Penang formed a specialist hunter-killer platoon. They are very good and had some remarkable successes.'

'I am not sure that I agree with that system,' said Robson. 'All platoons should be hunter-killer platoons. Every soldier who enters the jungle must be jungle-wise, a skilled marksman with first-class fire discipline, fit, and imbued with the offensive spirit; they must all be specialists in this type of warfare. I have no worries about keeping my men in the forests, but I am concerned about the ever-present problem of depriving the bandits of food. What is being done about the Sakai aborigines? I understand that they are now supplying the bandits.'

Jimmy Potter said, 'We are building a system of forts, or rather stockades, deep in the jungle, manned by policemen and soldiers and supplied by the Royal Air Force. These places fulfil two minor functions in that they serve as military bases from which to conduct offensive operations and also as rallying points for any Sakai who may be under intimidation. But much more important they provide a means by which we can reach the hearts and minds of these people who have been very much neglected in the past. There are fifty thousand of them in the country, you know; they live in intolerably primitive conditions and need all the help we can give them.'

Lieutenant-Colonel Robson returned to his battalion's camp. En route, he passed a small convoy of 3-ton trucks crammed with soldiers and escorted by armoured cars, driving at full speed out of the town. His adjutant explained the need for this sudden sortie:

'There has been an incident at the Lenggeng Pass,' he said, 'the first for some time, I understand. The bandits stopped a bus, tied a number of passengers into their seats and set fire to it. I thought the Politbureau had put an end to atrocities, but here is one which will not help their cause with the people. We received the news remarkably quickly and there is a good chance of a follow-up.'

'Who is in charge of the party?'

'Lieutenant Chapman, sir.'

'Has he been told to track them down no matter how long it takes?' asked the CO.

'Yes, sir. They have taken five days' food and the RAF have been alerted for re-supply.'

'Good! And so we wait. Have the police been informed?'

'The report came from the police, sir.'

The first to return from Lenggeng was a Sergeant, with the vehicles and with two wounded soldiers. He reported to the Commanding Officer:

'We ran into an ambush just short of the pass, sir. They caught the leading vehicle, but the ambush was not very well sited and we reacted pretty quickly. We were out of the truck in a moment and there was some good cover at the roadside. Men from the following vehicles counter-attacked at once and the bandits fled as soon as Lieutenant Chapman threatened them; they were not a very determined lot. One bad bit of trouble, sir. A car carrying four civilians was mixed up in the battle and in the general confusion two were killed.'

'And who killed them, Sergeant?'

'I'm afraid that I hit one of them, sir. It was a mistake, of course. There was a hell of a lot of shooting going on and I couldn't see much.'

'You realise that you will have to stand trial for this, don't you, Sergeant?' said the CO.

'Yes, sir. What will the charge be?'

'It depends on the coroner; manslaughter possibly. Where are the two civilian victims?'

'The police are looking after them. An ambulance arrived on the scene pretty quickly.'

'All right, Sergeant; we will hold our own enquiry and get our facts straight. We will then obtain for you the very best defence available. Meanwhile, carry on with your duties, but I am afraid there will be no jungle operations for you until the affair is over.'

'Very good, sir,' said the Sergeant.

While his sergeant stood trial, Lieutenant Chapman ran down the guerilla band. He and his platoon came out of the jungle ten weeks later, with seven bandits killed and four captured to their credit. A week later the remainder of this particular band surrendered, flagging down a timber lorry and driving it into the police station at Seremban.

By early 1954 the government and the security forces had reached a most promising, yet most difficult stage in the campaign.

During the first three months of the year, several districts in Malacca, Trengannu, Perlis, Kedah and Negri Sembilan were declared 'white', indicating that they were entirely free from Communist activity, either covert or overt. Elsewhere, incidents affecting the population were few in number, except only in Johore and Pahang. As a result, the government was able to relax some of the emergency regulations while the numbers of suspects and sympathisers under arrest or detention fell sharply. The people revelled in a new sense of security as they found that they were able to go about their daily business without being either put upon by the Communists or subjected to controls by the security forces.

Deserted by their friends abroad, the members of the Malayan Communist Party had been driven ever deeper into the jungles. The armed guerillas had been reduced to some three thousand in number – since taking to the field in 1948 they had suffered 6,400 casualties in killed, captured or surrendered, against total casualties to the security forces of 1,563 killed. But the guerillas were still there, the majority ruthlessly held to their duties by the fanatical hard-core Communists. There could be no relaxation in the efforts to eliminate them and to secure the country against any possibility of a Communist come-back.

On May the 30th, 1954, General Templer handed over his duties and left Malaya. That he had suffered so few reverses, either political or military, during his time in office must be attributed to his wisdom and leadership, to his resolution and almost frightening energy. He had provided leadership of a quality which the Communists could not match.

His going was followed by a flurry of Communist-inspired incidents, but meeting firm counter-action it soon subsided. It was now left to the security forces, initially under British control, but from August, 1957, onwards under the direction of an independent Malayan government, to root out what remained of the evil. The process, continuing on the same lines as those originated by General Briggs, as improved upon and executed by General Templer, took another six years to complete. It was not until July 31st, 1960, that the emergency was formally brought to an end. By this time a remaining handful of dejected and starving guerillas had taken final refuge beyond the border in Thailand; even there they were not to be left in peace.

The following facts and figures illustrate the effort required, in man-power and money, to force a victory over an isolated revolutionary movement once a situation has developed in which armed guerillas have taken to the field.

Throughout the emergency some 12,000 armed guerillas passed through the ranks of the Malayan Races Anti-British and Liberation Armies. When the emergency ended, 500 of these remained; the rest had been accounted for by the security forces, the majority of the 6,170 killed falling to British and Gurkha regular troops.

Ranged against them were security forces numbering, at their peak, 350,000 of whom 40,000 were regular troops, the remainder policemen, special constables and Home Guard. The ground troops were supported by an air force which carried out over 25,000 strike sorties, dropped 33,000 tons of bombs and fired nearly 100,000 rockets. A sizeable fleet of the Royal Navy patrolled the seas to prevent the smuggling of arms to the insurgents. The enormous disparity in numbers was forced upon the security forces by a combination of many factors, the most important of which was the terrain. Each contact made with the armed guerillas in the jungle cost 1,000 man-hours, each confirmed killing 1,500 man-hours.

The total cost of the emergency amounted to 1,470 million Malayan dollars (approximately £180,000,000); no estimate can be made of the economic damage inflicted upon the country.

But whatever these figures may show, the campaign in Malaya demonstrated above all else that it is men who win wars against guerillas; leaders with active brains and fit bodies who can make good plans and who possess the confidence and energy to implement them; civil administrators who have the people's welfare at heart and will work ceaselessly for the people's good; policemen who deal firmly with the guilty while retaining the friendship of the innocent; airmen who can sustain long hours of search for infinitesimally small targets in a featureless terrain and then hit them when found with discriminating and pin-point accuracy; soldiers who can carry the war deep into the guerillas' strongholds, proving themselves more skilful, fitter and tougher than their opponents while at all times, and if necessary in the face of extreme provocation, conducting themselves honourably towards and in sight of the citizens among whom they live.

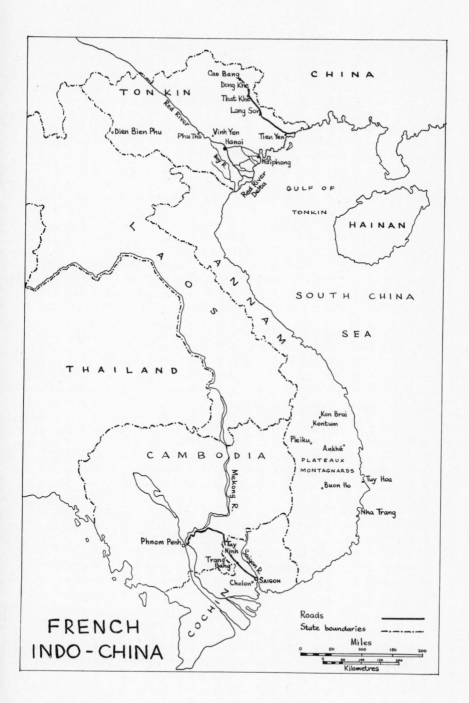

CHINA

TONKIN

Cao Bang
Dong Khe
That Khe
Lang Son

Red River

Dien Bien Phu

Phu Tho

Vinh Yen
Hanoi

Tien Yen

Haiphong

Red River Delta

GULF OF

TONKIN

HAINAN

SOUTH CHINA

L   A   O   S

A
N
N
A
M

SEA

THAILAND

Kon Brai
Kontum

Pleiku
Ankhé

CAMBODIA

PLATEAUX

MONTAGNARDS

Tuy Hoa

Mekong R.

Buon Ho

Nha Trang

Phnom Penh

Tay
Ninh

Trang
Bang

Cholon
SAIGON

Saigon R.

C
O
C
H
I
N

FRENCH
INDO-CHINA

Roads
State boundaries

Miles
0   50   100   150   200

0   50   100   150   200
Kilometres

Chapter 10

Introduction to Indo-China

Prior to World War II, French Indo-China – called the Indo-Chinese Federation – consisted of three protected kingdoms – Laos, Cambodia and Annam, one protected territory – Tonkin, and one French colony – Cochin. At the outbreak of war the French were compelled to withdraw their best troops to the European theatre, so that after the French defeat by the Germans in 1940 the countries of Indo-China were left wide open to Japanese pressure. By the end of 1941, shortly after Pearl Harbour, French Indo-China was as much a Japanese-occupied territory as any that she had overrun with her armed forces, although the French internal administration remained, together with a small number of French colonial troops.

In 1945, before final defeat, the Japanese killed or imprisoned the remaining French elements in the country. This political master-stroke gave the signal to various nationalist and Communist groups to reorganise their parties with a view to taking over the country on the defeat of the Japanese. But the only group with the necessary strength and with sufficiently purposeful leadership fully to exploit the situation was the Communist Party, under their Moscow-trained leader, Ho Chi Minh. On 6th August 1945, the first atomic bomb fell; on the 7th, Ho Chi Minh's guerillas, previously armed with weapons provided in turn by the Americans, by the Chinese nationalist forces operating on the border and by defeated Japanese soldiers, became the 'Vietnam Liberation Army'. During the following days the 'Vietnam People's Liberation Committee' came into being and by the 25th of August, only two weeks after Hiroshima, the Communists controlled all of Vietnam, the new name given to the old territories of Tonkin, Annam and Cochin. This Communist movement, this power which sought to step into the shoes of the French, was the Vietminh.

An extraordinary situation now developed which defies detailed description. A British force of 2,500 men under General Gracey landed at Saigon on the 25th of September to occupy an area larger than Korea, while Chinese Kuomintang troops occupied the northern part of Vietnam. General de Gaulle, then Premier of the French government, was temporarily excluded from these plans, but none the less despatched French troops to the country by any means available. The French Expeditionary Force under General Leclerc, who alone appreciated the importance of speed, arrived in Saigon on the 20th of October and during the following five weeks secured all the key points in an area of 70,000 square miles, although less than a division in strength. The Vietminh disbanded their 'divisions' and 'brigades' and resumed guerilla warfare.

The French were again in charge, more or less. With the Vietminh's agreement, they landed more troops in Hanoi. However, political squabbles between the French and the Vietminh soon led to an atmosphere which became so explosive that it needed only one spark to set off a general conflagration. The spark was provided in Haiphong where the Vietminh, for insignificant reasons, set up road blocks and then attacked the French bulldozer crew sent to clear them. In return the French shelled the city, whereupon the Vietminh assaulted French installations throughout Indo-China. It was 19th December 1946 – the war between the Vietminh and the French had begun.

At the beginning the French position seemed hopeless. The bulk of their troops were confined in small garrisons thinly spread over the huge area which was Indo-China. It was only skilful use of massed fire power, armoured units and air transport, of paratroopers and strike aircraft, that saved them from immediate disaster. But they were too weak to be able to dislodge the Communists from their mountain strongholds. The situation slowly developed into stalemate.

Over the ensuing years, while sustaining intense political and some military activity, Ho Chi Minh reorganised his army on a regular basis. From 1949 his endeavours were greatly assisted by Mao Tse-tung's victory over Chiang Kai-shek in China. There on his borders was the sanctuary that Ho Chi Minh needed, a base for rest and re-training, a source of ammunition, equipment and instructors. By 1950 the Vietminh in the North possessed thirty regular battalions under command of their famous General, Vo Nguyen Giap; in the South a large number of guerilla units were operating under Nguyen Binh.

Despite the wide dispersion of their forces the French, throughout three and a half years of guerilla fighting which varied from month to month in intensity, persisted in maintaining a line of block-houses along the Chinese border with a view to cutting the Vietminh off from Chinese aid. By the autumn of 1950, General Giap was ready to launch a full-scale attack and he selected as his first objective this vulnerable line of outposts.

Narrative 9

Indo-China—1950 to 1954—

PART I

'She saw her sons with purple death expire
Her sacred domes involv'd in rolling fire
A dreadful series of intestine wars
Inglorious triumphs, and dishonest scars.'

POPE

I sit in the dug-out, wilting in the midday heat. There is barely room to stretch out, so I sit with my knees drawn up under my chin, the sweat running off my face and pouring in rivulets down my legs, leaving runnels in the grime. The atmosphere is almost insufferable; no air enters the tiny slits through which the machine-guns are trained. The nights are cold, the mornings full of mist, but the days are unbearably hot. My head is heavy with fatigue, my eyes glazed.

The bunk on which I crouch is a wooden board raised six inches off the ground, with a blanket spread over it. My pillow is a pack stuffed with a green towel; I have this behind my back. Round me are the earthen walls of the dug-out, each two metres high, each three metres in length. It is just possible to stand upright under the low roof. Against one wall the ammunition is stacked – ten thousand rounds for the machine-guns. Beside them are boxes of FOM rations, with a paraffin stove perched on top which we use for cooking when we can be bothered to cook. At the foot of the wall opposite is the bunk of my Second-in-Command, Sergeant Duroc.

There are four such bunkers on the perimeter of the post, with a fifth, a larger one, in the centre; six of my men live in that stinking hole – with the radio.

If I look out through the slit – I spend a lot of time looking out through the slit – I can see only as far as the jungle, one hundred metres away. The ground between is cleared, the trees hacked

167

down and used to build the bunkers, the shrubs and grass kept down by daily toil. Between the bunkers and the jungle are three rows of barbed-wire entanglements; near the edge of the jungle is a fourth row, festooned with empty food cans which give us warning if anyone approaches. We listen all night for the clanking of the cans, telling us that the Viets are closing in, but the clanking can also mean the presence of some wild beast or the stirring of the night breeze.

If you climbed a tall tree in the jungle you could see range upon range of high mountains running away to the north and to the east over the border into China. Looking back into Tonkin, if some other mountain range did not intervene, you would see the flat lands of the Red River Delta, the 'rice bowl' of north Indo-China. But we never climbed the trees. Our job was to defend Post No. 30 – no name, just a number. Perhaps we were registered on some map at the headquarters in Hanoi or Haiphong, or some-where back there, but here in the ground we were only a losing number in a numbers game.

If you walked up the trail for two kilometres, going either north-west or south-east, you would come upon another post, just such a one as mine – No. 29 or No. 31 – but we seldom walked there. When we did we found only another handful of Frenchmen or Legionnaires or native Vietnamese troops, all as bored and as tired as we were. Perhaps if they had been attacked the night before, and still survived, there would be stories to hear, but none that we had not heard before. We confined our walking to patrols in the jungle by day, looking in vain for the presence of Viets, or to cutting the grass and maintaining the wire round the post. There was no movement outside the post at night for by night the jungles belonged to the Viets.

Duroc stumped in through the narrow doorway, back from a patrol to the nearest village three kilometres away. He eased off his pack and threw his jacket on to the bunk, first using it to wipe the sweat from his torso. His body stank. I must get the men down to the stream for a bathe. I should have done this yesterday, but of course there is always tomorrow, provided the Viets do not intervene.

'What's the news?' I asked.

'Bad,' he answered. He lit a cigarette and started burning off the leeches from round his private parts.

'What bad news can there be?' I asked him.

'No chickens! No eggs! No cigarettes! The headman is away.'

'Where? He has never been away before.'

'The people are silent, turning their backs.'

'How about your little woman?'

'No play. Always before I had only to jingle my money and her clothes were off and she was down on her back before I could get my flies open. But today she is ill; she cannot help me, she says. No, we have lost contact. The Viets are now dictating when you can get your bloody oats.'

'Did you get to questioning any of them?'

'Oh, yes! The men took a couple out and beat them up, but not a word. See no evil, hear no evil, speak no evil. They didn't look so good as they crawled back into the village. I doubt if the woman will live; she passed out before we left.'

The moment of truth. We no longer held authority over these people; the Viets were around, cowing them into submission. It would be as much as their lives are worth, little as it is, to help us now. We had not seen the kids near the post for two weeks; I should have thought out the implications of this, but clear thinking is at a premium in this deadly climate.

'You brought nothing back then?' I asked.

'Oh, yes! Chickens and eggs. They wouldn't accept payment so we took them. You've got to have something to relieve the monotony of these dreary FOM.'

Six months and eighteen days on dried rations. Yes, you needed something to relieve the monotony. I stretched out on the boards. Duroc removed his boots and socks and started burning off the leeches from between his toes. They, too, needed a wash.

Why do we fight this war? Whom do we fight? I am a French officer, aged 33, still a Captain and in charge of this miserable little post of fourteen men, an important post they tell me! I have been in this country for four years, living and fighting in the jungles, with only an occasional vacation in Hanoi or Saigon where you drink like a fish until it is time to go back, visiting the sleazy joints to get rid of your spleen on some icy-hearted bar girl who is counting her money or addressing prayers to whatever bountiful god she worships, even while you wrestle with her delicate and delightful body. Is this what we are fighting for – the delights of civilisation?

Within a few months of the end of World War II anti-French slogans began to appear in all the villages. Somebody was promising the people a better life, something to fight for. This is what they read; this is what they heard from agents planted in their villages, or from their headmen. Those who doubted the words were chopped down, their families slaughtered. Fear took hold of the jungles. People became silent.

The fight is strange. There are no objectives, but the enemy is here. Our friends are killed, their houses burned; convoys are shot up, soldiers murdered; mines and bombs explode everywhere, killing men, women and children. The enemy melts away, either into the jungles or into civilian clothes. The people are silent, so we have no intelligence.

There is no uniformed army to defeat and so end the war. The rules have changed. Everybody is a fighter, with or without uniform. Those who do not carry weapons gather information or deliver food and messages, or simply remain silent. When we appear we see no weapons, only smiles, if we are strong enough to earn them.

Although we are tough our ideals prevent us from taking hostages or eliminating whole villages, although we know that they shelter the enemy. The Communists know this and play upon our idealism, and so involve us in the numbers game. With hands tied behind our backs we require enormous numbers to defeat the Viets. But the people at home in France, many Communists themselves, will not provide us with the men we need.

We have no support from people abroad who believe that we are fighting an old-style colonial war; even our own people make collections for the 'heroic resistance' of the Vietnamese people. Only we soldiers in the jungles know, yet we cannot spread the truth because a democratic machine is not geared to make full use of propaganda. But the Vietminh are so geared and are backed by a machine, political and military, carefully built by one of the greatest powers in the world.

These thoughts make our lot hard to bear as we breathe the stifling air in this deep forest. How lonely is the fight! We will fight it anyway, even though our units are organised for warfare in Europe.

We hold the towns, the roadways, the sea lanes and the airways. We appear to hold everything but we hold nothing because the enemy is everywhere. The Viets leave the highways, but we are bound to them by the need for fuel, ammunition, supplies and food. If we leave the road, our vehicles bog down in the swamps. If we go on foot we are lost in the jungles, the mountains and the endless forests, where disease strikes us down in larger numbers than it ever does the Viets. Our strength is insufficient – only 30,000 men – to reconquer the whole country. But over whom is victory to be won? The Communists, the Vietminh, or twenty million civilians?

We keep order during the hours of daylight, for then our planes can fly, our vehicles move and our men search, but by night Indo-China belongs to the Vietminh.

The Viets have turned each village into a political and military entity, with its own Communist cell, its commissar, its own supply system and theatre of operations. Men, women and children carry arms, deliver supplies, bear messages, spread propaganda. We need half a million men, infantry men, specially trained for this type of warfare. But we will not get them.

Our modern weapons may help to capture and hold territory, but they cannot win over people. On the contrary, they repel them. The fighter-bomber deals out death with no discrimination, innocent and wicked alike falling to the hail of cannon-fire and in the fiery furnaces of napalm. The shell, fired from the long-range gun, cannot distinguish between the good people and the bad, nor often can the single bullet fired by a rifleman. Even against the known enemy the use of modern weapons is limited by cloud and rain, by the lack of roads and railways. They are useful for one half of the time over only one-tenth of the terrain. Machines cannot conquer in this type of war, only men.

But we will fight for this post, myself and my fourteen men, even though it is now of less value than the earth and the logs of which it is built. We no longer hold authority even over the people in the village down the trail; nor are we an obstacle to the Viets' operations in the jungles. Yet there are hundreds of posts like this, tying down to useless pieces of ground thousands of French and Vietnamese soldiers who should be in the jungles playing the Viets at their own game. But we will defend it; we have been told to.

Those in Hanoi and Saigon are still fighting in the style of World War II in Europe; the Maginot Line, the *Groupements*

Mobiles tied to the roads by their tanks and vehicles, the aeroplanes that cannot see into the dense forests, the sophisticated and
vulnerable lines of communication, large-scale pincer operations
and sweeps failing for inadequate intelligence or security. Only
up there in the high mountains are we pitting guerillas against
guerillas, but even there a lone corporal or a single sergeant is
attempting to retain the loyalty of the Monomes, the Hres, the
Boutes and the Alakhones and a hundred other tribes without
either proper political support or guidance.

I drag my way around the dug-outs alerting the men. The
attack will come soon, maybe tonight – the Viets always attack
at night – or if not tonight, tomorrow night. The men had heard
it all before; grumbling they go lazily about their tasks.

The sun goes down; the evening chorus assails our ears from
the jungle – a thousand million insects, birds and animals voicing
their separate desires after the silencing heat of the day. We man
our slits, and wait.

At 11 p.m. an early moon descends below the horizon. At
almost the same moment the food cans clank. Human or animal? –
we could not know. A pause while we relax. Then come the
mortar bombs, crashing and thumping upon the roofs, thin
coverings of logs and earth only a few inches above our heads.
We crouch inside. Then the dreaded cry *'Tiên-lên'* comes through
the darkness, telling us that the Vietminh Death Volunteers are
upon us. The machine-guns clatter, sending bright lines of tracer
through the night. Flares shoot up into the sky, lighting the
ground before us as they swing down on their little white para-
chutes. The Viets are blowing great gaps in the wire with explosives crammed into bamboo poles. They come swarming through
and we mow them down. But still they come.

Suddenly a loud explosion in the next-door bunker. The blast
fills our own, bringing with it clouds of dust and cordite fumes.
The atmosphere becomes unbearable. With eyes streaming, bodies
sweating and throats choking for want of clean air we peer out,
shooting in bursts at anything we can see.

I bend down to collect another box of ammunition when a
bazooka shell bursts in, a lucky shot that crashes through the slit
and bursts against the opposite wall. God knows why I was not
hit or deafened by the hideous noise. Duroc and another man
crumple to the ground. I have to get out before our own ammuni-

tion explodes. I stagger to the doorway through the pitch darkness and heave myself on to the parapet, rolling away from the hell beneath me. I lie quite still, gulping in the sweet night air.

There are Viets all round me; I can hear rather than see them swarming over the bunkers, cursing and shouting as they disentangle themselves from the wire. Crawling towards the central bunker I become aware of two others just ahead of me – Viets. I bury my knife into the first man's neck; as the other turns towards me, I smash my fist into his face. He is momentarily stunned. Withdrawing my knife I drive it into the nearest part of his body. I discover that I have skewered him right between the legs; then a desperate tug-of-war as I pull the knife out of his pelvis. To make quite sure I slit his throat.

I look up and listen. There is near silence; only the scuffling of feet as dark shadows flit across my vision, heading in the direction of the jungle. I roll away from the dead men; the Viets will look for them to carry them away. I lie as dead until all is quiet. There is little point in examining the post, but I do so; three bunkers shattered, one empty – maybe my men have evaded capture. In the central bunker no wireless set, only the signalman with a dagger protruding from between his shoulders. As I turn to leave I hear the death rattle in his throat – the death rattle of Post No. 30.

I move cautiously over to the jungle's edge, there to wait for the dawn. When daylight comes maybe a patrol will visit from the neighbouring post, if that has not also been taken out. At 10 a.m. a *Morane* flies over, dips and then returns to look again before hurrying back as the clouds come down over the mountains. I dare not show myself or wave; the Viets will also be at the jungle's edge, maybe two hundred metres away, just opposite, or maybe only a few yards from me. At mid-day I assume that no help will come and creep back deeper into the forest. I turn to make for base; fifty kilometres to go through rain-soaked jungles which are the playgrounds of the Viets, skirting villages which are Viet-dominated, with no arms, only a pair of worn boots on my feet and a knife in my hand. But I make it.

Back at base I discovered that between the 1st and the 17th of October Giap had attacked and destroyed all the French forts along the Chinese border. Fourteen battalions of regular Viet infantry and three artillery battalions had swept them away, despite the intervention of parachute battalions dropped in to reinforce the lost garrisons. At Cao-bang, Dong Khe and Lang Son, and at the posts in between, we had lost 6,000 troops and sufficient weapons and ammunition to equip a whole division of Vietminh.

And yet within a year another line of forts and bunkers was to be brought into being, the 2,200 pill-boxes of the 'de Lattre Line', designed to seal off from the surrounding Communist areas the 7,500 square miles and the eight million inhabitants of the Red River Delta, the great rice bowl of North Vietnam. The line was to lock up more than eighty thousand troops and thousands of automatic weapons, mortars and guns; yet as a seal it had no more effect than a sieve. Within a few months of its construction General Giap had more than 25,000 combatants fighting within the 'de Lattre Line' – regular regiments, regional battalions and *dai-doi Du-Kich* (militia).

But for myself I was finished with static soldiering, finished with any kind of soldiering for one whole year, except that even in hospital in Saigon there was no escaping the sounds of war or the atmosphere of moral decay. God knows what illness I had. I do not believe that it was ever diagnosed, but my own good health drove out whatever disgusting germs might have found their way into me. They could have been any of a thousand varieties which prey on the human body in this terrible climate.

When I started to move about again I was struck by the comparative freedom of life in Cochin compared with the restricted existence of a year before in the Red River Delta. The difference was marginal, a matter of degree, and was due to military successes achieved under France's very best combat commander, General Jean de Lattre de Tassigny, who had been appointed Commander-in-Chief, French Expeditionary Force, Extreme Orient, at the end of 1950.

Certainly he was responsible for the de Lattre Line, a system of fortifications which he designed as a springboard for attack but which, in the long term, proved so costly and ineffective, and which induced in the Army the 'fort' mentality. But in the north he had beaten off all the enemy's attempts to capture the Red River Delta. In these battles General Giap, spurred on by his successes on the Chinese border, made the crucial tactical error of pitting his armies against our masses of flat-trajectory weapons in the flatlands of the Delta. At Vinh Yen, against Haiphong and again on the Day River General Giap and his eighty-one battalions were soundly beaten.

General de Lattre, by new and unorthodox tactics, had also freed Cambodia and Laos from the grip of the Communists, except for a few, small guerilla-held areas.

Down here in Cochin large sweeping and extending operations, often preceded by encirclement of the enemy, met with considerable success so that pacification of many regions became a reality rather than the political pipe-dream of the past.

But on 11 January 1952, after little more than one year in office, General de Lattre de Tassigny died, his heart broken by the death of his only son in this wasteful and endless war. The General's death was not only a personal tragedy to every soldier engaged against the Viets, but was also disastrous to the conduct of affairs. Within weeks of his untimely end the Vietminh had made considerable progress in recovering those areas which they had lost.

At this time I was posted to an infantry outfit stationed thirty kilometres from the capital city. Late one Sunday afternoon, when the sweltering core of heat had left the day, I turned my back on the twin cities of Saigon-Cholon, the seat of French administration, the base for the war and the swill-pit for all that war had brought to the people.

Saigon was the typical French colonial city, with wide boulevards and imposing administrative buildings, tree-lined avenues and villas set in large and lovely gardens. Here European-style restaurants, cabarets and bars were filled to overflowing with officers, NCOs, and soldiers looking for brief moments of respite from the dangers and drudgery of the *padis* and the jungles. Down the boulevards and avenues flowed a never-ending stream of bicycles, taxis, cars and trucks, and the death-dealing *poussepousses*, all hurrying along at breakneck speed. Cheek by jowl with this spacious city lay Cholon, a swarming ant-heap of straw-thatched shanty towns, intersected by pitted roads and tortuous lanes lined with stalls and child-infested shacks. Here was a teeming world of Chinese drug-stores, chop suey booths, bars, brothels and dance halls, opium dives, bazaars and fly-blown market places where everything could be bought and sold – opium, drugs, gold and guns, chewing gum, women, children, military secrets, honour, life itself.

The Sodom and Gomorrah of biblical times, the Chicago of the 1920s, were oases of innocence and tranquillity compared with the Saigon of today. The motivating forces of the ceaseless activity were the war, which poured in an unending stream of commodities for sale and a constant supply of over-paid soldiers for the population to batten upon, and the over-valued piastre which brought fortune to swarms of businessmen, officials, pimps, pretty bar girls and raddled prostitutes. I was glad to leave, even though it was to join a battalion engaged only in piddling forays and pacification in Cochin, rather than in the real war which was being fought out in Tonkin. My military ardour had been somewhat restored by a year of rest, and by the successes of the French army under General de Lattre de Tassigny.

I drove out in the back of a truck along the main Saigon-Cambodia trunk road, a road so narrow and bumpy that a speed of more than fifteen kilometres an hour was out of the question. At each kilometre post (PK) was a watch tower, smothered in barbed-wire and earth-work defences and manned by the local militia, a body of uniformed men whose untidy appearance and unmartial attitude gave me little grounds for confidence.

The surrounding countryside of plantations and *padi*-fields seemed deserted, though here and there I saw groups of crumbling, thatched hovels swarming with naked children, pigs and chickens.

The battalion was stationed near Trang Bang in a camp of dirt and dust and wooden huts, hastily thrown up. On arrival I was given no specific command but was left free to look round and to get to 'know the form'. On my second day I heard that a platoon was leaving on patrol to a village suspected of harbouring the Viets; I asked to go with it. After making it clear that the platoon commander was in charge and that I was not to interfere except in emergency, the Commanding Officer sent me off.

The platoon paraded in combat dress, with ammunition belts and grenades buckled on, personal weapons crooked in the right arm. They looked suitably battle-hardened. We marched for an hour along primitive tracks before reaching the area to be searched, exchanging the inevitable camaraderie as we trudged through the heat of the morning.

As we neared the objective the platoon commander gave the signal to spread out and we then moved forward in formation and in complete silence. Progress through the tangled undergrowth and bamboo thickets was infinitely slow and arduous. Increasing heat and the vicious attacks of millions of red ants, whose bites were red-hot needles jabbing into every exposed part of the body. added to our discomfort. We sweated and struggled for an age until suddenly we broke out into a series of clearings where were built a few scattered *cainhas* (native grass-roofed huts), surrounded by plots of manioc and ground-nuts.

The different groups made straight for the *cainhas* to search and to bring out men for questioning, I myself accompanying the left flank group. First dropping off the Bren section to keep guard, we entered. The first two *cainhas* were empty, but for a few pieces of old and broken furniture and a scattering of cooking pots and water jars. In the third we found a frightened huddle of women and children. The sergeant searched each one, taking away any-thing of value. The last to come was a girl of sixteen or so. The sergeant stretched out his hand and in one swift movement ripped open her jacket and tore down her trousers. Pulling her to him, he started fondling her breasts, stomach and buttocks. I watched for a while and when he was about to throw her on to her back I reckoned that he had gone far enough. I pulled him off. Before she ran out of the hut, screaming and clutching at her torn clothing, he wrenched off her ear-rings. He looked surprised and disappointed.

'A little friendly rape will do no harm,' he said. 'Anyway, they are only *boun-youls* – who the hell cares?'

'No harm in frightening them,' I said, 'but you don't need to go all the way.' We moved on into the next shack.

The platoon commander then ordered the men to set fire to the *cainhas*, and columns of smoke and sparks climbed lazily into the hot and heavy air. The men slowly assembled from various directions bearing chickens and eggs and some other pitiful objects; two men were struggling with a young pig. We divided the loot and marched away.

Another village had been pacified.

The journey back was a hell of heat and toil and fiery red ants. Shortly before reaching the track which led back to camp the soldier on my right fell to the ground with a bellow of pain. I ran over to see what had happened. He had fallen into one of the covered, bamboo-spiked pits which abounded in the area; no animal traps these, but man traps prepared by the Viets and their sympathisers. A bamboo had passed clean through his knee joint. The platoon stopped and took up defensive positions while we extricated him and bound the wound. After six months in hospital the soldier returned to the unit with a limp for life.

Back at base we handed over to a detachment of the *Bande Noire* two men whom we had found in the village. Why they were there, God knows, for the people must have been warned of our coming – they always had warning. The two men were to regret whatever reasoning made them stay, for the *Bande Noire* had their own special and effective methods of interrogation. Their weapons were the rod and the boot, the steel rule tapping an exposed throat, electric shock treatment applied to the genitals. If a man knew anything the *Bande Noire* would get it out of him; they treated a surprising number who knew nothing.

Within half-an-hour of our return the alarm rang. Grabbing cartridge belts and weapons we dashed out on to the dusty parade ground, buttoning up our clothing as we ran. Within three minutes we were away, a small convoy, preceded by a mine-clearing detachment with an armoured car following, then a six-wheeled GMC with an ambulance and a Dodge bringing up the rear. As we crawled and jolted along the pot-holed, dust-laden roadway I found out what had happened.

The small post at Son Cat, a few kilometres away, had been attacked, was in flames and had lost radio contact. At three o'clock in the morning an adjacent post had heard heavy firing but had been unable to send anyone as they were short of numbers. A native auxiliary had escaped from Son Cat to report that the post had been overrun by five hundred Viets who had first infiltrated into the place and set fire to the buildings. The post was manned by two French NCOs and two dozen auxiliaries, all of whom lived there, the NCOs with their *congaies* or native concubines, the auxiliaries with their wives and children.

Fear of ambush and mines cut our speed right down so that we were three hours covering the seven kilometres to Son Cat. The Viets, of course, had gone, so we were able only to make a survey of the attack and the resulting carnage.

It had been a perfect operation and showed the infinite pains which the Vietminh took over both planning and execution. Outside, as throughout the whole of Cochin, they had organised bodies of regional troops, recruited from the local peasantry, who stayed in their home area to conduct local guerilla activity, to spread propaganda and to make life insecure for the forces of law and order. These regional troops supplied incoming regular troops with information about French posts and troop movements; they also supported the regular units in action.

Local agents had carefully studied the layout at Son Cat and the habits of the small garrison and their camp followers. They had then presented a plan to the Chief of the regional battalion who decided to attack when the time was ripe, in concert with a few regulars.

The time he chose was the first night after the arrival of a relief for the NCO in charge. The agents had studied the background of the new man and discovered that he had recently arrived from Africa; this was his first operational assignment in Indo-China. They had also suborned one of the auxiliaries who had a grouse, and he had provided them with any missing details.

The post consisted of a main defence tower with sheds and outhouses around it and a medley of huts which housed the auxiliaries and their families and the coolies who worked on the nearby rubber plantation. The whole was surrounded by a defence system of barbed wire, bamboo stakes and earth-works. The sole entry was by a gate which was closed at sundown.

In the early hours of the morning, a time at which vigilance is at a low ebb, the Viets crept up to the post. The auxiliary opened the gate and the enemy filtered through, quietly disposing of the sentries and taking their places. Others continued to infiltrate the post until the whole was surrounded, both within and without. During this time the NCO visited each one of the sentries but knowing neither his own men nor the Viets he had no cause for scenting danger.

Meanwhile other units were laying ambushes and mines along the routes by which relief columns might arrive. By 3 a.m. everything was in place and no one in the post was aware that an attack impended.

At a given signal the Viets stormed the buildings and within moments had mastered the garrison. Killing the NCOs in the first few seconds, they finished off the few auxiliaries who had any fight left in them after a short bout of vicious hand-to-hand fighting. The enemy then quickly withdrew, taking with them everything of value.

We found the NCOs dead and beheaded, a dozen auxiliaries dead, the remainder wounded. The womenfolk had been scalped or cut open, or both; the children killed. One of the women, her stomach ripped from pelvis to navel, was pregnant; she still lived, and in her arms she held a small child who had been slashed through the neck. There was no sign of weapons or radio; all had been taken.

This then was the pattern of war in Cochin throughout 1952 and 1953. The Viets had been quick to recognise the dangers inherent in our successful pacification of parts of the vast area, and had lost no time in taking counter action. They first took the important step of placing agents in the villages and districts and establishing cells which became centres for counter-pacification, for spreading propaganda and recruiting adherents to the Vietminh cause. Having once gained a firm political foothold they proceeded to the military measures leading to attack and destruction. Within a comparatively short space of time they had succeeded in terrifying the local people to such an extent that pro-French activity among the natives was virtually eliminated.

Throughout the whole of the twenty-two months during which I toured various parts of Cochin with my battalion I saw only one good civilian administrator, a man named Tougeron, who was District Commissioner of a large district in which for a time he was responsible for civil administration and development while we provided the military force. There were others, I know, as good as he, but they were too few in number.

His tasks were manifold, but in general included the settling of agricultural and forestry problems in pacified areas, the supervision of the application of law and order, and the refereeing of the constant clashes between the army and local authorities.

He was a man of integrity, charm and courage. He toured the district incessantly by jeep, with a small escort, frequently shot at, often mined, sometimes ambushed. By dint of his untiring energy and unflagging devotion he had managed to reinstate important farming areas which had for years been abandoned to warfare between the French and the Vietminh, at the same time winning over the sympathy of the people. As a result, he regarded any sortie by the army into areas which he had pacified as an act against the welfare of the people as a whole.

But the army was there to oust the Viet. To enable us to do so we must be allowed to place our soldiers, spies and interrogators, our bullets, bombs and napalm wherever we thought fit. It was accepted practice that we made off with everything moveable or saleable that we found in the course of patrols and operations. Individual raids by local commanders in need of cash were also frequent.

Tougeron managed somehow to curb the more flagrant forays into his pacified areas, but it was a bitter and constant struggle in which the victim was the peasant, pacified and looted by us, imposed upon by the Vietminh, in constant terror of every passing French patrol and of every Viet agent. Each new face meant a demand for subservience, goods and service, or worse, a battle over the peasant's own small-holding.

I knew Tougeron only for a short time, for he left our area of operations in July of 1952. At the end of two years in office he had succeeded in persuading the High Command to issue an order that disciplinary measures would be taken against any soldier who abused property outside official war zones, but this was small reward for so much gallantry and devotion to his people.

But in districts in which there were no such men as Tougeron the battalion commander was at one and the same time political chief, police superintendent, civil administrator and military commander, and yet, like most of us, the average CO was no more than a good professional soldier with a firm belief in the power of the sword and with some skill in wielding it against a uniformed and orthodox enemy.

Toward the end of 1953 the battalion was taken out for a period of rest, but I was not considered a fit subject for further relaxation – I had had my rest in hospital two years ago. Near Saigon, *Groupement Mobile* No. 100 (GM 100) was assembling and I joined one of the infantry units, the 1st Battalion of the Korea Regiment, on the day of the GM's activation – the 15th of November, 1953.

Groupement Mobile 100 was an elite force, every unit composed of skilled and experienced men whose training during the first two weeks of the GM's existence was both well-designed and thorough. An observer might think that two weeks was little enough, but to be drawn out of battle for training was a rarity in Indo-China. The prevailing theory was that the best training was to 'send 'em out to face the Viets'. Ten years of almost continuous fighting have proved to me, if ever proof were needed, that no training value whatsoever accrues to units while face to face with an enemy; rather skills and drills deteriorate for lack of supervision by officers and NCOs entirely taken up with the business of outwitting or fighting off their opponents. Other benefits accrue to soldiers in action – they learn to live rough, to sense and avoid unnecessary danger; their bodies become tough, their reactions quicken – but even these benefits are best absorbed during realistic training; the essential military skills must be, if the soldier is to hunt down and kill his enemy before he himself is killed

The composition of GM 100 was of great interest to me. The hard core of the formation was the Korea Regiment, of two infantry battalions. The soldiers were Frenchmen, except for two companies of Vietnamese recently incorporated. The Regiment included also the famous Commando Bergerol. To this hard core was attached a special task force of the 'Bataillon de Marche' of the 43rd Colonial Infantry, rugged and jungle-wise French and Cambodian troops; the 2nd Group of the 10th Colonial Artillery Regiment and the 3rd Squadron of the 5th Armoured Cavalry. The whole *Groupement* was vehicle-borne and contained 3,498 men in excellent mental and physical state; the majority had recently arrived in the country after several months of re-fitting in peaceful Korea. The men in this outfit were beyond compare, the equipment in first-class condition; the whole made up a magnificent war machine – for any other war but this.

After a dismal and abortive operation in the Saigon River Delta, GM 100 set out on the long drive to the Plateaux Montagnards, the highlands in the centre of Annam.

On the 17th of December we assembled at Buon Ho, a tea plantation hacked out of dense woods, and from there we took up the role of providing a mobile backbone for the defence of the whole huge area, a defence which had been depleted by the withdrawal of units for Dien Bien Phu.

To the north of us lay countryside of a grandeur and beauty which defies description, yet a territory full of foreboding for us men of the inaptly-named *Groupement Mobile*. The whole was a grand massif of rolling, jungle-clad hills, criss-crossed by miserable rutted and pitted dirt roads connecting the 'towns' and garrisons at Chéo Réo, Pleiku, Kontum, Kon Brai, De Kieng, Ankhé, and Plei Rinh. These roads, dust-laden in the dry weather,

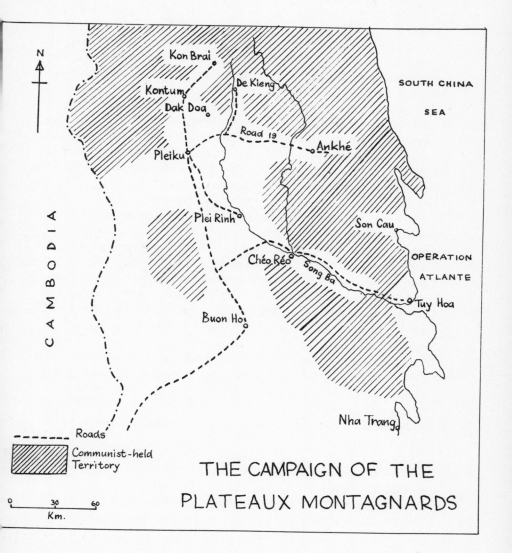

N

SOUTH CHINA

SEA

Kon Brai

De Kieng

Kontum

Dak Doa

Road 19

Ankhé

Pleiku

C A M B O D I A

Plei Rinh

Son Cau

Chéo Réo

Song Ba

OPERATION

ATLANTE

Tuy Hoa

Buon Ho

Nha Trang

- - - Roads

Communist-held
Territory

0   30   60

Km.

THE CAMPAIGN OF THE
PLATEAUX MONTAGNARDS

degenerating into quagmires of mud after rain, were lined by the tall trees and the dense undergrowth of the jungle, or by elephant grass three metres high. It was into this country that we of the GM 100 were to be launched, with our splendid vehicles, our heavy guns and tanks and our excellent communications against an enemy of fast-moving foot soldiers of the 108th and 803rd Regiments of the Vietminh army, whose men were locally re-cruited and knew every ridge and valley, every trail and pathway of the great Plateaux.

The first call came on New Year's Day of 1954. Chéo Réo needed reinforcing; the Viets were threatening. The long convoy lumbered down the seventy kilometres of wretched secondary road. Assembled in Chéo Réo by the 4th of January, we were then ordered to re-open Road 7 down to the south Annam coast. Slowly and methodically, in suffocating heat, we de-mined and re-bridged that eighty-five kilometres of so-called highway. In the midst of this operation we were joined by a Commando composed of mountain tribesmen under the command of a Captain Vitasse; they became our eyes and ears in the jungle. By the 28th of January we had linked up at Tuy Hoa with forces landed on the coast (Opération Atlante), but on the same day the 1st Korea were ordered to Pleiku, the 2nd to Kontum – journeys of 160 and 220 kilometres respectively, each few kilometres a separate operational move, with mine detectors and clearing squads in front, with infantry marching on either flank to guard against ambush, with vehicles limited to the speed of their protective detachments.

We had now been on the march continuously for thirty days and nights and the effects were beginning to show, although we had as yet made only one brief contact with the enemy. On this day Colonel Barrou, Commander of the *Groupement* wrote in his war diary:

'The most delicate problem remains that of the protection of the artillery and of the means of command and communication, since the largest number of infantrymen must be left free to search out the enemy and fight him.

'The very means of support and co-ordination which make the strength of the GM also create some enormous obligations in a mountainous area where roads are rare and of poor quality.'

During the next five months we were to learn the full implications of this masterly under-statement.

February 1st – A sudden move for the whole GM to join the 2nd Korea at Kontum. There the Viets threatened, and a state of near-panic existed among the civilian population. On this day a platoon of 2nd Korea was wiped out in a well-laid road ambush – 35 men lost.

February 2nd – All our posts to the north-west of Kontum were submerged by wave upon wave of enemy troops – 50 men lost.

February 5th – Dak Doa, twenty-eight kilometres to the south-east of Kontum, was attacked. All bridges to the north of Kontum were blown up. The Viets were squeezing us in.

February 7th – We evacuated Kontum and made a hasty withdrawal to Pleiku, where we grimly dug in.

February 11th–12th – Dak Doa attacked again and finally swamped by a full battalion of Viets – 80 men lost.

February 23rd – One platoon of my own battalion saved from destruction in ambush only by tanks of the 5th Armoured and strafing from fighter-bombers – 19 men lost.

March 1st – After one month of continuous probing and destructive attacks the Viets disappeared. Where have they gone? How do we find them? Airborne Group No. 3, three battalions strong, were dropped in to seal them off. The rain had turned roads into rivers of mud which our vehicles soon churned into bottomless quagmires. For fourteen days we pushed forward in desperation towards the paratroops. The enemy must be somewhere; but no, the feeling of emptiness, the horrors of the *guerre des grandes vides* – the war of the vast empty spaces – continued.

March 14th – The operation was called off and the paratroops withdrawn to be dropped into Dien Bien Phu.

March 15th – We had now been operating continuously for seventy-three days and nights, but today the monthly convoy must be escorted to Ankhé, 100 kilometres to the east. No doubt the Viets would be there before us. Lightly equipped, with no need to open roads nor to move upon them, like will-o'-the-wisps they could move faster than any motorised force opposed to them.

March 22nd – The bivouac of the *Groupement Mobile* at Plei Rinh was heavily attacked by night. The main features of this onslaught were the violence of the enemy's mortar fire, the devastating effect of the Communist SKZ recoil-less cannon, the overwhelming numbers of the black-clad Viets who charged upon the sleeping garrison, and the desperate courage of the defenders who by dawn had driven the enemy back. With the daylight fighter-bombers appeared to reconnoitre, but found nothing. There was no follow-up.

The Viets suffered, but so did we – 36 killed, 177 wounded, 8 missing. The strength of my own battalion had now shrunk, since leaving Saigon, from 834 to 532 men, while casualties in the other infantry units of the GM had been no less severe. There were no reinforcements in sight.

April 1st – No sooner had we evacuated the wounded from Plei Rinh, and replaced the ammunition and fuel expended, than there came a *cri de coeur* from Ankhé. A protecting detachment at the Deo Mang Pass had been overrun the day before, and the Viets now threatened the main garrison. The slow and fatiguing business of moving the convoy of trucks, guns and tanks over 140 kilometres of roadway started again. I myself was with one of the four companies responsible for opening the road as far east as Post Kilometre 11 (PK 11). There we met up with an infantry force operating out of Ankhé. The convoy passed through and then began the well tried and oft-repeated telescoping process, as one company passed through another on the way back to base, a precise and tedious drill.

As we reached PK 15, safe at last so we thought, all hell broke loose. With no warning whatsoever rifle and machine-gun fire streamed into the company's vehicles. With the road blocked by the leading truck and the column brought to a standstill, the shrill cry of '*Tiên-lên*' rent the air and Viet regulars of the 108th Battalion charged in from the thickets. We fought them off, God knows how, until the tanks of the 4th Tank Platoon rumbled on to the scene with all guns firing. The Viets turned on the tanks like maddened animals, crawling all over them until beaten off by desperate hand-to-hand fighting. Then, looking up, we saw the *Mouchard,* the tiny observation plane, and behind it the B-26s diving down from the blue sky in the light of the setting sun. For once the spitting cannon and the black canisters of napalm found a target, for the Viets had broken off the fight too late. The small clearing filled with sheets of flame surmounted by a pall of black smoke. On the heavy air hung the smell of frying flesh and the stench of burning gasolene.

By dark the wounded and dead had been loaded up and we began again the tiresome business of retreat. We were not to be left alone, for the Viets came out of the darkness, swarming again over the tanks, to be shaken off only by the 'cleansing' process whereby each tank lit up the one before and sprayed it with machine-gun fire. It was not until midnight that we staggered into the defensive perimeter. Our saviours, the tank crews, had spent from nine to twelve hours shut into steel hulls with an interior temperature of 110° Fahrenheit. We lost 90 men that day. My own company was now reduced to a total strength of only 67.

April 9th – But our mission still stood – the defence of Ankhé – and there we finally assembled. There followed a long period of respite during which morale, as so often in a defensive position not under imminent attack, began to drop off. On the 8th of May a Communist's loud-hailer told us: 'Soldiers of Mobile Group 100! Your friends in Dien Bien Phu have not been able to resist the victorious onslaught of the Vietnam People's Army. You are much weaker than Dien Bien Phu! You will die, Frenchmen, and so will your Vietnamese running dogs.'

The French soldiers bared their teeth in what had become the symbol for a smile; they swore and expressed a hope, now that Dien Bien Phu no longer needed them, that reinforcements might come our way, but they were to hope in vain. The Vietnamese troops, and we had many in Ankhé, including the 520th Tieu-Doan Kinh-Quan (TDKQ), nominally a commando battalion, saw the news in a different light. Deserters multiplied; self-inflicted wounds, sickness, slackness, all the symptoms of a lowering morale became apparent. By the time the Communists were ready for a final push into the Plateaux Montagnards we knew that we could no longer hold Ankhe. The French High Command had reached the same conclusion.

June 24th 1954 – The military evacuation of Ankhé began at 03.00 hours. Prior to this a large airlift of C-47s and Bristols had taken out 1,000 civilians and all essential equipment. We watched the air evacuation with interest. We ourselves, of course, could not leave by air; there was the small matter of the tanks, the guns and the vehicles.

The Vietminh also watched the airlift, and drew their own conclusions. We, the *Groupement Mobile*, would eventually follow and there was only one route which we could take – Road 19;

intelligence reports told us that the whole of the 803rd Regiment was converging upon it.

Plans were made to hasten the withdrawal, but additional speed on jungle-enclosed mountain roads entails less security en route. Our first objective was PK 22, where another Mobile Group, No. 42, and the 1st Airborne Group held a defensive perimeter into which we were to withdraw.

The *Bataillon de Marche* of the 43rd Colonials led the way, followed by the 2nd Korea; then the interminable convoy of vehicles formed by the engineers, the armour, the headquarters, the artillery and the hospital. My own battalion, 1st Korea, drew up the rear. All the infantry were dismounted, screening the vehicles. Behind us struggled three hundred civilians who had been unable to find places on the airlift; if the Viets were in any doubt these people would be able to keep them in touch with our movements. But, in any case, there was no hope of secrecy.

For our own intelligence we had placed Vitasse's Bahnar tribesmen in the jungles to the north; any Vietnamese troops approaching the road would inevitably have to cross their path. Overhead were the *Moranes*, the *Mouchards* and the fighter-bombers.

We moved ponderously across the semi-open plain surrounding Ankhé. On reaching Kilometre 6 the rear-guard received fire from automatic weapons. We fanned out and adopted the well-practised drill of leap-frogging, but as suddenly as they had attacked so the enemy faded away. After only half an hour the march continued.

Two kilometres, and one and a half hours later, the *flechettes*, poisoned darts from the tribesmen's blow-pipes, flew into the column. We retaliated with a wild burst of firing, hurling grenades at every clump of bushes. Once again the enemy flitted away in silence.

The convoy reached PK 11, whence the road was lined by thick jungle and overhung by high cliffs, providing an ideal ambush site at every twist and turn. For this different terrain Colonel Barrou reorganised the column into four self-contained elements, each with its own infantry and artillery. We resumed the march, a *Mouchard* overhead, fighter-bombers on call at Nha Trang. Only 11 kilometres to go; maybe this time we would make it.

But almost immediately we received important information; from Captain Vitasse – 'Important Vietnam elements three kilometres north of Road 19'; from the *Mouchard* – 'A Viet column at Kon-Barr, eight kilometres north of PK 11'; again from the *Mouchard* – 'Rocks are placed across the road at Kilometre 15, but otherwise the area seems clear.' The 105 mm guns, still at PK 11, and B-26s called up from Nha Trang, bombarded the enemy column at Kon-Barr.

What now happened at Kilometre 15 is pieced together from various official reports and the stories of survivors. Although intimately involved myself, I saw and heard little beyond what was passing on my own small part of the battle-field. When fighting in close country one sees only the piece of ground to left and right and immediately in front. One is concerned only with one's own command, with the bullets, shells and bombs which are falling upon one's own men. The hectic business of locating the enemy and conducting the fight allows little time for fear, and none at all for thought beyond one's immediate task. The eyes and ears form vague impressions of what might be happening to 43rd Colonial or 2nd Korea, to the tanks or the guns, but such impressions are immediately set aside in the interest of concentrating one's whole being upon the task in hand.

Near Kilometre 15 the road emerged on to a small plain, covered with elephant grass over two metres high. As the 43rd came on to the plain, a slight wind stirred. There was no one in sight, no beasts, no birds. Some instinct told the men that the place looked much too calm. The leading company disappeared into the high grass, cutting across an arc made by the road. Once inside they could use only their ears to discover what was going on around them, and their ears told them that they were not alone on the plain. The constant clacking of the grass, as they themselves stood still to listen, told them that the Viets were in there with them.

The information came too late. At precisely 14.20 hours the Viets turned their machine-guns upon the 43rd Colonials, and the men knew that *Groupement Mobile* No. 100 was caught again. They went into action as the book told them, forcing their way forward through the dense grass, looking for the enemy and killing him, hand-to-hand, where they found him.

At the same moment the engineers and headquarters convoys reached the ambush site, to be smothered in clouds of dust and shattered metal as salvo upon salvo of artillery and mortar fire rained down. Tanks, half-tracks, engineers' vehicles loaded with explosives, and the radio trucks, were in a moment reduced to blazing wrecks. The wireless sets, the only means of control for Colonel Barrou, were put out of action.

The headquarters company of 2nd Korea, supported by shells from the last surviving M-8, counter-attacked an enemy-held crest, but only to be wiped out in the hail of small-arms fire. At the same time our Vietnamese truck drivers and the whole of the 520th TDKQ rushed pell-mell from the battlefield and disappeared.

It was now 15.00 hours and at this moment my own group arrived at the hideous scene, 2nd Korea preceding us by a few minutes. The 2nd charged straight up the road, opening a path through the wrecked and still-burning vehicles to join up with the 43rd Colonial at the head of the column. Meanwhile we of the rear-guard took up a defensive position.

At 15.30 our guns came into action, firing at point-blank range against waves of Viet infantry. The B-26s swept over, but the battle was by now so closely joined that the deadly cannon found their mark impartially among both friend and foe. The battle froze while they swooped and swerved overhead, the men of both sides clamped to the ground within metres of each other and feeling equal hatred for the destructive machines overhead and for the men who flew them. I heard a calm voice on my radio: 'This goes to show you again – the whole aerial warfare business is not quite perfected . . .'

Dusk fell; pressure from the Viet infantry slackened, but the mortar bombs still whined and burst among us. By this time there were more than one hundred wounded in the improvised dressing station and if they were not soon moved they would die. But it was clear that we could not hold our position throughout the night, nor, without a single truck able to move along the road, could we carry them out. The agonising decision was taken to abandon them where they lay, sheltered behind over-turned trucks and an ambulance. With drugs and food, with volunteer medical men to attend to them, we left them in charge of Major Varme-Janville. They were later to die in the hospital at Ankhé, or in the course of the long death march to the prison camps.

The remnants of GM 100 collected themselves for the breakout. We stumbled through the twilight, not to the west towards PK 22, but due south into the pitch darkness of the jungle. Only in the shelter of these mighty trees and dense thickets had we any chance of escaping the clutches of our enemies. We walked into jungle so thick as to make the progress of a large body of troops impossible. In groups of platoon size we hacked a way through the wall of undergrowth and darkness, parting the bushes with bayonet, knife and bare hands, every step a nightmare of fear and extreme exertion.

Hundreds of men were lost during the night. By dawn the enemy were all around us, and we were compelled to beat off no fewer than four separate attacks. As the Viets disappeared for the last time the trees thinned and we saw again the blue sky and felt the breeze upon our sunken cheeks.

The survivors literally fell into the arms of the paratroopers of the 1st Airborne Group.

Groupement Mobile No. 100, the best fighting formation in Indo-China, had ceased to exist at Kilometre 15. Where had we failed? How was it that we had allowed the Viets to involve us in a war of attrition, ourselves always on the defensive while the enemy clawed at our resources, month by month, until finally destroying us in a trap of steel? Those fine vehicles, those guns, those tanks, those road-bound monsters which had in a space of six months travelled 3,500 kilometres in areas of intensive combat, were our undoing. The effect which they had on the mental attitude of our leaders, myself among them, the limitations which they imposed upon our tactics, the insatiable demands which they made upon our means of supply, played into the hands of an enemy no less brave or skilful than ourselves.

In the dense jungles and vast forests of South-East Asia, and in the high mountains, there is no substitute for the combat infantryman, for the fit, highly-skilled and well-trained jungle fighter who will go deep into the forests and there out-stay his enemy.

Machines cannot win this war, whether in the wild terrain where people are few, or in the fertile plains where the multitudes sweat and strain – only men.

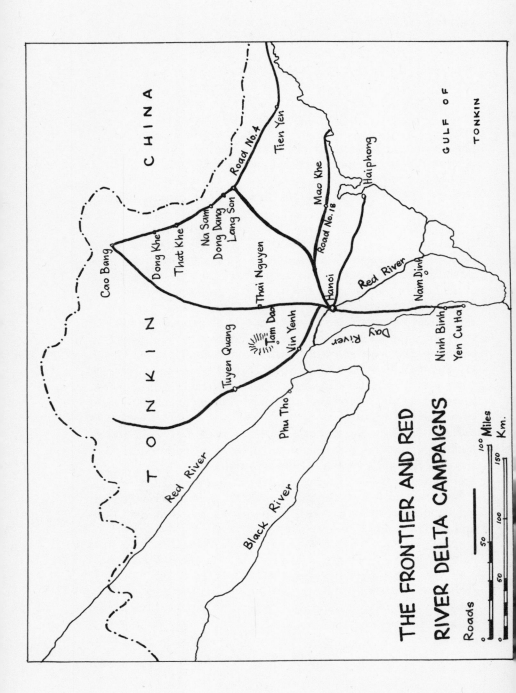

THE FRONTIER AND RED
RIVER DELTA CAMPAIGNS

Roads

0   50   100 Miles

0   50   100   150 Km.

Indo-China — 1950 to 1954 —

PART II

'The People's army is the instrument of the (Communist) Party and of the revolutionary State for the accomplishment, in the armed form, of the tasks of the revolution.'

VO NGUYEN GIAP, Vietminh Commander-in-Chief, in *People's War – People's Army*. Hanoi, 1961.

Uncle Ho gave the order to all the army men and civilian workers in the Cao Bang and Lang Son provinces: 'In this campaign you must win at any cost,' he said.

It was some few weeks before September 1950, the month for the opening of the great offensive to liberate the region bordering on China. All the people were determined to go through the test of blood and fire to carry to victory the men of the Cao Bac Lang army, for the people had suffered for many years from the exactions of the colonialist enemy. No labour would be too much for them, no hardship beyond enduring if it resulted in the liquidation of the French Imperialists. There were slogans everywhere, written in charcoal, lime and red earth, on the trees, on the rocks, in the rice fields, on the stones on the mountain-sides and on the walls of the caves. 'We must win', said the slogans.

Political cadres visited every hamlet and village, and even the lonely huts deep in the forest, to organise the people for war – the entire population. They forged into one united force the men and women of the Red Man minority from the mountain tops; those of the tribes of the Nung and Tay, the men tall and lively, the women in tight-sleeved gowns; the Man Lai girls who wore full skirts and grey low-necked jumpers revealing the lines of their beautiful breasts; and the people of the Kinh majority from the Delta. The mountains and forests were disturbed by the ceaseless activity of a teeming crowd, all working for victory. It was as though the giant trees themselves were on the march towards the enemy posts at Cao Bang, Dong Khe, Na Sam and Dong Dang, and towards the famous highway No. 4 – the 'Bloody Road' of the French colonialists.

How much do the French know of our preparations? They must guess that we are making plans for battle, but the night and the forests cover much of our revolutionary effort. How can they assess the full grandeur and strength of our north-eastern people? At night the lorries are loaded with timber by tired men who have only sufficient strength to pile one log upon another before dropping to the ground in a deep sleep as soon as the task is completed. At night thousands of men and women break stones for the roads leading over the mountains and through the jungles – new roads for the avenging army. At night, and in the fogs of the morning a gigantic labour force, unimaginable in concept yet carefully organised and systematically controlled, prepares the way for the army men by making new roads, building bridges and carrying forward all kinds of supply. The enemy might know something of our work in the day-time for then their planes can see into the open areas, but how can they visualise our labour at night?

The time for reconnaissance has come. The battalion commander and the commissar met the group leaders in an observation post only one kilometre away from Dong Khe.

'We can see nothing,' said an observer, 'but a post of the *puppet troops* is over there, nine hundred metres away'. We could hear the *puppet troops* singing.

The intelligence officer said, 'The town is over there facing us'.

We waited. A fresh breeze fanned our faces and the fog began to thin out, the wind tearing it to pieces which eddied up and down the green valleys. Suddenly the town was laid bare. We could see the post of the *puppet troops*, the main defences which were our target for the attack and the living quarters – white-walled, red-roofed houses among green trees with the Road No. 4 winding into and among the buildings.

The intelligence officer, who had left the town only the evening before after living for three days within the perimeter, gave us details of the layout and the defences, while the battalion commander looked carefully through field glasses. We walked down the hill to a house built on poles where we washed our bodies and clothes and grilled maize. The commander said, 'All is quiet in Dong Khe; the enemy will now be reporting that there is no action in the area!'

The time for meetings has come. We gathered together to make plans for defence against aircraft and parachute troops, to discuss mobile warfare which was new to most of the army men who had only recently been converted from guerilla into regular units, and to plan a campaign of unremitting attacks. At the meetings, also, wrong ideas were adjusted and the personal troubles of the army men were looked into – matters concerning promotion, health, family problems and love affairs. We discussed such affairs as the attitude of certain officers, the allocation of loot won in previous campaigns, the stripping down of equipment so as to make it light enough to carry over the difficult terrain, the replacement of leaders who might be wounded or killed, and the handling of recruits. Everyone spoke his mind and all came to know each other. Councils were elected to promote a democratic way of life in the army.

New units and new equipment provided both trouble and much pride among the army men:

'There are many cannons now,' said one, 'and they are big ones. There are also plenty of "sweets" to feed to the French'.

'The infantry too have artillery,' said another. 'The SKZ recoil-less guns are as powerful as elephants, and how accurate is the fire that we can pour into the enemy from our mortars!'

'Beware!' said the commissar. 'Our brothers in China are generous and have given freely of their armament. We need plenty of weapons to defeat the enemy, but what is more important for us revolutionary men? Why, our morale of course!'

We hung our heads and tried to think it out.

Outside a grotto a group of artillery men studied the range-finder, a new instrument, sleekly black with shining lenses.

'Level,' cried one.

'Bring the barrel a bit higher . . . now a bit lower,' ordered the battery commander.

'Very complicated,' said one of the gunners. 'It is accurate enough to aim through the barrel. We will study the instrument when the battle is over'.

'The range-finder is more accurate,' said the battery commander. 'We must learn now how best to use it.'

The artillery men grumbled and scratched their heads, examining the instrument in their clumsy hands. The artillery donkeys grazed nearby, the donkey boys squatting beside them with folded arms. The animals had brought great joy to the men and had become a part of their fighting life; they were fat and sleek and ready for the fray.

The fifteenth day of the seventh lunar month – the rice plants were in ear, some even laden with grain, but still no order to start the operations. The fighting men were becoming impatient. Why is it that the High Command does not give the order to advance? With such equipment there is no reason not to fight; with such supplies no number of enemy can prevent victory; yet the rice bags in the grotto were emptied and filled again.

News spread that the Commander-in-Chief, Comrade General Giap, was at the front talking to men and units. Then we heard that President Ho Chi Minh himself was to visit the front. Unbelievable. It would take him eight days to reach us here in the Cao Bang province, travelling on foot, carrying his own mat and rice ration just like us.[1]

'Uncle Ho is coming,' we said. 'We will surely fight.'

The enemy reinforced Cao Bang, Dong Khe and That Khe, the *Tabors* arriving in great numbers; so much the better for us. There will be more enemy to kill and it is better that they should not withdraw; but when will the fighting start?

'Think it out for yourselves,' said one who pretended to be a military expert. 'We will not start before the rains come, you'll see. The Vietminh soldiers are masters of attack on rainy days and the Frenchman's aeroplanes cannot fly among the clouds.'

Another regiment came and yet another and another, all fully equipped. Trung Khanh[2] and Quang Uyen[2] became crowded with people and beasts. Night after night an endless stream of lorries ran to and fro. The air raids increased in intensity.

A letter came from President Ho:

'Dear fighters,
    In the National Defence Army, Local army organisations, Guerilla and militia units, we are resolved to win this battle.

---

[1] The Vietminh Resistance base, located between the provinces of Tuyen Quang and Thai Nguyen, was 300 kilometres distant from Cao Bang.

[2] Two districts in Cao Bang province.

In order to win it, fighters at the front must have a determined will, and be very brave. Whoever achieves great exploits will be rewarded by the government.

Beloved fighters, units must emulate with units, regions must emulate with regions. With the emulation movement for killing the enemy and scoring exploits the Frontier Campaign will certainly be victorious.

Let all the fighters advance! Triumph is awaiting you. I am longing to reward you.

With wishes of affection and determination to win,

HO CHI MINH'

The political commissar gathered all the men of the unit in front of the grotto:

'Have you read Uncle Ho's letter, comrades?' he asked.

'Yes, we have.'

'Are you determined to kill the enemy?'

'Yes, we are.'

'Then good luck to you all, comrades! You must bear in mind that Uncle Ho closely follows the battle'.

The army, pledged to kill the enemy, began its great move. As we marched forward the French bombers came overhead, shedding their loads of thunder and lightning. All was confusion, with army men and civilians running everywhere for cover, but the jungles held us in their sweet embrace until the flying monsters could be seen and heard no more. The units collected on the road again and advanced in the setting sun, walking under smoke- and dust-laden branches with their scorched and faded leaves curling in death. The road was marked by tall poles shining white in the lowering evening light; beside the poles stood the carriers, drawing aside to make way for the soldiers. Women looked out from isolated houses built on bamboo poles, recalling the happy days when our men were stationed among them.

'Brothers, kill the enemy for me!' cried one.

Then the landscape faded out of sight and pitch darkness fell upon us; but the forward movement continued.

The next day we eagerly awaited those of the people who carried our supplies. Are there women among them? Are they beautiful? Are they healthy? They soon arrived, men and girls all of the Tay minority, the men fine and upstanding, the girls shy.

'It must be hard for you to follow the army,' we said. The men said nothing; the girls blushed and giggled.

'Why do you laugh?' I asked.

'We do not speak the Kinh[1] language,' answered one, a young beauty.

'Not to speak the Kinh language is not to love one's country,' I said.

'Not to speak the Thô language is not to love one's country,' said she.

We laughed and came to know these strangers. We were one big family of civilian workers and army men.

The morning of the 14th of September. Today we were ordered to start on the long and immensely difficult march to the forming-up position for the attack. The road was crammed with people – infantrymen, engineers, artillery men, cooks, wireless operators, scouts, political commissars and cadres, staff men. It seemed that the very jungles and mountains themselves were moving along with the soldiers and civilian workers.

'The infantrymen must lead,' cried an officer.

'Hurry up! Hurry up, you heroes!'

'Get the donkeys out of the way, then.'

'Look at that one, old and one-eyed; he must be due for retirement soon.'

The infantrymen broke into a run, although laden down with bags of rice, rifles, water gourds, ropes, hand grenades, knapsacks, baskets on carrying poles and all the paraphernalia of battle. Our hats were camouflaged with twigs and branches from the jungle.

Still running we came to a long row of huts camouflaged with banana leaves, with fireplaces where the fires had died out. The rinds of pumpkin and papaw were scattered on the ground. A blue streamer hung from a hut bearing in white the slogan: 'Determined to win President Ho's Prize'. We looked up and read the slogan and ran on yet faster. Sticks clacked, leaves rustled.

We jogged forward with the civilian workers amongst us, Tay girls carrying heavy cases of cartridges, young Man with silver rings round their necks and their bodies sweating. Some sang while they marched.

A man at my shoulder said, 'Here is Hoa'.

'Who is she?' I asked.

[1] The Kinh language is the national language of Indo-China.

'She carries the wounded; she has been in battle before.' I looked at Hoa. She was very beautiful and had long black lustrous hair. I said, 'You will come with me, please'. I wanted her.

'I will come with you,' she said. 'I will feel safer beside a great warrior of the people.'

I marched on, chin held high, with Hoa beside me; the load seemed lighter and the way less steep.

Another streamer hung on a tree at the side of the trail, with the slogan: 'Keep the discipline of the battle-field'. A soldier stubbed his toe against a stone and uttered a low groan, then moved on muttering, 'Keep the discipline of the battle-field'.

We were now exhausted with the running, but a murmur went up and down the line: 'Why don't you keep going? That's an order from the company commander'.

At night-fall the building of huts started. The kitchen had been erected; smoke arose and a smell of roasting meat. Two soldiers were sitting by the fire boiling rice gruel. In a cave nearby, where boxes of cartridges were stacked, some girls lay sleeping on a stone slab like fairies in a wood. A bright star shone through slits in the leaves above. Everybody was waiting for a meal.

When we had eaten I took Hoa into the forest to rest; she was warm and soft to the touch. We woke at midnight. In the cave the political instructor was holding a meeting.

'For the first time in the history of the Vietnamese resistance,' he said, 'we fight by day. This is a great honour. We will attack Dong Khe at 6.30 in the morning on the 16th. Thirty hours are left for us to complete our preparations. Keep this information secret. See to it that we camouflage to the utmost. Bring only one change of clothing and a blanket to the front. Be kind to those civilian workers who take part in the battle'.

Preparations continued busily for the rest of the night. At daybreak a scout left with a guide to look out the way we should take. They returned in the evening and told us that the way was long and arduous.

What a night for the march to the front! No light, no moon, no stars. The march was terribly slow, interrupted, confused. At every step there was an obstacle, a fallen tree, a dense thicket, a steep and slippery slope. The rain fell, thundering on the leafy canopy above our heads. We met two guerillas returning from the front line.

'Is it far from here?' we asked.

'Yes, it is'.

'Is the road difficult?'

'There are too many slopes'.

Out of the jungle came a group of civilian workers, groping for a way through the mud, panting, crying. A carrier lost his balance, slipped and held up the whole column.

'Come on! Keep going! Keep going!' said the officers. 'We should have been in position by 10 o'clock, yet it is already midnight'.

We strained forward, tapping on the ground in front with sticks as the jungle grew thicker and the night darker. The guide had attached a piece of luminous bark to his hat; we watched this bright spot threading its way up and down among a multitude of silhouettes. We were stupefied with fatigue.

The guide drew us on until we came near to the place. Here the road was less hard and we saw sleeping on the road-side in the tiger grass several men wrapped in blankets, like heaps of snow in the mist. A figure sprang out of the darkness and told us that this was our position.

'Our unit arrives only two hours before the operation,' said the company commander. 'All other units seem to be ready in their positions'.

At daybreak the objective was clearly seen – Dong Khe, white and red spots across the valley. The artillery men were not yet in position, but the Operational Command ordered that the attack should go forward. Then suddenly we heard a shout, 'No. 1 gun – fire!' and with the shout the battle began. The enemy artillery answered; planes rent the sky, circling, strafing. Almost at once dead and wounded strewed the ground and the nurses threaded a cautious way up and down the bloody slopes and among the broken limbs.

On either side of Dong Khe the shock troops waited for the order to attack, hidden under the leafy trees. Camouflaged soldiers lay alone or in groups, most of them in newly-dug holes with their legs sticking out over the top. Hanging on the trees were hand grenades, rifles, water bottles, towels and satchels. Some slept, some wrote in their diaries, some picked guavas by the bank of a stream.

The company commander, Captain Nam, returned from reconnaissance. 'The army has annihilated the Phia Khoa post after three assaults,' he said. 'We must fight hard this afternoon. We have first to destroy the outer posts and then attack the centre. The task is heavy but it is a fitting task for us shock troops. I pledge that I am determined to command you until its fulfilment.

'The enemy has dropped supplies by parachute on Dong Khe. They may even launch a counter-attack, but we will meet any attack that may come'.

'Good!' shouted the men.

A group of women workers arrived. 'Welcome to the stretcher bearers,' we cried.

'Where is Hoa?' asked one of the soldiers.

'She is there, hiding behind Thao'.

At 5.30 p.m. on the 16th of September we attacked Dong Khe. We assaulted with fury, rushing in upon the post. Machine guns and cannons mowed down many of our number, but the remainder dashed up the slopes and occupied the northern outpost. Many died, but always there were more to replace them and the acts of heroism were too many to tell. The battle raged throughout the night but by morning the main post still remained in the hands of the French so that we were compelled to withdraw. What confusion there was, with all the officers in doubt as to what to do! The outpost became a shambles.

'Let us stay where we are'.

'The attack was intermittent'.

'It was not continuous'.

'The fire was not concentrated'.

'We have not the knowledge or we would not have attacked as we did, but we will not make the same mistakes again'.

The planes strafed all day long while we waited for night-fall.

The orders came for the second attack and our guns began to fire even while the King Cobra aircraft were circling overhead. Cannons, recoil-less guns, mortars and machine-guns of all sizes crackled and boomed. Flames shot up into the sky. The shock troops advanced, pouring forward in an irresistible mass. The enemy withdrew to the main post, but not before more than half of our company had been killed. The remainder were exhausted.

The Operational Command threw in reserves while we rested briefly. Then we poured more troops into the school, more into the bus station and finally penetrated the main post.

'We will take Dong Khe tonight at any cost,' we cried.

Captain Nam dashed ahead of his company to hurl a grenade into the loophole of a concrete post. Machine-guns sprayed bullets into his body while inflammable bottles broke around him, bursting into flame. Captain Nam staggered. 'Liberate Don Khe!' he cried. 'Long live President Ho!'

'Nam is dead,' we wailed, but the deputy commander shouted, '*Tiên-lên! Tiên-lên!*' and suddenly Dong Khe was ours. What a marvellous victory for the liberation army! All faces beamed with delight. I wondered where Hoa was for I had not seen her since the battle started; but she would find me, I knew, once her duties were done.

By the 17th of October we had annihilated the enemy throughout the whole length of Road No. 4. News of the victories passed among the people in swelling waves while talk of the liberation of new lands and towns spread like a sea of happiness.

Political cadres hurried from village to village and from town to town arranging committees to clean up the area and organise the people for further struggle, while the army pursued the enemy into the mountainous regions and helped the guerilla units to eliminate them piecemeal.

With my company I travelled from one end of the highway to the other. Cao Bang was flooded by the rains; a vehicle depot and workshops had been established at Nam Nang; at Dong Khe there was not a tree nor a building left standing; That Khe nestled in a valley of golden ripe *padi*; the posts of Khau Trich and Chap Gaio stood on their mountain tops. The road came alive with vehicles threading a way through the debris of battle. A convoy of traders' horses entered Binh Gia; the valley of Bac Son was red with the patriotism of the heroes of the past. Now the children ran here and there on their way to school. Vu Le was a burnt forest, the trees black columns, yet the houses were in order and crowded with refugees.

Everywhere people were returning to their homes. The frontier district knew peace again, molested only by the enemy's aircraft strafing towns and roads; but the roaring of the planes was no more than a cry of distress from a beaten foe. Every town and village erected its own triumphal arch; in every place mottoes hung on gaily-coloured streamers:

'Welcome to the carriers at the front!'

'Spare rice for the army!'

'To serve the front is to kill the enemy!'

The army were to be given only a short respite for on the 10th of January we moved down to the plains of the Red River Delta, a massive force of eighty-one battalions. A new motto was on the lips of every man: 'President Ho in Hanoi for the Têt.'[1] Little did we know that we were advancing into the mouth of hell.

I shall never forget the terrible exertions and the hopeless fears and frustrations of those six months of slaughter between January and June of 1951. No matter which way we turned in those open, flat plains we could not avoid the deadly fire from the enemy's machine-guns, rifles, tanks, mortars and artillery. As we debouched from the hills towards Vinh Yen, to hurl ourselves bodily against the defences, the enemy at first gave way. Down into the plains we followed, employing no tactics other than attack by human waves, there to be met by a wall of flame descending from the sky. The heavens were blackened by clouds of aeroplanes diving upon us, releasing canister after black canister of the deadly, terrifying napalm. As the first one fell upon us, I heard one man cry, 'Is this the atom bomb?'

'No,' answered another; 'it is napalm'.

For four days we attacked, withdrew and attacked again among the low hills surrounding Vinh Yen, but no weight of numbers nor all the acts of heroism would carry us through that wall of fire and steel, nor could we prevail against the courage and obstinacy of the colonialist defenders. We fell back into the protection of the woods of Tam Dao, but even as we fled rocket and cannon fire thundered about our ears. Then the enemy's guns and mortars found us, cutting us down by the hundred, to be followed by their fast-approaching infantry. The enemy showed no mercy and if we stood to defend ourselves we died; only by fleeing could we live to fight again.

In the offensive against Vinh Yen the People's Army lost 6,000 men killed and 500 captured and failed in the bid for Hanoi. We gave small return for the magnificent efforts of the civilian workers who worked two *million* man days and brought to the battle area five *thousand* tons of rice, ammunition and weapons.

But we were not to be brought down by one single defeat. Inspired by our great Commander-in-Chief, we moved down for

[1] Têt is the Chinese lunar New Year, generally falling in mid-February.

an attack on Mao Khe, which was to be but a preliminary to an onward triumphant march to the port of Haiphong.

At two o'clock on the morning of March the 28th, screaming the famous war cry of the People's Army, we rushed in upon the defences which were held by paratroopers, *puppet soldiers* of the *Thô* partisans, and a number of *Tabors* and armoured cavalry. Again we employed no tactics. Wave upon wave of heroic army men shattered the bunkers and defences, but the colonialists shelled and mortared even as we closed with their own men, while an endless stream of bullets and canisters issued from the tanks and tore into our ranks. At dawn, those of us who lived – and there were few – dragged our weary limbs out of the village and into the shelter of the wooded hillocks beyond. There the planes caught us in retreat, and we were again burnt up in the awful fire.

Yet a third time the Operational Command committed us to battle in the open plains, ordering us to attack the French positions on the Day River from the south and west. After an unimaginably difficult march we were thrown in upon the defences around Ninh Binh where the battle raged to and fro for days and nights on end. The colonialists brought tanks and massed artillery against us and, finally, their armoured boats and massive air strikes smashed the civilian workers who were ferrying supplies across the river in a brave but vulnerable little fleet of junks and *sampans*. Without these supplies we could fight no more, even though we still possessed the hearts of tigers. Once more, on the 18th of June, we withdrew into the shelter of the jungles.

The political instructor called together those who had survived and we discussed the battles:

'We need anti-aircraft guns,' said one. 'We cannot live beneath the fire from the sky'.

'We need more artillery, more bazookas,' said another, 'to kill the armoured tanks'.

'We need time,' I volunteered, 'to learn the tactics of the open plains. Too many die when we rush in where angels fear to tread'.

'Equipment is more important,' cried another. 'The colonialists are fighting with guns and tanks and radios provided by the American Imperialists. We must have better'.

'But what is more important than all these things?' asked the political instructor.

'The morale of the army men,' we cried.

At one such meeting the men of the unit decided that I should become an officer. I was filled with pride that they should show such confidence in me and I determined to fight even harder for the freedom we all lived and longed for. When I told Hoa, who had survived with me the dangers of the previous six months, and who now carried a rifle instead of a medical satchel, her eyes shone with gladness.

'You have indeed found favour with the people,' she said. 'They will send your name to Uncle Ho as a great hero among the army men. Second-Lieutenant Thao – that is good!'

When I became an officer I was at once instructed to take the long journey into the South. I was glad in my mind to leave behind the regular unit campaigns in the Red River Delta and to return again to true guerilla fighting which I understood so well. But I was sad in my heart to leave behind my good friends, although many lay buried in heroes' graves in the rice-fields and on the mountains in the North.

I asked if I might take Hoa with me since we were now regarded as man and wife (there would be time to marry when victory was won) and imagine my unbounded joy when the Operational Command issued us both with the black uniform of the guerillas and sent us together on our way.

With a small group of fellow army men, and a political cadre of six young men who had recently completed a training course in China, we took the long, winding trails leading through Laos and Cambodia, all the time marching south and guided at each stage by local men and women.[1]

After six weeks of steady travelling through the beautiful countryside we came out into the spacious plains of Cochin. I made for the district of Trang Bang, thirty kilometres from Saigon, a district which I knew well for I was born in a small village nearby and moved to the North only at the beginning of the freedom war.

The Operational Command had received news that the colonialists had succeeded in 'pacifying' much of Cochin. Their soldiers had conducted large 'sweeping' operations and had driven the guerillas out of the rice-growing areas back into the jungles. Their intelligence spies and traitors had betrayed many Party cells and

---

[1] The route taken by Thao and Hoa and their companions is today known as the 'Ho Chi Minh Trail', by which the North Vietnamese feed men and supplies from their recruiting centres and factories in the North to the 'fronts' in South Vietnam.

those heroic men and women were now suffering in detention camps. Their civilian administrators had moved in behind the armies – some, indeed, had never left their posts – and were restoring the colonial regime in 'settled' areas, and the guerillas were unable to operate in these areas for fear of betrayal by the puppet councils set up by the French. Uncle Ho in his wisdom had decided to send out the cadres to reorganise the regions of Cochin and to stir the people to action against the hated enemy.

Hoa and I, and one of the cadre men, ended our long journey in the *dinh*, the community house, at the large village of Tay Ninh in the Cao Dai territory, a place conveniently situated on the edge of a forest of abandoned rubber plantations. There we removed our guerilla uniforms and donned peasant clothes. The following day we moved into the house of one of the village men who, with his wife, was languishing in a French gaol. We soon became part of the friendly community and within a few days the people had accepted us as brothers and sister in the struggle for freedom.

When we had been in Tay Ninh for three days we called a meeting at which the local Party men told us about the situation in the district. The picture was black indeed. A Legionnaire battalion was stationed in Trang Bang, with a detachment of the dreaded *Bande Noire*, and were making frequent excursions into the villages, each time indulging in rapine and plunder before carrying off victims to the interrogation centres. The Party men pointed out that such behaviour antagonised the people towards the colonialists and enabled the liberation front to maintain its organisation, but the alertness and the constant patrolling of the soldiers made it impossible to operate against them. The village cells were in being but could work only in the utmost secrecy. The people of the regional battalions lived and worked in their homes but their weapons were hidden away and they were unable to fight openly against the enemy troops. It was difficult to collect the rice tax for the guerillas who were forced to remain concealed in the jungles without enough food.

The Trang Bang district was bounded on the east by the Saigon river and to the east of this river, around the Rubber Empire plantation, the situation was even worse. There the colonialist administration had set to work, first arresting all Party members and then 'settling' the region. The people went about their day-to-day business in peace, kowtowing to the colonialists, knowing that French army troops would not be allowed to enter the area to inflict hardships upon them, while the guerillas would not make war across the land for fear of betrayal by a people who had come to reject them. On the edge of this region, near the Saigon river itself, lay the important village of S . . . S . . . where the headman was a puppet of the colonialists and set a bad example to the people by collaborating with the enemy.

The meeting continued far into the night as the local Party men and the cadre man who had come with us discussed what was best to do. I said little, for this was not so much an army affair as a matter for the political organisation, and Hoa squatted nearby quietly listening. Her presence was a great comfort to me and during our few moments of rest, when we were alone together, her gentle and generous love overwhelmed me, pushing into the background the cares of war.

The two Party men, first looking to me and Hoa for agreement, decided that we must quickly stage an attack on an enemy post near Trang Bang in order to encourage the people, and must also make an example of the village of S . . . S . . . in order to remind the people of their duty to the liberation front.

For several weeks Hoa and I gathered together the guerillas in the jungles. They were a hungry and dispirited lot and the cadre man spent much time giving them news of our glorious victories on the northern front, and telling them about the new activities which we had planned for Cochin. We arranged a line of supply through Tay Ninh so that rice became a part of each day's diet instead of the jungle-grown fruits and berries on which they had previously existed. It took time to restore the morale of the guerillas and it was not until early in 1952 that the local Party men sent a courier into the jungles, instructing us to take action against S . . . S . . ., and later to attack the enemy post at Son Cat.

We set out gaily for the river's edge. It was good to be going into action again after the many weeks of waiting. As we marched we sang the famous Hey-ho song of the guerillas, beating time with our hands:
'Grenades and rifles
To kill the French,
Hello, brothers,
Hello!
Cudgels, grenades,

Grenades, rifles,
Cudgels, grenades, rifles
To kill the French.
Hello, brothers'.[1]

At night-fall we took to the water – four men to each of ten dug-out canoes – and paddled slowly south, in complete silence. Before daybreak we were hidden in the jungle on the river bank and there we stayed until darkness fell once again to cover our movements. At dawn on the following day we came to within three kilometres of S . . . S . . . Here, on the right bank of the river were the rice-fields of the Trang Bang district and, on the left bank, an abandoned rubber plantation. We concealed ourselves in the thick undergrowth, once again to await the coming of darkness. It was dangerous for us to move in the day time, but at night, even in these 'pacified' areas, the land belonged to the guerillas.

At 8 a.m. we heard the sound of an engine in the sky and looking up saw a small reconnaissance aeroplane which the French call the *Morane*. It circled round for a few minutes, then flew away to the south. Looking out across the river we saw the young people of a nearby village racing across the fields towards the river bank. They waded and swam over to disappear into the shelter of the same rubber plantation in which we were hiding. We gave them no sign of our presence for we knew that they had been warned that the Legionnaires were approaching on one of those forays which the French call *ratissages* – mop-ups.

It was not long before a swirling cloud of dust foretold the approach of vehicles. The soldiers climbed out of the trucks and spread out round the same village from which the young people had so recently escaped. They advanced steadily across the *padis* until one final rush carried them into the village itself. No shot was fired, no word spoken; the whole operation was completed in silence. Then we heard a babel of voices carried across on the gentle breeze as the French parleyed with the old men and women and children. We heard also an occasional shriek as a group of rough-looking men entered the *cainhas*. After thoroughly searching every household the Legionnaires left, taking with them ducks and chickens and any small trinket which took their fancy.

[1] This simple ditty is attributed to Van Chung and was popular during the revolution.

Even as we relaxed from the tension of watching we again heard aeroplanes in the sky, two 'box-cars' flown by pilots of the American Imperialists. Somewhere out of our range of vision there was an army post where supplies were to be dropped. We saw in the distance the huge white and yellow flowers blossom out and descend gently to the ground, and even as we watched the 'box-cars' appeared suddenly over our heads as they swung away to return to base. Filled with excitement, mad after the weeks of frustration, the guerillas fired up at the slowly-moving planes. This was madness, but no orders from myself, nor from the cadre man stopped the shooting until the planes were small grey specks in the blue sky.

We had achieved nothing by the shooting and had only revealed our hiding place, and our worst fears were realised when three bolts of gleaming metal shot across the heavens. But instead of turning upon us, the fighter-bombers dived straight down on to the village of S . . . S . . . We saw the black canisters drop out of their bellies, heard the whoosh-whoosh of the napalm bursting on the ground, then saw the black smoke rising. But the fighter-bombers were not yet finished; they returned, spitting flame and shot from machine-guns and cannons. We could imagine the terror in the village as the people ran here and there for shelter, while flames consumed their houses and bullets ripped into their fleeing bodies.

'The colonialists have done our work for us,' said the cadre man.

'No need to go in there,' said a guerilla.

'At dark we will go,' said the cadre man. 'They need our help and we must in any case make an example of the headman and his woman'.

'Is there to be no end to the slaughter?' I asked. 'I have lived among strife and bloodshed for five years now'.

'That is bad talk for a guerilla fighter,' answered the cadre man. 'We must march ahead under the Party's banner until final victory is won'.

I felt humbled and turned to Hoa for comfort. I determined to carry out better the tasks that lay ahead.

We walked into S . . . S . . . at dusk and the horror that met our eyes and nostrils was beyond description. The *cainhas* and many larger buildings were piles of ashes. Corpses of men, women and children lay everywhere, contorted in the agony of their fiery death. Some who had been wounded were crawling towards the *dinh,* which had somehow escaped the onslaught, moaning and crying out at each painful movement. On the warm night air hung the stench of blood and frying flesh.

The cadre man called us to order and we set about clearing up the horrid mess. As if they had known of our coming the survivors crept warily back to their broken homes. The cadre man collected them together.

'Look what your protectors, the colonialists, have done!' he said . . . My attention wandered and I could not take my mind off the gruesome task that lay ahead. I heard him again as he finished his harangue. '. . . There are two traitors of the people among you who have collaborated with the enemy and brought you nothing but misery. These two are your enemies and must be punished'.

He pointed at the headman and the woman who cowered beside him. 'Take them away,' he ordered. 'As for the rest of you, the men come with me; the women stay here'.

We dragged them out to a nearby copse of trees and tied them up with arms and legs outstretched, first tearing off their clothes. The village men assembled to watch the punishment in the light of a bonfire which we had made. One guerilla fighter stood at the side of the headman, another at the side of his woman, each handling a sharp knife. The cadre man explained to the people once again why it was necessary to punish collaborators. At an order the knives cut into the quivering flesh. The man screamed as a strip of skin was torn off his body from shoulder to waist; the woman cried out as the knife dug into her belly. The skinning continued until both were stripped clean from shoulder to waist level.

'We will leave them there,' said the cadre man. The men of the village who had watched in silence stumbled back to the *dinh* to find the broken bodies of their loved ones. The work of clearing up went on until daybreak.

At dawn we threw the two corpses into the river, together with the millions of ants which seethed over their bare flesh. Then the guerillas departed, leaving the cadre man to complete the organisation of the people. It was now the turn of Son Cat.

A week later the guerillas came to the meeting place, on a dark and moonless night, to find that all was ready. Our agents had spied out every detail of the French post which was held by puppet troops with European officers. The regional battalion commander had decided upon the moment for attack. A puppet soldier opened the gate to the guerillas and by 3 a.m. all was in readiness. The attack was swift and ruthless. We killed all the French and *puppet troops* in the first few minutes of the fight, and when their women-folk rushed upon us, begging for mercy, we hacked them down and ripped open their bellies as a sign that there was to be no mercy for those who lived with traitors. Within the hour all was done and the guerillas were racing for the river bank, laden down with weapons and ammunition carried from the post, and, more important, a precious radio set.

We spent the remainder of the night putting as great a distance as possible between ourselves and Son Cat. By dawn on the following day we were back in the safety of the jungles, flushed with triumph.

'It is good to be back in action again', said one.

'We have struck two mighty blows for the liberation', said another.

'We must learn to use this radio,' said a third.

'The most important thing is the guerillas' morale', said I, looking at Hoa and welcoming her agreement. 'A short time ago we were in low spirits; now we are happy. You will see how the situation down here changes as we march ahead under the Party's banner.'

Oh! What changes we wrought during the ensuing two years as we ranged over the plains and jungles of Cochin. We revived the determination of the people and re-organised them to carry on the war against the colonialists. As our efforts bore fruit the French army and the *puppet troops* discovered that they were unable to operate by day without their every plan and move first being made known by the people to the guerilla forces. By night the enemy were brought to a standstill, for in the darkness the land belonged to the Vietminh.

In the space of time our liberated areas grew larger and stronger and were freed from invasion by the enemy. More and more regions fell into our hands until the control of the crack-brained government in Saigon became control in name only, even though they retained possession of the large towns and, at immense cost in the blood of their soldiers, of the main lines of communication.

But I myself was not destined to see the culmination of our plans for Cochin. In the summer of 1953 the Operational Command, guided by the wisdom of Uncle Ho and Comrade General Giap, decided to mobilise a major force of the Vietminh People's Army for an assault on Dien Bien Phu. With the faithful Hoa, who loved me as deeply as I loved her and who had survived all the dangers and hardships of the southern campaign, I made the long journey back to the northern sector.

The 'Road to Victory' ran through the wild mountains for four hundred kilometres from the depots of of Phu Tho to the battlefield of Dien Bien Phu. The people, answering the call of the Party's Central Committee – 'All for the front, all for victory' – gave of their manpower and wealth, devoting millions of man-hours and untold labours to the construction of the great highway. Although under constant attack from enemy aircraft, and subjected to every hardship by the vagaries of the weather, our people toiled by night and day to carry supplies to the army men fighting heroically against the colonialists' last stronghold in our country. So many were they, and so constantly in movement, that it seemed as though the very forests themselves were moving along the trail, bearing the needs of our freedom fighters.

To the flanks of the 'Road to Victory' lay the high reaches of the uplands and there, in the deep forests, the enemy had established guerilla units of puppet tribesmen led by Europeans of the group which the French called the *Groupement de Commandos Mixtes Aéroportés*.[1] The Operational Command deployed a force amounting to twenty battalions in strength to protect the road and our civilian workers from the assaults of these traitors, and it fell to my lot to join their company.

Rain and mud, mud and rain as we advanced into clouds of mist. Deep squelching holes appeared in the trail where a herd of elephants had gone before us. It was still raining when we crossed the river, swollen by the downpour. *Lianas* were thrown across with hooks to catch in the trees on the other side. Then we had to swim, clutching at the *lianas* which tore the skin from our hands, and fighting against the rushing water. So we dragged ourselves over, sometimes floating, sometimes disappearing under the

---

[1] The *Groupement de Commandos Mixtes Aéroportés* (GCMA), whose name was changed in December 1953 to *Groupement Mixte d'Intervention* (GMI), is the equivalent of the 'Special Air Service' (SAS) in the British Army and the 'Special Forces' (SF) in the American Army. The Groupement's role was to recruit native guerilla forces to operate permanently in enemy-held territory.

swirling river. Our equipment was soaked, but every guerilla fighter reached the other side with his gun firmly clasped in his arms.

We began to climb to the heights of the plateau, clambering round the side of the ravine, still in pouring rain. We had been on the march for seven exhausting days, for seven cold and sleepless nights. Our spirits were held up only by the news of the heroic armies' successful assaults at Dien Bien Phu, of which details were passed along the jungle trails by word of mouth from man to man, from woman to woman. 'All for the front, all for victory!' Yet there was a limit to human endurance and I wondered when the men and women in my patrol would reach that limit. There were two days of fast marching before we reached our objective.

We came to a beaten track on the hillside, quite wide but enclosed by thickets. And there came the ambush, just where it was most likely to succeed. The first bomb fell five metres ahead of me, the second some distance behind, both exploding at the same time. The explosion flung Hoa into my arms. Pushing her aside, I shouted my orders and the guerillas yelled even louder, charging into the thickets. I brought the machine-gun into action, using a corpse for cover. Bullets crackled all around and I hoped that my men would not shoot each other.

One of the enemy saw me and called out, 'Surrender, Vietminh!' I shot him down, making his head burst like a pumpkin. After a little while I saw shadowy figures running away into the misty rain. The firing died down. The action has lasted for no more than five minutes.

I knew what was waiting for me behind; Hoa was wounded, but I had to see to my men. We counted our dead and those of the enemy. It had been an equal battle, but whoever lost or won, it still meant death for some.

Hoa lay against the thicket with her stomach ripped open by a grenade splinter; dark blood was oozing from the wound. I had a stretcher made with two bamboo poles and a blanket, but before her brothers put the damp blanket round her, I took Hoa into my arms and put my cheek, damp with mist and rain, against hers. Although she could not hear, for she was now dead, I murmured into her ear: 'Hoa, darling, sweet lover and companion, even the moment of triumph is the hour of darkness for us. But you are already in the light and joy of the eternal land where there is no more hunting, no more killing, no more guerilla warfare'. What is guerilla warfare? Simply, it is the death of Hoa.

As we marched off into the mist I thought I could hear far away in the west the booming of artillery fire, sounding as the last defiant cries of the doomed garrison of Dien Bien Phu.

Chapter 11

Epitaph for Indo-China. Kenya, Cyprus and Cuba. Introduction to Algeria

'It doesn't take a majority to make a rebellion; it takes only a few determined leaders and a sound cause.'

H. L. MENCKEN: *Prejudices.*

EPITAPH FOR INDO-CHINA

Anyone reading the mass of literature which has been written about the campaign in Indo-China must be tempted to arrive at the conclusion that the French made all the mistakes while the Vietminh knew all the answers.

Certainly over a period of almost eight years the French suffered a series of military defeats which finally undermined their position in the key Red River Delta to such an extent that they were forced to come to the conference table at Geneva and, on July 20th, 1954, to conclude a cease-fire which ceded to the Vietminh the whole of Tonkin and that part of Annam north of the 17th parallel. But during those eight years of suffering and slaughter both contestants made many errors in military tactics and in regard to their dealings with the population.

The Vietminh fell far short of having things all their own way. The fact that the people of the South even today, thirteen years after the end of the war in Indo-China, are fighting against Communist infiltrators from the North clearly demonstrates that the Vietminh failed to gain the allegiance of the Annamese and Cochins. On the various battlefields the Vietminh lost enormous numbers of men and women fighters, but these they were able to replace with new recruits whom they could train, from 1949 onwards, in the sanctuary provided by China, and whom they were able to equip with war material provided by Mao Tse-tung's government.

The French, on the other hand, in spite of a number of psychological errors, managed to retain the loyalty of large numbers of the people, particularly in the South, until towards the end when the population came to appreciate the inevitability of a military defeat for the French. The fundamental cause underlying all the difficulties encountered by the French in Indo-China lay in the fact that the French nation, itself in the throes of recovery from the political and economic consequences of years of Nazi occupation, were unwilling to pour into Indo-China the enormous quantities of men, money and material required to ensure outright victory, or even sufficient to enable the French commanders to conduct operations on equal terms with the Vietminh.

The political consequences of the campaign should be viewed in the light of the hard fact that in 1945, after the defeat of the Japanese, Ho Chi Minh and his Vietminh established full administrative control over the whole of Tonkin, Annam and Cochin, an area today known as Vietnam. Had the Vietminh been allowed to consolidate their position, there is little doubt that Laos and Cambodia must have fallen to Communist pressure, a situation which would have given the Communists dominion over the whole of the Indo-Chinese peninsula. A glance at the atlas will show what further gains might then have accrued to Communism in South-East Asia.

Since World War II a number of revolutionary guerilla actions have arisen outside Asia, some under the aegis of international Communism, others purely nationalist in character.

KENYA – 1952 – 1955

In Kenya there was open rebellion between the years 1952 and 1955. Although fostered underground by its leaders for many years before they showed their hand, the *Mau Mau* movement from the outset had very little chance of success. The cause of independence from the European thieves who had stolen their land, which the rebels presented to the people, was embraced by only one of the tribes of Kenya, the Kikuyu, a tribe of one and a half million people which lived in a native land unit on the forested mountains of the Aberdares, to a large extent surrounded by neighbouring tribes, the Embu and Meru, who showed only a lukewarm attitude towards the rebellion. The *Mau Mau* leaders' sole assets were excellent guerilla terrain and an apparent shortage of numbers in the government's administrative and security services, but they failed fully to capitalise even on these advantages and the rebellion was conducted in such crude fashion as to have little hope of success against resolute and sophisticated opponents.

Throughout the year 1952 the *Mau Mau* leaders actuated intimidation and murder in the Kikuyu land unit, directed against government officials and Christians, making it increasingly clear that they meant business. As a result of these activities a state of emergency was declared in Kenya in October of that year and the police, informed by a good intelligence service, promptly incarcerated the majority of the rebel leaders.

The government then established a command structure based on the 'Three Service' committee system. A war cabinet was formed which had as its members the Governor, the Deputy Governor, the Commander-in-Chief and the Minister without Portfolio. At provincial and district level emergency committees were organised to plan the anti-guerilla war, each committee consisting of the senior civilian administrative officer as chairman and senior police and army officers as members. The police and army officers were, however, responsible to their own immediate superiors for the execution of plans.

At no time during the emergency in Kenya was martial law, declared, the security forces at all times operating within the law, which was adjusted to suit the military situation by the passage of various emergency regulations. In this situation the legal status of the security forces had to be very clearly laid down and made known to every member from the Commander-in-Chief to the policeman on the beat and the private soldier. Their status was simplified by defining certain areas throughout Kenya into three categories: 'prohibited areas', which were 'out of bounds' to all law-abiding citizens and where the security forces enjoyed full freedom for developing military operations; 'special areas' where the security forces had the right to challenge anybody and to fire if they did not halt; and the remaining areas where the security forces had only the same powers in preventing crime as policemen in normal times.

The government also set up a counter-guerilla movement in

the form of a Home Guard, recruited from resident Europeans and loyal members of the Kikuyu tribe. The Home Guard eventually spread throughout the land units of the Kikuyu and the neighbouring tribes, and when later it became necessary for security reasons to collect the scattered population into safe villages, they were concentrated on the posts already established by this force. The African, accustomed to living with his family in his own hut on his own land, bitterly opposed this compulsory movement into villages, but he eventually came to accept its lasting advantages as the administration developed facilities such as schools, churches, medical centres and sports grounds which he had never known before.

In April 1953, only nine months after the start of the rebellion, the Commander-in-Chief, General Sir George Erskine, was able to take the military offensive. He selected as his first objective the rebels' strongest point, the very heart of Kikuyu-land. He selected this most difficult area because he was confident in his own military strength and because his war cabinet had agreed on the vital necessity of firmly establishing the Home Guard in the area. Full-scale military operations followed in the Kikuyu land unit between June 1953 and March 1954 which succeeded in considerably reducing the rebels' influence. Elsewhere the Commander-in-Chief reduced numbers of troops to a minimum while the strength of the police force was building up.

In April 1954, General Erskine switched his attention to the capital city of Nairobi where the *Mau Mau* had obtained a firm foothold. In two months an operation code-named 'Anvil' cleared the city of all Kikuyu who could not show a real and useful reason for being there, and completely disrupted the central direction of the *Mau Mau* movement, a shock from which the rebels never recovered.

The authorities in Kenya were now placed in a somewhat difficult situation by their own successes. The operations to date had done much to re-establish political and administrative control in the areas concerned, but the government were not yet able to hand over to the police and Home Guard complete responsibility for security and so release troops for further mobile operations in the sparsely inhabited forest areas where the *Mau Mau* still held sway. For a period of seven months, therefore, the army concentrated on training the Home Guard and assisting the police in controlling the native land units until these two organisations were ready to accept full responsibility for security.

During this period the *Mau Mau* bands were not left undisturbed in their hiding places in the forests. They were kept on the move and under constant strain by bombing and cannon fire from slow-flying aircraft of the Royal Air Force – Harvards and Lincoln bombers. These particular aircraft proved most suitable for the task, their slow rate of flight combined with various bombing aids giving them a capability of discrimination in target selection and extreme accuracy in attack both by day and night and in all weathers. It was, however, difficult to determine the effect of these air strikes; the authorities could only assess results from such indirect signs as an increase in surrenders, a drop in the rebels' morale and prisoners' reports.

At the end of 1954 the army were once again turned loose in the forests and in four months of continuous fighting dealt the guerilla bands a series of heavy blows, inflicting severe casualties which the *Mau Mau* could not replace. The tactics pursued by the army required special training and equipment and high-class junior leadership. The tactics were in effect guerilla tactics, the fighting unit being a patrol of six or seven men, normally aided by white hunters, native trackers or dogs. The soldiers were lightly equipped yet stayed on patrol for many days, their administration being provided for by special rations, air drops, bases established deep in the forests, by porters, pack animals and by many other expedients.

By May 1955, the *Mau Mau* rebellion had been mastered. That it survived for so long as two and a half years was mainly due to the time taken to recruit and train new men into the administrative and security services in Kenya in order to produce the strength required to meet an emergency situation, and by the magnitude and type of terrain in which the campaign was conducted. To find, surround and eliminate a guerilla band in the forests on the Aberdare mountains would tax the skill, patience and endurance of the finest warriors. That such operations were successfully achieved, not once but many times, is a tribute to the qualities of the civilians, policemen and soldiers involved, and particularly to those of the junior leaders at section/squad and platoon level.

CYPRUS – 1955 TO 1959

In the Mediterranean island of Cyprus an organisation calling itself EOKA (*Ethniki Organosis Kyprion Agoniston*) took up arms under the leadership of the Archbishop of Cyprus, Makarios, and the Greek Colonel Grivas, against the British-controlled government in the island. They adopted a cause which made an immediate appeal to two-thirds of the people of Cyprus – self-determination and union with Greece (*Enosis*).

Cyprus is a most unlikely place for a successful guerilla campaign. A small island of only 3,572 square miles, consisting mainly of open plain, it has no inaccessible terrain at all, although the Troodos mountains in the south-west provide a modicum of cover for guerilla bands. There are five towns, all quite small and by no means over-populated and the communications throughout the island are good.

Two-thirds of the population of 510,000, the Greek Cypriots, were a volatile and emotional people who, after centuries of domination by foreign powers shunned responsibility in public affairs, were poor organisers and technicians and preferred to do nothing until told. Lovable, hospitable and generous to a fault, these people were by no means ill-disposed towards the British overlords whom they were expected to fight. The remaining third of the population were Turkish Cypriots who had in the past lived in amity with their Greek Cypriot compatriots, but rather than espousing the cause of EOKA vigorously opposed it, seeing in it a threat to their own rights on the island.

The Greek Colonel, George Grivas, appointed to take military command of the rebellion, stepped into this unpromising arena on 9 November 1954, when he landed secretly on the coast near Paphos. For five months he built up, trained and equipped a small force of terrorists, no more than one hundred strong, and made preparations for insurrection and sabotage. Throughout this time the under-manned intelligence services of the government were unable to gather more than an inkling of what was afoot and could not provide sufficient proof of clandestine activity to enable the administration to take stern measures.

On 1 April 1955, EOKA struck. There followed two years of violence and crime of every kind. Initially EOKA selected their targets at random intending only to make a noise in order to draw attention to their case. After a few weeks, with this mission successfully accomplished, they turned their weapons against the police force and 'traitors', this latter term embracing all those who helped the government, in whatever capacity. EOKA's weapons, in common with other revolutionary forces resorting to terrorism, were riot and arson, the bullet, the bomb and knife, and they quickly succeeded in winning over the active support of the Greek Cypriots by means of terror combined with intense propaganda directed upon the island by radio broadcasts from Greece.

It was not until two years later that the security forces, distracted by having to mount a large-scale operation into Suez from Cyprus, brought the militant arm of EOKA to heel. By March 1957, Colonel Grivas' armed guerillas had nearly all been captured or killed, his courier system was in disarray and many of his more active sympathisers in detention. This favourable state of affairs had been brought about only by an enormous disparity in numbers. The armed men of EOKA at no time numbered more than 1,000, while the security forces at their peak numbered 30,000, the majority of these regular sailors, soldiers and airmen. The need for such an overwhelming superiority was occasioned by the nature of the topography and economy of Cyprus which made it impossible for the security forces to separate the guerillas from the people who supported them.

The defeat of EOKA's military arm (the top leaders were still free) did not at once provide an answer to the problems which beset the island. An uneasy armistice was agreed to in March to give the politicians an opportunity of hammering out a solution, but there were many interests to be considered other than those of the people of the island. The two great NATO partners, Greece and Turkey, were vitally interested in the future of Cyprus and took up apparently irreconcilable attitudes, while over the negotiations hung the threat of international Communism.

As the political discussions dragged on, EOKA recouped their organisation and strength under cover of the armistice and struck again in the late summer, but were again brought to heel within a few months. Even so, it was not until March 1959 that the problems of the island were temporarily solved when Archbishop Makarios was returned from exile to become the chief Greek Cypriot representative in the new government. In December of that year he was elected President of Cyprus.

The armed guerillas of EOKA had succeeded by terrorism in drawing the attention of the world to the Cyprus problem and by so doing had helped to achieve one half of the aim to which they aspired – self-determination for the people of Cyprus. Mao Tse-tung claims that political power comes out of the barrel of a gun. There is, however, one unfortunate legacy resulting from the methods adopted by EOKA in that, during those four years of struggle, the Greek Cypriots incurred the suspicion and hatred of their Turkish Cypriot compatriots, leaving an uneasy political situation on the island which even today is a special concern of the United Nations Organisation.

CUBA – 1956 TO 1959

In 1956, at the other side of the world, Fidel Castro secretly landed in Cuba with a small band of followers, intending to overthrow the Batista regime which then governed the country and substitute for it a Soviet Republic. He was, however, betrayed to government forces and narrowly escaped with his life. He retired into the Sierra Maestra mountains whence he began a relentless guerilla campaign. The gradual degeneration of Cuba into a police state under the authoritarian rule of Batista brought many people over to his cause and by December 1958, he felt strong enough to stage a full-scale attack. In a lightning guerilla campaign he brought down the Batista regime and in February 1959, became Prime Minister.

The guerilla war in Cuba was notable for the marked lack of military skills or offensive spirit in the soldiers of either side.

The *Fidelistas*, never more than 15,000 strong and only half this number in uniform, were completely lacking in the basic military arts or in any experience of fighting as a co-ordinated force. Their tactics, based on excellent intelligence provided by the villagers, were confined to road ambushes which were seldom carried to close quarters; to patrols whose sole object was to fire at some isolated target far removed from the main communication arteries; to cutting off the town and village *cuartels* (fortified barracks) by destroying the roads leading into them; to 'assaulting' the *cuartels* by rifle and machine-gun fire only; and to rapid withdrawals in the face of superior force. The armament, personal equipment and logistics of the *rebeldes* were extremely primitive.

They depended upon their enemy and a few adventurous smugglers for every item of war material; for food and clothing they relied upon the villagers.

The *Batistianos*, although well-equipped, suffered from a near-paralysis of the will to fight at all. They answered the guerillas' tactics by fleeing from ambush sites as fast and as far as available transport would carry them; by huddling inside their *cuartels* waiting for the next inaccurate air drop; by occasional 'sweeps' in search of the *Fidelistas* which generally resulted only in the flight of a number of innocent civilians to join the *rebeldes* and the destruction or confiscation of their property. Batista's soldiers were supported by B-26 bombers which by their presence in the skies succeeded in terrorising the rural population, but served no useful military purpose other than that of providing improbable targets for Castro's riflemen.

This short campaign was noted for its incredibly high rate of ammunition expenditure and its abnormally low number of casualties. It was enough for Fidel Castro that he had the people on his side and was opposed by a weak and inefficient regime which had virtually worked its way out of office before the guerilla war started. Castro had only to stir the people to action.

The danger of Fidel Castro's triumph and subsequent rule in Cuba lies in the fact that he is a self-avowed Communist, intent on spreading the socialist revolutionary spirit throughout South America. His mouthpiece on the subject of guerilla warfare is Doctor 'Che' Guevara whose writings are worthy of study, particularly in South America.[1]

ALGERIA

In addition to these guerilla wars in Kenya, Cyprus and Cuba a number of minor guerilla actions have taken place in other parts of the world since 1945. They were minor only in relation to the numbers of people involved, but they were important to the countries concerned and in most cases to neighbouring countries also. In Algeria, however, the French nation and the French armed forces became involved, only a few months after the heroic

[1] *Che Guevara on Guerilla Warfare* has been translated into English and is published by Frederick A. Praeger Inc. in America and by Cassell and Company Limited in London...Guevara was reported killed in South America late in 1967.

but disastrous battle at Dien Bien Phu, in an insurrection which grew to terrifying dimensions and was conducted with the utmost determination and savagery by the two contestants, the FLN (National Liberation Front) on the one side, and the French in Algeria on the other.

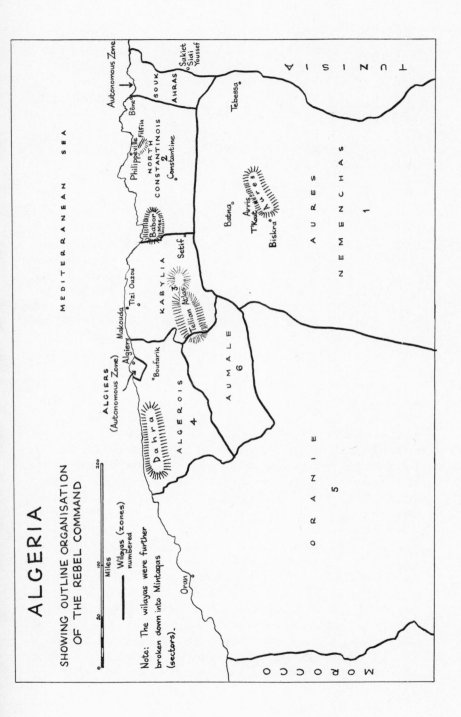

ALGERIA

SHOWING OUTLINE ORGANISATION
OF THE REBEL COMMAND

Miles

Wilayas (zones) numbered

Note: The wilayas were further broken down into Mintaqas (sectors).

MEDITERRANEAN SEA

MOROCCO

TUNISIA

Oran

ORANIE
5

ALGIERS
(Autonomous Zone)

Algiers
Boufarik

Dahra

ALGEROIS
4

Makouda

Tizi Ouzou

KABYLIA

Tellian Atlas
3

AUMALE
6

Setif

Babor Mts.

NORTH
CONSTANTINOIS
2

Philippeville
FilFila

Constantine

Autonomous Zone

Bône

SOUK
AHRAS

Sakiet
Sidi
Youssef

Tebessa

Batna

Arris
T'Kout
Aures
Biskra

AURES

NEMENCHAS
1

Narrative 11

Algeria — 1954 to 1961

*'From hence let fierce contending nations know
What dire effects from civil discord flow'.*

JOSEPH ADDISON 1672 – 1719

I am a Colon and a farmer, a Pied Noir. My farm, which covers
one hundred and twenty hectares and is situated seven kilometres
outside the town of Algiers, was first bought by my grandfather,
then a young man. He toiled for forty years to win crops from the
barren soil, and when he died he left to my father a lovely and
fruitful place. My father continued to modernise methods of tillage
and to improve the produce from the land, and when he was
drowned at sea in 1946 I took over the farm and all its responsibilities.

As a family we are not alone in paying careful attention to the
welfare of our employees, most of whom are Algerian Moslems.
We care for them not only for humanitarian reasons but also
because we consider that we, like them, are Algerian, although of
French European stock. It is true that both my grandfather and my
father married Frenchwomen (I am as yet unmarried) but the very
roots of our being are in Algerian soil and the fact that we, as a
family, retain French citizenship is due more to a sentimental
loyalty to our country of origin than to the dictates of our hearts.

It has often been said, and it is an argument that can hardly be
denied, that the problems which arose in Algeria during the terrible
years between 1954 and 1961, arose from the fact that in a total
population of ten million there were one million and seventy
thousand non-Moslems, mostly of French European stock yet all
at heart Algerians. Furthermore, this minority was not to be found
only in privileged positions in the community; they were to be
found among the street-sweepers, labourers and truck drivers as
well as among the craftsmen, artisans, managers and senior
administrators. It is not strictly accurate to say that the population

of Algeria consisted only of Moslems and non-Moslems; there were other sects, creeds and religions, but since these others made no important contribution to the lamentable story which I am now to tell, I shall refer to the population under these two headings.

Revolution, bloodshed and resistance to law and order has from the beginning of time been the lot of the Algerian people, the country being conquered and colonised in turn by the Carthaginians, Romans, Arabs, Spaniards, Turks and French. The French conquest started in May of 1830 and was completed in 1871 when a French administrative system was imposed upon the country which was grossly over-centralised, inefficient and led to severe evils.

At the end of the second war in Europe, there were two thousand officials in the town of Algiers, while out in the country the *Communes Mixtes* were understaffed. The French administrator of Arris, in the Aures Mountains, exercised control over seventy thousand people in an area half the size of Southern France with the help of only one secretary and a handful of gendarmes. He had, therefore, to administer his commune through tribal chiefs – the Bachagas or Caids – many of whom were unwelcome to the populace and many of whom used their terms of office only to amass wealth.

The administration, by its electoral system, also ensured that the interests of the powerful non-Moslem Colon minority, of which I was a member, took priority over the requirements of the Moslems. I criticise this system only in retrospect; at the time, and before the bloody revolution, it seemed to me quite fair although somewhat ineffective.

Nationalism had for many years been latent among the Moslems but from 1922 onwards it was given voice and direction by such men as Emir Khaled, Abd El Kader's grandson; Messali Hadj, the extremist; Sheikh Abd-el-Hamid Ben Badis, the founder of the Ulemas Association; and Ferhat Abass. The movement flourished in the political and economic vacuum which existed in Algeria after the fall of France to the Nazis in 1940.

At the end of the war in Europe, on May the 8th, 1945, there occurred a dreadful and unlooked-for explosion of human emotions. In Setif thousands of Moslems paraded, cheering, shouting and waving banners with the slogans: 'Down with Colonialism'; 'Free Messali Hadj'; 'We want to be your equals';

and 'Long live a free Algeria'. Shots were fired into the crowd by panic-stricken policemen and there followed wanton and savage attacks on non-Moslems, of whom twenty-nine were killed and fifty wounded. By noon the violence had spread to the wild Babor Mountains of the Kabylia, where Moslems roamed the countryside killing, pillaging and burning.

Retribution came quickly, ferocious, stern and indiscriminate; martial law in Setif; summary executions throughout the countryside carried out by Senegalese, Spahis and Foreign Legionnaires; rough justice meted out by non-Moslems without authority. In one village after another thousands of Moslems were killed – the exact number will never be known. Ferhat Abbas, now looked upon by many Moslems as their leader, was gaoled and with him 4,560 Algerians.

Whatever the cause of the Setif uprising there is no doubt in my mind that its bloody aftermath gave the Algerian Nationalist movement a new and revolutionary determination. Those moderate men who had hoped for progressive evolution had their hopes dashed to the ground; those who were thinking in terms of an armed uprising had been presented with a cause, the first essential ingredient for a guerilla movement.

After Setif the French government made efforts towards a more liberal and embracing form of government for my country, but their efforts failed in the face of non-Moslem resistance. We scoffed at the ideas put forward for an *Election à L'Algérienne* but while we scoffed a group of young political agitators were taking the part of the Moslems, among them Ahmed Ben Bella, then twenty-eight years old.

These young men believed that discussion, pleading, argument and moderation would never take effect and that the sword must prove mightier than the pen. Using as cover Messali Hadj's legal party, the Movement for the Triumph of Democratic Liberties (MTDL), they set about raising an *Organisation Secrète* (OS) and a small clandestine army of some five hundred men. In the early stages they took no overt action against the state except in Oran where Ben Bella himself led a masked raid against the central post office in 1949, stealing 3,070,000 francs for the movement. Despite the air of secrecy, however, the plot was uncovered by the French police in the spring of 1950.

Two years later I was directly drawn into what proved to be a long and bloody struggle. Persuaded partly by my interest in the history of Algeria and partly by my knowledge of Moslem people and customs, the government enlisted me into the intelligence service so that, on a cool spring morning in April, 1952, I handed over the farm to my brother Maurice and drove to the government offices in Algiers. My work there brought me in contact with political, police and military intelligence and, as the revolution developed, it took me into many parts of the country.

Although not in possession of all the facts, during my first two years in office I watched the development of the Moslem underground organisation, first under the *Club des Neuf* (nine young men of considerable drive and energy, six resident in Algeria, with Ben Bella and two henchmen in Cairo) and later, under the *Comité Revolutionnaire Pour L'Unité et L'Action* (CRUA). These men divided the country into six *wilayas* (zones) and appointed commanders to recruit men, disseminate propaganda and suborn the people. Then, on 1 November 1954, only a few months after Dien Bien Phu, the terrible war broke out.

It is true to say that during the last two and a half years during which the revolutionary organisation had been preparing itself for bloodshed, we who knew of its existence failed to take proper action against it. We placed too much confidence in the break-up of the *Organisation Secrète*; we failed to infiltrate the movement with agents and spies; we failed to play on the different viewpoints of the plotters and so set one against the other. Politically we failed to divorce them from help or sympathy from countries outside Algeria (though this, in the light of their cause, may well have been impossible), nor did we succeed by liberal measures in alienating from them the Moslem people. Although we in the intelligence services knew much of the revolutionaries' aims and activities we could not produce sufficient proof to secure drastic action.

It was in the early hours of the morning that the peace of Algeria was shattered. One hundred and fifty rebels closed on the Benchaiba farm in the Aures Mountains to pick up weapons and spread out over the countryside, some to attack the gendarmerie in T'Kout, others to blow up the lead mine at Ichmoul, others to attack the French army barracks at Batna, the largest town in the area. Elsewhere, too, soldiers were killed, buses ambushed and policemen and government officials murdered.

We were left in no doubt that a central organisation had planned these dreadful crimes. A pamphlet appeared in thousands summoning the Moslems:

> 'Side by side with our brothers to the east and to the west who are dying that their fatherlands may live, we call on you to re-conquer your freedom at the price of your blood. Organise yourselves to give aid, comfort and protection to the forces of liberation. To take no interest in the struggle is a crime; to oppose it is treason. . . . Long live the Army of Liberation; long live independent Algeria.'

Other tracts and proclamations announced the creation of the National Liberation Front (FLN), who defined their aims as national independence through the restoration of the Algerian state within the framework of the principles of Islam, and the preservation of all fundamental freedoms without distinction of race or religion. The FLN was to be supported by a National Liberation Army (ALN).

These sentiments were supported from Cairo: 'At one o'clock this morning', a bulletin announced, 'Algeria began to live a worthy and honourable life.'

We reacted immediately to the threat. Police and army sprang into action against the armed bands while reinforcements were despatched in an ever-increasing flow of transport aircraft by the Mendès-France government in Paris. Arrests were made in every *préfecture*.

On 15 November I accompanied a battalion whose task it was to comb out an area in the Kabylia where the rebel leader Belkacem Krim had been reported. I lay down with the soldiers that night, to be assaulted by the harsh cold which grips the countryside of Algeria so suddenly and so surprisingly in the autumn. Shortly before dawn, after a sleepless, restless night and after a hasty breakfast of *jus* and *boule*, we slung on our packs, loaded our weapons and drove away up the rutted track towards our first objective, Makouda, where the *fellaghas* had been spotted the day before.

An icy wind lashed our bodies, exposed as they were in the open trucks. A drizzle drifted down out of a grey sky, while the dawn mist shrouded the countryside. No one spoke. The trucks ground to a halt as the track came to an end. The mountains hung over us, grey, gloomy, forbidding; the rain fell remorselessly, soaking everything; the cold became more intense. We trudged off in a long straggling line down a muddy track into a deep canyon. Then the officers murmured, and the whole column came to a halt. We stood like stakes in the ground as hour after hour went by.

The men were young and new to fighting, but the initial excitement and thoughts of adventure slowly seeped out of them as the rain and cold soaked into their shivering bodies. Where were the *fellaghas*? Was this war – standing in the cold and wet, waiting, waiting? They would find out during the next few years that this indeed was war – guerilla war – waiting in every conceivable position which the human body could adopt, standing, crouching, kneeling, lying, on the blazing sands of the deserts, on the rock-hard sides of the mountains, in the forests, in the cramped quarters of the shanty towns, in the stinking *mechtas* of the *douars*.

But now we knew only that somewhere out there in the mist, somewhere beyond Makouda, other soldiers were sweeping slowly and laboriously across the broken countryside, looking for an elusive foe, coming nearer and nearer to us – the line of 'stops'. Throughout the day no one spoke, no one either ate or drank; there was barely a movement in the waiting line of wretched men. As evening began to close down we suddenly heard the rattle of light machine-gun fire, and all at once we became alert. When rifles answered the automatics the urge to dash forward on to the unseen battle-ground became almost more than we could bear. Yet we stayed, held rooted to the ground by the invisible and soundless force of discipline. Then the firing died away and night fell deep down into the canyon. The battle had been fought without us.

Four more hours of waiting, then the high command, perhaps realising the impossibility of trapping a band of rebels by night in their own mountains, ordered a withdrawal. The whole unwieldy column launched out into the darkness, and God! what a night we spent, plunging about the mountainsides, searching in vain for a way out. At last, with every man in a state of exhaustion, we came upon a narrow, twisting *oued* and staggered down its length, stumbling over shifting boulders and razor-sharp rocks while up to our waists in icy water. It was not until the light of dawn touched the grey skies that we saw the trucks for which we had been looking.

As for the *fellaghas*, they had gone. Troops sent in to search the area in daylight found no dead nor wounded, nor any single person who would admit to their having been in the area.

In spite of many operations of this nature, in spite of innumerable arrests and exhortations to peace, ambush, murder, arson and sabotage continued throughout the countryside, while the whole apparatus of a counter-revolutionary organisation was called into being.

On 26 January 1955, Jacques Soustelle took up office as Governor-General.

He was at once faced with imposing difficulties. The Mendès-France Government, which had appointed him, fell, to be replaced by one with differing North African policies. Both Moslems and non-Moslems opposed the policies for which he stood, expressed in the one word 'integration'.

He, himself, was appalled by the extent of the widespread guerilla warfare, which claimed as victims both Moslems and non-Moslems; he was disturbed by Algeria's poverty, by its top-heavy administration and by the poor results of police action and the army's large-scale operations.

But the FLN were no respecters of persons; from the day Soustelle landed, they further intensified their murderous activities. As the months went by the rebellion spread alarmingly from the Aures Mountains into Southern Constantine and beyond.

It was perhaps unfortunate that in order to meet these increasing threats Soustelle, as one of his first public actions, was compelled to urge on the French National Assembly the passing of a State of Emergency Bill, a bill which in practice allowed comparatively minor officials to impose restrictions on public life, thus threatening the normal rule by law. Prefects could restrict movement of persons, establish special security zones, send suspects into enforced residence, authorise night searches and arrests and control public means of communication; military courts were set up to try persons. There is no doubt that some adjustment to the normal processes of the law was forced upon the administration by the total lack of witness to any crime committed by the FLN. The police and army, depending as always upon support from the judicial system, were paralysed in their efforts to maintain law and order by the rebels' ability to shelter behind the law knowing full well that citizens were afraid to bear witness to crime. Even so, another nine months were to elapse before the emergency regulations strengthened the arm and the will of the judiciary.

At the same time, Jacques Soustelle attempted to reform the administration, to streamline departments, to de-centralise and to give increased responsibilities to Moslems, but every one of his reforms had to be fought through the non-Moslem groups, the most powerful of which were the *Rassemblement des Français D'Afrique du Nord*, the *Union Française Nord Africaine*, and the *Vigilance Africaine*.

Soustelle established the *Sections Administratives Spécialisées* (SAS) and the *Sections Administratives Urbaines* (SAU), under which army officers were brought in to reinforce the administration. The organisation of the SAS was entrusted to General Parlange who evolved a system with excellent intent but one which carried with it mixed blessings. Situations inevitably arose where the tasks of the local army commanders, whose interests lay only in destroying rebels, conflicted with those of junior military SAS officers, whose interests lay in the welfare of the local people; equally inevitably the latter took second priority.

In the midst of these reforms and changes there occurred, on 20 August 1955, a series of uprisings which filled the non-Moslems with anguish and horror. The FLN, who had always sought for a general insurrection, selected the day for slaughter to coincide with a similar demonstration in neighbouring Morocco. While two thousand Berber tribesmen were turning Oued Zem[1] and Ait Amar[1] into a nightmare of death and destruction, thousands of maddened Algerian *fellaghas* set upon everything French.

The city of Philippeville bore the brunt of the onslaught. I moved down there on the day before the massacre, lodging in the barracks outside the town where a parachute regiment was stationed. Imagine it! – the troops were confined to barracks, so that there was not a soldier in the streets. Quite early in the morning, about two hours after daylight, we heard a strange sound issuing from the town. Many of the men still slept, and none was aware of the significance of the sound they heard until a frenzied civilian came running into the barracks. Undeterred by sentries or officers, by wire fences or locked doors, he burst like a madman into the commanding officer's office and poured out his horrible tale.

[1] Two places in Morocco.

The *fellaghas*, coming down from the mountains, having given prior notice of their coming, whipped up the fury of the Arab citizens by the cries of a holy war and unleashed them upon the Europeans. Mad with fury, they started killing with rifles, grenades, knives, stones, sickles and sticks. For a whole hour they slaughtered men, women and children without pausing for breath.

Within three minutes the whole of the battalion, many of the men half-dressed, were on their way into the town, but it was already too late. There was nothing but bodies to see in the streets; bodies still bleeding but already swarming with flies; the half-naked bodies of women clutching the pale corpses of their strangled children; bodies mutilated beyond recognition. The only moving creatures were the dogs, furtively licking up all the blood they could find. In the houses it was even worse, men and women lying naked on the sheets, hacked and slashed with sickles and *douk-douks*.

The rebels, when they saw us coming, fled from the town, taking with them those civilians who had been involved in the massacre. The latter, however, encumbered by their *burnouses*, were too slow in their movement. We shot them down at point blank range. While half the battalion pursued the enemy into the hills, helped by planes, the remainder searched the town to find terrified Arabs huddling under any available cover – at the end of alleyways, in the *mechtas*, under rubbish heaps, even in the cactus hedges. For two hours the town echoed with the sound of automatic and rifle fire. Then the order came to take prisoners. Several hundred were carted off to the barracks in the Caserne de France, but by dawn it had become impossible to hold them prisoner any longer for fear of reprisals by those Europeans who had escaped the massacre. The battalion's machine guns were lined up opposite the crowd of madly-yelling *boukaks*. Ten minutes later the bull-dozers were digging ditches for the corpses.

I thought that I had seen the ultimate in horror, but this was reserved for the mining village of El Halia in the Fil Fila Hills, east of Philippeville. Here the Moslem employees hurled themselves against the European community attached to the mine, brandishing sticks of dynamite, bottles of gasolene, drums and axes. They proceeded to butcher all the men they could find, then turned upon the women and children, literally hacking them to pieces. Thirty-seven children perished, including ten under fifteen years of age.

Soustelle visited the scenes to see for himself the charred and mutilated remains of non-Moslem dead; the streets still strewn with corpses; the *scènes de carnage* which had been houses; the Europeans who had been spared huddling together in the town halls giving vent to their grief and despair. It is possible that from this moment his attitude hardened towards the Moslems of Algeria.

Certainly he applied immediate and drastic counter-measures to the area concerned. He appointed Colonel Georges Camille Meyer as both civil and military commander in the Philippeville and Collo districts. He improved the administration and he posted in reinforcements of both police and soldiers. Yet nothing that he could do hindered, at least for a time, the atrocious and brutal actions of non-Moslems driven mad by fear and thoughts of vengeance, nor the continuing depredations of the Algerian rebels themselves.

Terror and death stalked the streets, while normal life came to a halt. Shops closed; traffic ceased; people spoke only in whispers; civilians armed themselves without authority and opened fire at the drop of a hat; the slow poison of fear and mistrust infected every mind. Fear-crazed Moslems, dreading alike the vengeance of non-Moslems and retribution for non-cooperation with the rebels, took to the countryside and wandered hither and thither in vagrant, bewildered crowds.

At this moment the rebels were given encouragement when their case was brought before the United Nations. An Afro-Asian motion stating that colonial rule had prevented the Algerian people from exercising their right to self-determination, and stressing the 'imperious necessity for negotiations between the French Government and true representatives of the Algerian people' was admitted by the Assembly. Thus stimulated, the rebels extended their activities over the whole of Algeria, even into the Oran department, hitherto a haven of peace and security. The end of 1955 saw the rebellion stronger than ever.

Throughout this fateful year political efforts to crush the rebellion, beset by the instability of the French government and resulting prevarication, failed to match the military effort, itself hampered by inherent weaknesses.

After Philippeville Soustelle showed signs that he was at last assimilating the realities of the Algerian situation (I write as a non-Moslem), but in January 1956, there was yet another change of government in France and the new socialist leader, Guy Mollet, appointed in his place Robert Lacoste, the labour leader, after the non-Moslems had thrown out his first nominee, General Georges Catroux.

Although I would not have said so while in the grip of the emotions of the time, it has since become clear to me that no agreement could be reached over Algeria, nor a stop put to the bloodshed, while the non-Moslem minority in the country dictated the terms and while governments in France shifted so swiftly in their policies from one extreme to another.

But more ominous even than non-Moslem intransigence was the handing to Colonel Meyer of both military and civilian responsibilities in Philippeville. At a lower level army officers of the *Sections Administratives Specialisées* and of the *Sections Administratives Urbaines* already held powers of life and death over the citizens within their small areas of responsibility and here, in Philippeville, we took a second important step towards the transfer of governmental policies from civilian officials to military men.

In any case, it appeared doubtful whether the army was able to deal with the military problems posed by the techniques and tactics of the rebels, let alone with political problems as well. With their efforts spread all over the country, with many units tied down to roads and railways by their heavy equipment, even though supported by aircraft and helicopters they seemed unable properly to control the activities of the armed gangs. Even the famous *Septième Division Méchanique Rapide* found its new equipment inadequate for this type of warfare and while such magnificent units roamed the countryside in search of rebel bands, these same bands began to take control of mountain areas. We had not yet arrived at the best means of adapting our machines to the terrain, nor had we yet adopted an orderly strategy.

Meanwhile outside support, so urgently needed by the rebels, continued to increase throughout 1956. By April, both Tunisia and Morocco had achieved independence and were providing sanctuaries into which the rebels could withdraw for rest, training, re-arming and re-equipping. A steady flow of arms crossed both borders into rebel possession.

By this time, also, two years after the outbreak of terrorism, the rebels had succeeded in gaining the co-operation of the whole of the Moslem people, not by persuasion but by direct terrorism. The official casualty list covering the first stage of armed revolt showed 8,650 civilians killed, of which 7,450 were Moslems! The rebels had successfully persuaded each Moslem citizen that if he helped the government in any way he would certainly die, whereas, if he helped the rebels he might, if caught, be imprisoned by the authorities for a limited time. Moslems were left little choice. With the people behind them the rebel leaders now took the fateful decision to attack the towns, a decision which recoiled upon them in a way which those whose brain-child it was could not have foreseen.

But before dealing with the events of 1957, I should outline what we knew of the rebel organisation at that time.

The beginnings, as I have explained, were small and were planned by the young men of the *Club des Neuf*. The rebellion was set in a country which at that time was of no great interest to the world at large, so that sympathy for the rebels came only from Cairo, Morocco and Tunisia.

In Algeria the people lived in tribes and sub-tribes, most of them divided against each other by centuries of feuding. To counter the threat of dissension the *Club des Neufs* divided the country into six districts (*wilaya*) each one with its own appointed leader, and the young men of the club pledged themselves not to take any decision without consulting all district leaders.

However, as time went by, this practice became impossible as some leaders were killed in action and others arrested. By August 1956, only two of the original leaders remained active in Algeria, Belkacem Krim of *Wilaya* No. 3, and Larbi Ben M'Hidi of *Wilaya* No. 5. Other leaders, including the unquestioned chief, Ahmed Ben Bella, formed the FLN's *Délégation Extérieure* in Cairo, dealing with finance, arms, supplies and diplomacy.

By 1956 new leaders had appeared, among them Ramdane Abbane, a sombre personality dedicated to removing by force an occupation imposed by force. He it was who dominated a meeting of 250 rebel chiefs in a deserted hut in the Soummam Valley in the summer of 1956, a conference which members of the *Délégation Extérieure* were unable to attend for reasons of security, but which none the less took far-reaching decisions.

The delegates established an overall execution and co-ordination committee (CCE), and a form of sovereign parliament entitled the *Conseil National de la Révolution Algérienne* to represent the people as a whole. But it was Abbane who forced through decisions which subordinated the *Délégation Extérieure* to the forces of the interior, decreed that collective leadership should be accepted at all levels and insisted that all military decisions should be dictated solely by the political aim.

Ben Bella, on learning of these decisions some months later, took Abbane to task for breaking solemn promises previously given, but it was not until a year later that he was able to bring down his determined colleague.

With their organisation complete, and in a moment of emotional exhilaration brought on by the fact that they had been able to stage a major policy conference on Algerian soil and under the noses of the French army, the rebel leaders decided to adopt indiscriminate terrorism in the towns. The battle of Algiers was thus launched with the intention of bringing the city to its knees.

I was aware, as indeed were my colleagues in the intelligence services, of the pressures besetting the leaders of the rebellion throughout its first three years of life, and it was a constant source of surprise to us that the rebel organisation had survived in face of comparative isolation from world opinion, in the light of the differences of opinion held' by its leaders and against the intense pressure brought to bear upon it by the government of Algeria and by the French army. That it survived these testing years was due to the dedication of its leaders and to the support for their cause which they obtained from the Moslem population by the straightforward method of killing those Moslems who did not espouse it.

By the end of 1956, the FLN was strong, highly-organised and well-equipped. Their leaders had mobilised a balance of world opinion in their favour while opinion in France itself was delicately balanced between the rebels and their opponents. In Tunisia, and to a lesser extent in Morocco, the FLN had sanctuary – there were no fewer than twenty thousand men of the National Liberation Army either training or resting in Tunisia at the end of the year. Arms flowed freely across the borders.

And on October the 27th, 1956, an extraordinary incident convinced the FLN that there was no chance of negotiating a peace. On that day, an aeroplane carrying Ben Bella and members of the *Délégation Extérieure* from Rabat to Tunis, there to take advantage of the good offices of the Moroccans and Tunisians in negotiating peace, was ordered down by my own organisation on to the airfield at Algiers, there to be met by armed soldiers and police who took Ben Bella into captivity. The news of this arrest was greeted in Algiers with wild joy, in Tunis with consternation, in Paris in wonderment, in Morocco as an affront to the king whose guest Ben Bella was; but however received, French and Algerian governmental support of the action, though tacitly given, made it clear to all that the FLN were to be allowed no peace-making in Algeria.

In this situation the rebels, now deploying an army of eight thousand *Moujahidine* (regulars) and twenty-one thousand *Mousebbelline* (auxiliaries), backed by an armoury of twenty-two thousand weapons and supported by the Moslem people, carried the war into the capital city. The *Bataille d'Alger* was to change the situation beyond recognition.

The Casbah in Algiers, to many a place of mystery and romance, was no more than a festering canker attached to the heart of a civilised city. Within its walls, crowded into squalid houses, tenements, cafés and brothels, lived the majority of the city's Moslem population, 450,000 in number. The crumbling buildings, tottering over narrow, fly-blown streets and rubbish-filled yards, were connected by an elaborate network of secret passages and stinking alley-ways. Inside this natural hiding place there lurked four thousand terrorists, their efforts directed by Yacef Saadi and his henchman Ali Ammar, known as 'Ali la Pointe'. Their weapons were the knife, the sub-machine gun and the bomb; their methods murder, mutilation and arson; their aim, to bring the city to its knees. Against them, on January the 7th, 1957, Robert Lacoste pitted General Jacques Massu and his Tenth Paratroop Division.

The parachute troops, given responsibility for all police and security measures in the city, were to stamp out terrorism by any means. I was temporarily posted to one of Massu's battalions as their intelligence adviser – I knew a great deal about Yacef Saadi and his methods. The battalion lived in decaying tents, pitched in drunken disarray on a barrack square. From this base they ceaselessly patrolled the town by day and night in groups of four to twelve men. Blindly entrusted with keeping an eye on the entire population, they soon assumed a free hand to apprehend anyone without explanation. Themselves the only representatives of law and order, no one, nor anything escaped their scrutiny. No person could refuse their demands; no building could bar its doors to the all-seeing, ubiquitous men of the parachute division.

They would lay their hand on the shoulder of any citizen and watch the terror in his eyes. In the middle of the streets, they would stop trembling men and women and search them from head to toe – how much nicer if the women were young and their bodies soft and naked under their dresses. They would enter any building by day or night – they became adept at silent entry – to drag the sleeping inmates outside and comb the place out from top to bottom, leaving behind a chaos of scattered clothing, broken goods, ripped mattresses and shattered furniture. They would rush into cafés, restaurants and brothels, like bunches of cowboys into some Western saloon, and search all who were there before withdrawing with their terrified prisoners. In the Casbah and throughout the town, the paratroops raided and searched, arrested and killed, innocent and guilty alike suffering from their depredations.

The prisoners were taken to the interrogation centres – there was one in each company lines and many others specially designed for the more valuable prisoners. In these places, their bodies assaulted by ice-cold water, by flailing fists and booted feet, their genitals, hearts and throats subjected to shock treatment from naked electric flex, their puny frames imprisoned in coffins for day after agonising day, their battered flesh scarred and bruised from maltreatment, those who had information to give, gave it, while those who had none soon reached that stage of physical and mental collapse in which the only recourse was the *corvée de bois*, the 'timber fatigue', from which they never returned.

In February, the FLN called a general strike in the city – the response was almost total. The paras, armed with automatic rifles, broke into the huts of Arab labourers, smashing in every door which did not immediately yield, dragged the wretched men from their beds and gave them two minutes in which to dress and go out to work. Closed shops were re-opened by the simple method of driving light tanks through the iron shutters and forcing the shopkeeper down to his counter from an upper room. Yet the strike lasted for several unpleasant weeks.

Algeria became one vast and tortured battle-ground, the citizens imposed upon by three armies, the rebels, the non-Moslems and the paras. In the end, we saw everything in the Casbah – even actual terrorists, who would greet us with a hail of fire before being cornered in some stinking garret or rat-infested attic. On these occasions we despatched them simply by blowing up the whole building. Only when intelligence coming out of the torture chambers became more precise, only when sheer terror drove the Moslems to betray each other were the paras able to confine their tactics to the guilty – but by then it was all over.

Within nine months of his appointment to the task General Massu had virtually eliminated the FLN organisation in Algiers and had brought the Moslem population under control.

At the same time the French army, now in massive numbers throughout the country and assimilating a power of their own at once political, psychological and military, were eliminating the rebel bands one by one, arresting or killing the FLN's most able and dedicated leaders and bringing the organisation into disrepute. The rebels had no answer to the numbers of infantry deployed against them; to the convoys of tanks and armoured cars which patrolled the roads; to the squadrons of armed helicopters which enabled infantry to surround any given place without warning while the rebels were pinned to the ground by fire from the sky; to the might of both the attack and transport elements of the French Air Force. Both climate and terrain favoured the use of certain machines at maximum efficiency, while numbers held secure those areas which had been cleared of rebel activity.

It was fascinating to watch from a central position the disintegration of the FLN armed forces, albeit at immense cost to France in terms of financial expenditure and military effort. But it became clearer with each passing day that with sanctuaries to their east and west the FLN could never be entirely eliminated while the spirit of their leaders remained alive.

Steps were taken to lessen the efficacy of the sanctuaries, particularly that offered by Tunisia. On February the 8th, 1958, we bombed the Tunisian frontier village of Sakhiet Sidi Youssef, a rebel position from which armed forces raided into Algeria. The incident excited world opinion to extremes of condemnation and caused the government in Paris to accept the good offices, in negotiations between themselves and Tunisia, of Robert D. Murphy, the United States Deputy Under-Secretary of State, and Harold Beeley of the British Foreign Office. Their findings made many recommendations but were rejected by the National Assembly, the rejection bringing down Premier Gaillard's government, thus leaving France once again in a political vacuum.

Meanwhile the army in Algeria took the matter of the frontier into its own hands and, with the aid of thousands of labourers, constructed the famous Morice Line, an edifice of wire, concrete and mines interspersed with all sorts of obstacles, stretching for hundreds of miles along the border and manned throughout its length by soldiers and police. But even this Morice Line failed completely to close the border to rebel movement.

I flew up to watch its construction, where the Roman walls of Tebessa gleam every evening like burnished gold in the glow of the desert sun. In this circular furnace of a town the soldiery were in process of taking over from the Arab population, whose hostility was engendered by the proximity of the Tunisian border, which offered a secure retreat in case of reprisal.

Arriving as dusk was falling, I walked through the narrow streets. Within moments I had counted thirteen explosions in various parts of the small town. Then a fire started, the smoke obscuring the already dim streets. The rebels, crossing the border from Tunisia, had penetrated the town and, first producing automatic rifles from underneath their *burnouses*, urged on the population to attack the soldiery. There was indescribable confusion. The yelling, frenzied, uncontrollable crowd, seething with violence, set upon two policemen and tore them limb from limb. Unarmed, I ran, hugging the grey walls of the alley-ways until I came across a group of young soldiers encircled by a crazy mob. We backed away, nonplussed, until Legionnaires and Colonials arrived as from nowhere. A fantastic *mêlée* then ensued, with bullets whipping everywhere and cutting the mob down in swathes; then it was the Arabs who retreated.

The fire continued to rage right across the Arab quarter. Explosions tore windows from their fittings, supports from underneath tumbledown shacks. The crowds dispersed, the rebels fled, but all was not yet done. The systematic repression began, and as the blaze reached higher into the sky, thousands of little black smuts floated down on to the corpses as they were thrown into the streets.

Political instability in France itself, and the very considerable political powers which the French army, now numbering well over half a million men, had taken upon themselves in Algeria caused further desperate tension and anxiety. As the year (1958) moved into the month of May the people of Algeria, cast down into the depths of despair, wondered what hope they could still cling to. The wildest enterprise stood some chance of success; lunatic phrases were given earnest consideration; kindness, common sense and the tenets of law were forgotten in the upsurge of unruly fanaticisms.

When Robert Lacoste was relieved of his post as Governor-General, on the 8th of May, his place was taken by General Raoul Salan, the Supreme Commander of the Armed Forces. Together with General Massu he set up a Committee of Public Safety in Algiers which was later extended to all the provinces. These committees were brought into being against a background of massive and emotional demonstrations, involving over 100,000 non-Moslems and Moslems, which continued throughout the month. The committee members, joined on the 17th of May by a previous Governor-General, Jacques Soustelle, could not but draw comfort from the cries of the mob: 'Massu to power!'; 'All Moslems are behind us,'; 'Long live French Algeria!' and, finally, '*L'Armée au pouvoir!*'

On the 13th of May the Committee of Public Safety despatched the following telegram to President Coty of France:

'We inform you creation civil and military Committee Public Safety in Algiers presided over by myself, General Massu. By reason gravity situation and absolute necessity maintenance order and to prevent effusion blood we require formation in Paris of a government of public safety alone capable of preserving Algeria integral part Metropolitan France.'

On the following day the Committee formulated its aim: to restore law and order and bring a government of public safety into existence in Paris, if possible with General de Gaulle as Premier. On the 20th of May the Committee members solemnly declared for the integration of Algeria with Metropolitan France. On the 23rd of May they statutorily voted themselves into existence.

Meanwhile, in Paris, politicians sought in vain for the means to form a government. It was not until the 15th of May that General de Gaulle formally offered his services to his country: 'I am ready,' he said, 'to assume the powers of the Republic'. He repeated this offer on the 19th of May before an audience of a thousand journalists and guests at the Palais d'Orsay Hotel in Paris: 'The moment seemed to me to have come when it would be possible for me once again to be directly useful to France'.

Finally, between the 27th of May and the 4th of June, General de Gaulle formed his new republican government and was invested as Premier.

On the 4th of June General de Gaulle flew to Algiers in a Caravelle jet airliner to be greeted by a popular outburst of spontaneous joy and enthusiasm. The opening sentence of his speech, delivered from the balcony of the Government General building and addressed to a vast multitude, was well-chosen: 'Je vous ai compris,' he said – 'I have understood you'.

But two significant facts emerged from his speech, namely, the praise that he gave to the French army for what they had done and his omission of the cry which had long been fashionable in Algeria: 'Long live French Algeria'. After the first impact of his personality had worn off, after time had been taken for thought his words were met with hostility by the Moslems, with doubt by the non-Moslems.

By this visit to Algiers on 4th June 1958, General de Gaulle took his first step along the hard road to peace, upon which he was to be dogged by continual opposition from Moslem and non-Moslem, both of whom distrusted his avowed intention to bring about the 'peace of the brave' under the 'white flag of truce'.

De Gaulle appointed a new Commander-in-Chief, General Maurice Challe, and a new Delegate General, Paul Delouvrier, at the same time removing from Algeria many of those army officers who either could not or would not espouse his policies.

He made overtures to the rebel leaders, though none were acceptable since they were hedged about with provisos. He obtained the backing of the Algerian people for his return to power by means of a referendum, the validity of which was many times called to question.

But the turning point in the negotiations, which he followed through with patience, sound judgement and inflexible purpose, was his famous speech on 'self-determination', in which he virtually adopted the rebels' own cause, although suspicion and past practices closed the eyes of the FLN to the vital importance of what he had said. But the eyes of the armed services and non-

Moslems opened wide, and they determined to resist by every means the implementation of the new policy.

At the same time as de Gaulle was restoring some sort of sense to our political affairs, the army began its 'West to East' programme against the rebels. One of the early operations took me to the Saida sector of the Western Tellian Atlas range, to the west of the Wadi Mina, where a reconnaissance plane had spotted tracks passing across the scrub on the lower slopes of the mountains, and into the forests on the upper slopes. My information was that a *Katiba* was on the move.

A helicopter force had been assembled; we were going to tackle this group of rebels from the air. The plan was made in meticulous detail from a close study of large-scale photo maps; no other reconnaissance or preparatory activity took place in the target area.

At 3.50 in the morning, the first wave of troops took off in American-built H-34 helicopters, and headed for distant dropping zones. At 4.50 the dropping zones were bombed by twin-engined attack bombers – B-26s, while slow-flying Thunderbolts and T-6 trainers strafed the hills and canyons all around. Finally, armed helicopters which we called 'Pirates' shot up the area immediately round the DZs, dropped smoke, and ordered the troops to land. The Pirates circled nearby during the landing to keep the enemy pinned down.

The soldiers had woken in their beds at 3 a.m.; by 9 a.m. the encirclement of the enemy on these high afforested mountains was complete. Then the searching and the fighting began, with Thunderbirds and T-6s above to give support, and with Pirates searching the canyons and rough places, at one place even shooting into caves below overhanging cliffs. By the end of the day, one hundred and ninety-seven terrorists had been killed and a further sixty taken prisoner.

The care we had taken to plan the operation from photographs without showing an apparent interest in the ground itself had paid a handsome dividend. A prisoner told us that sentries were posted with powerful binoculars who would have given the *Katiba* due warning of the approach of soldiers over the ground; the *Katiba* would then have disappeared.

This, then, was one of many such operations which, combined with final clearing and consolidation of each area gained, and following a logical sequence of area selection from west to east, succeeded, by the end of 1960, in reducing the FLN's army to no more than 9,000 men, separated from the population and broken up into small bands with most of their weapons buried for lack of ammunition. The rebel leaders in Algeria were at the same time cut off from any form of communication with the *Délégation Extérieure*, and the borders were closed to infiltration.

The army's efforts during these last three years were directed in accordance with the theory and practice of *guerre révolutionnaire*, a doctrine which had been evolved during the agony of Indo-China. There the French army had been defeated by a cunning and numerous enemy, the Vietminh. While suffering on the water-logged plains and in the foetid jungles, French soldiers of all ranks felt, rightly or wrongly, that they had not been properly supported by their own people at home. They had been able closely to study their enemy, not only by dint of engaging him on the field of battle, but by observing also the methods he employed to win over the civilian population in the country in which he was fighting. In prison camps which housed thousands of Frenchmen they viewed at close range the psychological methods employed in a war of revolution.

The French army, impressed by the complete integration of military and political forces at all levels throughout the Vietminh organisation, formulated their own theory of revolutionary warfare; in brief, this can be summed up as an integration of partisan warfare with psychological warfare.

To enable themselves to accomplish such strategy and tactics, French army officers called for two conditions; first that the government and nation should give complete support to the armed forces, wherever engaged; and second that the armed forces should themselves experience revolutionary changes in their concepts of duty and ethics as well as in their tactics.

When rebellion broke out in Algeria the implications and practices of the new ideas had been embraced by a number of the most senior officers in the armed forces, and were shortly due for inclusion in the curriculum of military academies.

It would take a whole book to analyse in detail the French army's view of revolutionary war and its application to the revolution in Algeria. Its assessment of action and successful reaction in revolutionary war might be plotted as follows:

The Revolutionaries	The Counter-Revolutionaries
1 Formation of propaganda and agitation cells.	Police and intelligence activity; strengthening of military and administrative controls; propaganda; social, economic and political reforms.
2 Expansion and co-ordination of opposition; riots and sabotage.	
3 Intensified propaganda; terrorism, minor armed actions, guerillas; diplomatic activity.	Mobilisation of state's physical and political resources; attack on the subversive infra-structure; organisation of self-defence units; education and re-education programmes; re-settlement of population; re-conquest of liberated zones; isolation and destruction of enemy forces; diplomatic activity.
4 Creation of liberated zones; installation of provisional government, gradual change from irregular to regular warfare.	
5 Regular warfare fully developed; diplomatic activity.	
6 Regular warfare fails, reversion to guerilla warfare.	
7 Reduction of liberated zones; small-scale guerilla warfare.	Reduction of the regular and auxiliary military effort; continuation of reforms and re-education; evolution of a new order.
8 Propaganda, agitation, sabotage, terror.	

It has been clearly demonstrated that the Algerian and French governments' reaction to phases one and two of revolutionary activity failed. Initial outbreaks of terrorism were met only by police and intelligence activity and by a certain strengthening of military and administrative control, but the seeds of good propaganda and of social, economic and political reform fell upon the stony ground of the non-Moslem's intransigence, ground which unstable government in France found too hard to plough.

By 1957 enormous numbers of men, huge sums of money and immense resources of energy were required to counter stages three and four of revolutionary activity. The French army were by then conducting the campaign much in the way they thought fit, and I saw in Opération 'Pilote' an example of the French army's doctrine of revolutionary warfare in action. As its name implies, the operation was experimental, but its success led to a general application of the techniques involved.

Pilote was conducted in the Dahra Mountains of Oran with the aim of setting up a Moslem politico-administrative superstructure which would enjoy the confidence of the people and be favourable to France.

The area, 1,700 square kilometres in extent, consisted, in the north, of a coastal strip of fertile plateaux and, in the south, of an area of steep and rugged mountains intersected by few roads or paths. Of a total population of 120,000, 3,000 were non-Moslems living almost exclusively in the fertile region.

On March the 22nd 1957, this area was placed under control of the Colonel Commanding the Fifth Cavalry Brigade who had under his command a motorised cavalry regiment, an armoured squadron, a mobile security group, two infantry battalions, a battery of guns, an airborne commando group and two counter-guerilla nomad companies. He had the backing of several psychological warfare teams, seven SAS teams, and one hundred million francs which was made immediately available to him.

He launched simultaneous operations against the rebel infrastructure and armed bands in the area, and within three months had weakened rebel influence to such an extent that he was able to initiate his psychological warfare effort.

Retaining the mobile military units in the area to retain security, the colonel set about the constructive task of pacifying the area. Drawing on friendly elements and former internees who had been re-educated and separated from their revolutionary beliefs, he established, with the co-operation of the SAS teams, chiefs and assistants in all the towns and villages. These chosen men first attended a course at Rivoli, where they were given fifteen days' basic training in civics and where they assimilated the roles they were expected to play. All were Moslems.

At the same time, district commanders increased the military potential by arming and forming self-defence units in those *douars* which were friendly.

This constructive process of handing over local politics, administration and defence to the Moslems themselves continued over a period of fourteen months. Meanwhile communications, buildings, and social and medical services were improved throughout the area by army engineers, army-organised civilian workers, youth councillors and army medical teams, all drawing on the huge sum of money made available to the operation.

Opération Pilote involved intense military and administrative effort and the expenditure of enormous sums of money. It was held up by the army as a remarkable stroke of counter-revolutionary warfare and certainly for a time it restored peace to the area, but within six months the rebel organisation was once again active there, not in the same strength as it had been before, but none the less active and apparent. The French army had been able to offer the people improved conditions of living, but within an existing political framework; it was far beyond the powers of the local commander to change that framework.

The framework was finally changed by General de Gaulle, but not until after he had mastered the intense, almost desperate resistance of his own armed forces and the non-Moslem *Pieds Noirs* to his policy of independence for Algeria, and not before he had also allayed the suspicions of the Moslems themselves. The dreadful 'week of the barricades' – a week of riot and mad slaughter in Algiers which followed on General Massu's return to France on January the 24th 1960, the revolt of his senior service officers, the activities of the infamous OAS,[1] any one of these events might have deterred a less determined man.

It was not until the 18th of May, 1961, after seven bitter years of struggle, that de Gaulle finally succeeded in bringing the rebel leaders and French negotiators to a conference at Evian which was to result in a cease-fire in Algeria and a prospect of true and lasting peace.

---

[1] The OAS was a guerilla organisation established in Algeria by those most violently opposed to de Gaulle's policy. The movement stood little chance of success because its leaders commanded the support of only a small minority of the population.

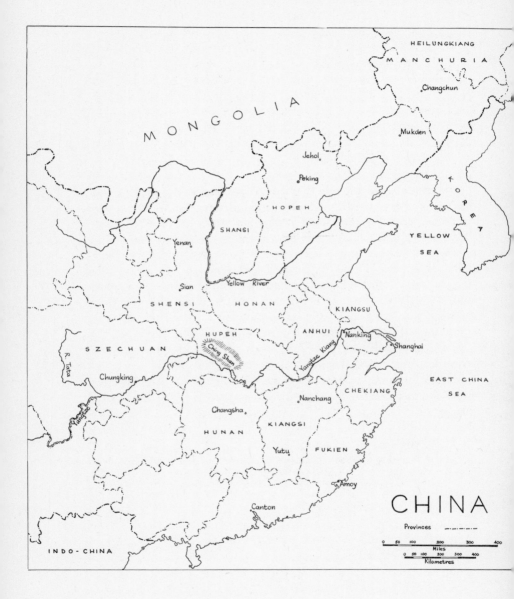

HEILUNGKIANG

MANCHURIA

Changchun

MONGOLIA

Mukden

Jehol

Peking

HOPEH

YELLOW

SHANSI

SEA

Yenan

Sian

Yellow River

SHENSI

HONAN

KIANGSU

HUPEH

ANHUI

Nanking

R. Tatu

Chu Shan

Shanghai

SZECHUAN

Yangtze Kiang

Chungking

EAST CHINA

SEA

CHEKIANG

Nanchang

Changsha

KIANGSI

HUNAN

Yangtze

Yutu

FUKIEN

Amoy

Canton

CHINA

INDO-CHINA

Provinces

0 50 100   200   300   400
Miles

0 50 100   200   300 400
Kilometres

Chapter 12

Summary of Communist revolution in China — 1921 to 1949

The most protracted of guerilla wars, and the most successful in terms of the achievements of the guerilla effort, was fought out in China between 1921, when the Chinese Communist Party was founded under the leadership of Professor Ch'en T'u-Hsiu (with Mao Tse-tung, then a librarian at Ch'en's university; Chou En-lai, a student in Paris; and the warrior Chu Teh as founder members) and 1949, when Mao Tse-tung came to power as leader of the Chinese people. There are no other historical examples of guerilla hostilities as thoroughly organised from the political, economic and military standpoint as those in China.

For the last twenty years of this long-drawn-out struggle, the Communists were in fact led by Mao Tse-tung as their political chief and military theorist, with Chu Teh as his military commander. In 1937, in his pamphlet *Yu Chi Chan* (Guerilla Warfare), Mao set out the principles by which he and Chu Teh conducted war against their enemies. This volume has since been widely distributed in 'Free China' and has received world-wide recognition as a modern classic on the subject.

The following chapter gives an abridged version of the views propounded by Mao Tse-tung in his pamphlet. They must, however, be read with the greatest caution, because although they lay down various principles which might well be relevant to guerilla warfare anywhere and at any time, the principles are applied by Mao to the specific environment of China during the Revolution, an environment which includes factors of history, time, space and multitudes which are not to be found anywhere else in the world. Mao himself writes that the theory and practice of warfare – and in this he includes both revolutionary and guerilla warfare – must be applied to the prevailing situation; that strategy and tactics which may apply to one situation may not be suitable for another. It is important, therefore, to understand what was the environment in which Mao led his people and armies to victory and the ways in which it changed from year to year throughout the protracted struggle.

China, the battle-ground for Mao Tse-tung and his opponents, is a country of vast magnitude which includes an infinite variety of terrain – areas of highly developed farmland; a few densely populated cities; interminable plains, immeasurable rolling grasslands; high plateaux and deep valleys of broken and rugged landscape; towering mountain ranges; unfathomable forests; unbounded space. In this country lived more millions of people than in any other country in the world, a multitudinous nation nine-tenths of which lived at barely subsistence level in the rural under-developed parts, with totally inadequate means of communication and transport.

These millions of country folk existed under an agrarian system of extreme feudalism, oppressed by exacting landlords, ravaged by rapacious brigands, raided by the numerous armies of the war-lords who warred across their lands, and subjected to every extremity of nature – drought and flood, cold and heat, storm and tempest. To them one day, one month, one year of danger and drudgery followed another; time was of no importance. To many death was a happy release from the burden of living. Yet, hungry and illiterate, enslaved by a hard environment, the majority lived by one of the most sophisticated codes of human behaviour known to man – namely '*li*'. This way of life had been developed over the centuries, and was given expression to by Chinese scholars and prophets among whom the best-known is Confucius. It is impossible fully to define this code in a few words; even to name it a code is incorrect. It is manners, custom, ritual and moral code all mixed together; it has a communicative, artistic and social function; it is a habit in which every person is trained from the day he or she shows the first glimmerings of understanding. To maintain '*li*' is the only criterion of right or wrong and in this it benefits even those who can understand neither the law nor philosophy. '*Li*' and Communism were not going to be easy bed-fellows.

Here, then, was an ideal setting for a protracted guerilla war – a vast and timeless land, a numerous and scattered people, an under-developed economy, inadequate communications; even '*li*' could be eliminated in time if the right means were chosen.

1921 to 1929

Mao Tse-tung stepped into this arena as a confirmed Communist in 1921, at a time when China was undergoing a period of war-lord rule, although Sun Yat-sen was nominally head of state with his government based in Canton. In this same year Sun Yat-sen travelled to Shanghai to meet a Russian envoy named Joffe, and accepted from him an offer of Russian aid for his country while agreeing to accept the friendship of the Chinese Communist Party and to re-name his own political party the Kuomintang, or Nationalist Party. This alliance, uneasy as it was, brought down the majority of the war-lords, chiefly by means of the 'Northern Expedition' which set out in early 1926, after the death of Sun Yat-sen, under the leadership of General Chiang Kai-shek. The expedition successfully concluded, the General, on March the 26th, 1927, broke with and proscribed the Communist Party, killed all those leaders on whom he could lay his hands, expelled all Russian advisers from the country and formed his own right-wing Nationalist Government with its seat at Nanking.

With the war-lords beaten, with the Communist Party driven from power, with the workers in the teeming cities suppressed, there was hope for stability in China. But on August the 1st 1929, a part of the Fourth Army, one of Chiang's best fighting formations, mutinied at Nanchang and under Chu Teh's leadership formed the Red Army of China. Chu Teh, following Russian advice (the Russians knew no more about China than anyone else and could not imagine a revolution without the proletariat) attacked the cities of Changsha, Canton and Amoy. At each place he was defeated with great slaughter and, driven into the mountains of Kiangsi and Hunan, eventually fled with the remnants of his army to the almost inaccessible mountain stronghold of Chingkanshan. There Mao Tse-tung awaited him, and there on the mountain Mao set up a new regime, based on the peasants, with guerilla warfare as its defence and 'Land to the Tiller' as its creed.

1929 to 1936

Mao Tse-tung now had a military force; he quickly gained the support of the peasants in North China; and he had an enemy –

Generalissimo Chiang Kai-shek. The revolution which had been under way for so many years since the fall of the Manchu Dynasty in 1911 was far from over – it had merely taken to the hills.

Chiang Kai-shek at once turned his enormous armies, first against certain pockets of Communist rebels in South China and later in five major 'annihilation' drives, against Mao's armies in the North. But by the time the Kuomintang soldiers appeared in force on his chosen ground, Mao had gained administrative control over most of the province of Kiangsi and had set up Soviets in the provinces of Fukien, Hunan, Honan, Hupeh, Anhui, Szechuan and Shensi. But more important, he had won the people to his side. Lacking the support of the peasants, the first four of Chiang's annihilation drives proved expensive failures, but for the fifth assault he revised his methods in the light of experience. The Kuomintang armies completely surrounded an enormous area in the Fukien-Kiangsi district with a modern and well-equipped force of 900,000 men. Against these the Reds could muster only 180,000 regulars and guerillas and 200,000 lesser partisans, only 100,000 of whom possessed rifles. They had no artillery and were short of both ammunition and equipment.

Chiang's armies advanced upon the Reds from all directions at once, compressing them into nothingness with a contracting ring of iron – a 'fiery wall' – thus depriving the Communists of the advantages offered by their extreme mobility. At the same time the Kuomintang's soldiers denied their enemies the support of the peasantry by literally scorching the earth and depopulating the area – a million peasants were massacred in effecting this policy. Mao and his armies were put on to the defensive.

Chiang's assault started in December 1933; by October 1934, the Red Army had lost 80,000 men or more. Mao and his Commander-in-Chief, Chu Teh, saw defeat staring them in the face and reacted with typical energy and daring. Choosing the weakest part of the Nationalists' encircling forces – at Yutu – by use of deception and by forced night marches they assembled there 100,000 men, all unknown to the Nationalist High Command. The Red Army now engaged in nine major battles over a period of thirty-eight days and at a cost of 25,000 soldiers, but in the end they had broken out of the encirclement and, on 16 October 1934, began the 'Long March'.

The 'Long March' is the most remarkable example in the history of warfare of the survival of an army in retreat, and a most striking demonstration of the application of Mao's maxim, 'The first law of war is to preserve ourselves and destroy the enemy.' The Red Army, with no transport other than baggage animals – all of which died en route – retreated over a distance of 6,000 miles (Mao describes the journey as the '10,000-mile March'), at all times under imminent threat of attack, or engaged in fighting off Chiang's pursuing armies or the warriors of nomad tribesmen through whose territories they passed. During the retreat they traversed some of the wildest and most rugged country in the world; crossed two huge rivers, the Yangtze and the Tata, by the most primitive means; passed over the Ma An Shan Pass on the Great Snow Mountain, a crossing made in a single day because at night no man can live on the mountain for the violent winds, the lack of oxygen and the giant hailstones; and marched through the Grasslands of the Mantzu, an unmapped wilderness inhabited by fierce and hostile tribesmen. Finally, on 20 October 1935, 20,000 survivors crossed the border into Northern Shensi province, where at last they were beyond reach of Chiang's armies. Here the remnants of Mao's army joined with the 25th, 26th and 27th Red Armies who had maintained small bases in Shensi since 1933.

While the Nationalists and Communists had been engaged in internecine struggle, the Japanese had made inroads into China. First annexing the rich province of Manchuria, they then invaded Jehol and later extended their sway over North China until finally openly invading the whole country. The Communists, even while in the Fukien-Kiangsi area, had formally declared war on the Japanese, militarily an empty declaration since they were far removed from any areas where Japanese troops were to be found, but politically a valuable propaganda move.

By the end of 1936, with their reviving armies secure in Shensi, the Communist movement had developed into a strong party favouring both agrarian reform (a policy by now deliberately modified to regain support of the landlord class) and united resistance to the Japanese invaders.

During the same period, the Kuomintang had lost favour with a majority of people, including many in those classes of society to whom the Communists had previously made no appeal. They had failed to produce a constitution for civil government, thus alienating enthusiastic Nationalists and intellectuals; they had made no attempt to put into effect a policy of land reform, thus alienating the peasants; they had yielded time and again to the Japanese, thus failing to capitalise on the intense patriotism of the Chinese people and their loathing for foreigners who had for a century plundered their country.

1936 to 1945

The Nationalist Party, for nine years pursuing a policy of internal pacification before resistance to external attack, had succeeded neither in pacifying the guerillas nor in throwing out the Japanese. The Communists appeared to offer something better, and they further consolidated their position with the people by a psychological master-stroke. In December 1936, at Sian the capital of Shensi province, they captured Chiang Kai-shek. Chou En-lai (now in a senior position in the Communist Party), by threatening his life, compelled the Generalissimo to agree to an alliance which seemingly placed the Communist armies under his, Chiang's, strategic direction. This move excited the wonder of the peasants and held a fascination for the educated classes. To them the Communists appeared to have made a supreme sacrifice in the interests of the country; it was they who had brought about internal pacification in order to pursue the war against the foreign aggressors.

By the end of 1939 the Japanese had driven Chiang's Nationalist armies out of the rich and populated coastal areas back into the western regions of China. There, with Chungking as their capital, the Kuomintang waited on the events of World War II. In the north, on the other hand, with Yenan as their seat of operations, the Communists pursued a guerilla campaign against the Japanese with sufficient purpose to convince the people that theirs was the truly patriotic movement.

By 1941 there was growing dissension between the two parties. Both pursued the same aim, namely, the monopoly of power in China after the war, but along entirely different paths. The Communists, by agrarian reform and by a show of force against the Japanese, won over to their cause both the peasants and the educated classes, while building up an army of considerable strength. The Nationalists, by disregarding the interests of the peasants and by relying for political strength solely upon the educated, lost the support of the majority of the nation while their military strength suffered severe losses at the hands of the Japanese and gained nothing in morale from the passive role which the army then adopted. By the end of the war China was no longer one country but two, a resurgent Communist China in the North (controlling an area of 350,000 square miles, a population of 95 million and with an army of 900,000 regulars and 2,400,000 militia), a decaying and corrupt Nationalist China in the South.

1945 to 1949

The only hope for peace rested in an alliance between the two, but there was to be no such *rapprochement*, nor could there be while one stood for revolution and the other for reaction. Instead, General Chiang Kai-shek carried the war to the north in American aeroplanes (America and her allies instinctively supported the 'legally-elected' government) and there followed four more years of civil war in which Mao Tse-tung, co-ordinating the activities of swarms of guerillas with those of his regular army, defeated the Nationalist forces at every turn. The struggle ended with a tremendous sweep across North China by the Communist forces (Peking fell on 22 January 1949), the defeat and disintegration of two Nationalist armies at Mukden and Changchun, and a final victorious Communist campaign to the south of the Yangtze river which led to the speedy capture of Shanghai and the southern provinces.

Mao and his colleagues, Chou En-lai and Chu Teh, had accurately estimated the feelings of the people of China and had fully taken account of the ancient rule of Chinese history that only with the support of both the peasants and scholars can revolution succeed. The Nationalists had succumbed because throughout they had looked upon the peasants merely as a source of recruits and comforts for their armies, and because they later lost the scholars due to their own corruption and inefficiency. The fact that neither side offered the Chinese people democratic rule mattered not at all; the Chinese had accepted the autocracy of the Empire for thousands of years.

Narrative 12

Yu Chi Chan[1]

WHAT IS GUERILLA WARFARE?

'In a war of revolutionary character, guerilla operations are a necessary part. This is particularly true in a war waged for the emancipation of a people who inhabit a vast nation. China is such a nation, a nation whose techniques are undeveloped and whose communications are poor. She finds herself confronted with a strong and victorious Japanese imperialism. Under these circumstances, the development of the type of guerilla warfare characterised by the quality of mass is both necessary and natural. This warfare must be developed to an unprecedented degree and it must co-ordinate with the operations of our regular armies. If we fail to do this, we will find it difficult to defeat the enemy.[2]

These guerilla operations must not be considered as an independent form of warfare. They are but one step in the total war, one aspect of the revolutionary struggle. We consider guerilla operations as but one aspect of our total or mass war because they, lacking the quality of independence, are of themselves incapable of providing a solution to the struggle.

Guerilla warfare has qualities and objectives peculiar to itself. It is a weapon that a nation inferior in arms and military equipment may employ against a more powerful aggressor nation.

---

[1] The extracts in this chapter are taken from the translation of Mao Tse-tung's *Yu Chi Chan* (Guerilla Warfare) made by Brigadier-General Samuel B. Griffith of the United States Marine Corps (Retd.), as published in the USA by Frederick A. Praeger, Inc. and in London by Cassell and Company Ltd. The footnotes are by AFC.

[2] In this passage Mao refers to confrontation with the Japanese imperialists, as he does throughout his treatise. Mao's revolutionary war was, however, directed not only against the Japanese but also against the Chinese Nationalists. His and General Chiang Kai-shek's various attempts to create a united anti-Japanese front broke down on the political obduracy of both sides and on the opportunities for independent operations offered by the terrain and lack of communications in China.

When the invader pierces deep into the heart of the weaker country and occupies her territory in a cruel and oppressive manner, there is no doubt that conditions of terrain, climate and society in general offer obstacles to his progress and may be used to advantage by those who oppose him. In guerilla warfare, we turn these advantages to the purpose of resisting and defeating the enemy.

During the progress of hostilities, guerillas gradually develop into orthodox forces that operate in conjunction with other units of the regular army. Thus the regularly organised troops, those guerillas who have attained that status, and those who have not reached that level of development combine to form the military power of a national revolutionary war. There can be no doubt that the ultimate result of this will be victory.

Both in its development and in its method of application, guerilla warfare has certain distinctive characteristics. We first discuss the relationship of guerilla warfare to national policy. Because ours is the resistance of a semi-colonial country against an imperialism[1], our hostilities must have a clearly defined political goal and firmly established political responsibilities. Our basic policy is the creation of a national united anti-Japanese front. This policy we pursue in order to gain our political goal, which is the complete emancipation of the Chinese people. There are certain fundamental steps necessary in the realisation of this policy, to wit:

1 Arousing and organising the people.
2 Achieving internal unification politically.
3 Establishing bases.
4 Equipping forces.
5 Recovering national strength.
6 Destroying the enemy's national strength.
7 Regaining lost territories.

There is no reason to consider guerilla warfare separately from national policy.

What is the relationship of guerilla warfare to the people? Without a political goal guerilla warfare must fail, as it must if its

[1] The 'resistance against imperialism' mentioned here should not be confused with the resistance movements in Europe during World War II, which were wholly patriotic in content. The revolutionary guerilla resistance in China, in addition to its patriotic appeal, included an ideological content which the European movements lacked. The Russians demonstrated confusion on this very point in the advice they offered to Mao Tse-tung during the closing years of the struggle, in that they applied the Russian wartime situation to Chinese problems. Their advice was disregarded.

political objectives do not coincide with the aspirations of the people and their sympathy, co-operation and assistance cannot be gained. The essence of guerilla warfare is thus revolutionary in character. On the other hand, in a war of counter-revolutionary nature there is no place for guerilla hostilities.[1] Because guerilla warfare basically derives from the masses and is supported by them, it can neither exist nor flourish if it separates itself from their sympathies and co-operation. There are those who do not comprehend guerilla action, and who therefore do not understand the distinguishing qualities of a people's guerilla war, who say: 'Only regular troops can carry on guerilla operations'. There are others who, because they do not believe in the ultimate success of guerilla action, mistakenly say: 'Guerilla warfare is an insignificant and highly specialised type of operation in which there is no place for the masses of the people' – (Jen Ch'i Shan). Then there are those who ridicule the masses and undermine resistance by wildly asserting that the people have no understanding of the war of resistance (Yeh Ch'ing for one). The moment that this war of resistance dissociates itself from the masses of the people is the precise moment that it dissociates itself from hope of ultimate victory.

What is the organisation for guerilla warfare? Though all guerilla bands that spring from the masses of the people suffer from lack of organisation at the time of their formation, they all have in common a basic quality that makes organisation possible. All guerilla units must have political and military leadership. This is true regardless of the source or size of such units. Such units may originate locally in the masses of the people; they may be formed from an admixture of regular troops with groups of the people, or they may consist of regular army units intact. And mere quantity does not affect this matter. Such units may consist of a squad of a few men, a battalion of several hundred men, or a regiment of several thousand men.

All these must have leaders who are unyielding in their policies – resolute, loyal, sincere and robust. These men must be well-educated in revolutionary techniques, self-confident, able to establish severe discipline and able to cope with counter-propaganda. In short, these leaders must be models for the people. As the war

---

[1] Mao here precludes the counter-revolutionary from adopting guerilla hostilities as his main effort; he does not preclude the use of guerillas as a subsidiary means.

progresses such leaders will gradually overcome the lack of discipline which at first prevails; they will establish discipline in their forces, strengthening them and increasing their combat efficiency. Thus eventual victory will be attained.[1]

Unorganised guerilla warfare cannot contribute to victory and those who attack the movement as a combination of banditry and anarchism do not understand the nature of guerilla action. The whole people must try to reform themselves during the course of the war. We must educate them and reform them in the light of past experience. 'Evil does not exist in guerilla warfare but only in the unorganised and undisciplined activities that are anarchism', said Lenin, in *On Guerilla Warfare*.

What is basic guerilla strategy? Guerilla strategy must be based primarily on alertness, mobility and attack. It must be adjusted to the enemy situation, the terrain, the existing lines of communication, the relative strengths, the weather and the situation of the people.

In guerilla warfare, select the tactic of seeming to come from the east and attacking from the west; avoid the solid, attack the hollow; attack; withdraw; deliver a lightning blow, seek a lightning decision. When guerillas engage a stronger enemy, they withdraw when he advances; harass him when he stops; strike him when he is weary; pursue him when he withdraws. In guerilla strategy, the enemy's rear, flanks and other vulnerable spots are his vital points and there he must be harassed, attacked, dispersed, exhausted and annihilated. Only in this way can guerillas carry out their mission of independent guerilla action and co-ordination with the effort of the regular armies. But in spite of the most complete preparation there can be no victory if mistakes are made in the matter of command. Guerilla warfare, based on the principles we have mentioned and carried out over a vast extent of territory in which communications are inconvenient, will contribute tremendously towards the subsequent emancipation of the Chinese people.

[1] Those with little experience of revolutionary and guerilla warfare tend to mock at the Communist's system of 'inflicting' political commissars on military units. The need for them in a revolutionary army is here explained. There is food for thought as to whether or not counter-guerilla military forces should be provided with similar political guidance. It is often extremely difficult for a man trained to kill and destroy properly to interpret a situation met in the field and to take the right action in the light of the prevailing political climate.

National guerilla warfare, though historically of the same consistency, has employed varying implements as times, peoples and conditions differ. The guerilla aspects of the Opium War, those of the fighting in Manchuria since the Mukden incident, and those employed in China today are all slightly different. The guerilla warfare conducted by the Moroccans against the French and the Spanish was not exactly similar to that which we conduct today in China. These differences express the characteristics of different peoples in different periods. Although there is a general similarity in the quality of all these struggles there are dissimilarities in form. This fact we must recognise. Clausewitz wrote, in *On War*: 'Wars in every period have independent forms and independent conditions, and, therefore, every period must have its independent theory of war'. Lenin, in *On Guerilla Warfare*, said: 'As regards the form of fighting, it is unconditionally requisite that history be investigated in order to discover the conditions of environment, the state of economic progress, and the political ideas that obtained, the national characteristics, customs and degree of civilisation'. Again: 'It is necessary to be completely unsympathetic to abstract formulas and rules and to study with sympathy the conditions of the actual fighting, for these will change in accordance with the political and economic situations and the realisation of the people's aspirations. These progressive changes in conditions create new methods.'

If, in today's struggle,[1] we fail to apply the historical truths of revolutionary guerilla war we will fall into the error of believing with T'ou Hsi Sheng that under the impact of Japan's mechanised army, 'the guerilla unit has lost its historical function'. Jen Ch'i Shan writes: 'In olden days, guerilla warfare was part of regular strategy but there is almost no chance that it can be applied today'. These opinions are harmful. If we do not make an estimate of the characteristics peculiar to our guerilla war, but insist on applying to it mechanical formulas derived from past history, we are making the mistake of placing our hostilities in the same category as all other national guerilla struggles. If we hold this view, we will simply be beating our heads against a stone wall and we will be unable to profit from guerilla hostilities.

To summarise: What is the guerilla war of resistance against Japan? It is one aspect of the entire war, which, although alone in-

[1] The year of which Mao Tse-tung is writing is 1937.

capable of producing the decision, attacks the enemy in every quarter, diminishes the extent of area under his control, increases our national strength and assists our regular armies. It is one of the strategic instruments used to inflict defeat on our enemy. It is the one pure expression of anti-Japanese policy, that is to say, it is military strength organised by the active people and inseparable from them. It is a powerful special weapon with which we resist the Japanese and without which we cannot defeat them.

THE RELATION OF GUERILLA HOSTILITIES
TO REGULAR OPERATIONS

The general features of orthodox hostilities, that is the war of position and the war of movement, differ fundamentally from guerilla warfare. There are other readily apparent differences such as those in organisation, armament, equipment, supply, tactics, command; in conception of the terms 'front' and 'rear'; in the matter of military responsibilities.

When considered from the point of view of total numbers guerilla units are many; as individual combat units they may vary in size from the smallest, of several score or several hundred men, to the battalion or the regiment of several thousand. This is not the case in regularly organised units. A primary feature of guerilla operations is their dependence upon the people themselves to organise battalions and other units. As a result of this, organisation depends largely upon local circumstances. In the case of guerilla groups the standard of equipment is of a low order, and they must depend for their sustenance primarily upon what the locality affords.

The strategy of guerilla warfare is manifestly unlike that employed in orthodox operations, as the basic tactic of the former is constant activity and movement. There is in guerilla warfare no such thing as a decisive battle; there is nothing comparable to the fixed, passive defence that characterises orthodox war. In guerilla warfare the transformation of a moving situation into a positional defensive situation never arises. The general features of reconnaissance, partial deployment, general deployment and development of the attack that are usual in mobile warfare are not common in guerilla war.

There are differences also in the matter of leadership and

command. In guerilla warfare small units acting independently play the principal role and there must be no excessive interference with their activities. In orthodox warfare, particularly in a moving situation, a certain degree of initiative is accorded subordinates, but in principle command is centralised. This is done because all units and all supporting arms in all districts must co-ordinate to the highest degree. In the case of guerilla warfare this is not only undesirable but impossible. Only adjacent guerilla units can co-ordinate their activities to any degree. Strategically their activities can be roughly correlated with those of the regular forces, and tactically they must co-operate with adjacent units of the regular army. But there are no strictures on the extent of guerilla activity nor is it primarily characterised by the quality of co-operation of many units.

When we discuss the terms 'front' and 'rear' it must be remembered that while guerillas do have bases, their primary field of activity is in the enemy's rear areas. They themselves have no rear. Because an orthodox army has rear installations (except in some special cases as during the 10,000-mile march of the Red Army or as in the case of certain units operating in Shansi province) it cannot operate as guerillas can.

As to the matter of military responsibilities, those of the guerillas are to exterminate small forces of the enemy; to harass and weaken large forces; to attack enemy lines of communication; to establish bases capable of supporting independent operations in the enemy's rear; to force the enemy to disperse his strength; and to co-ordinate all these activities with those of the regular armies on distant battle fronts.

Further distinction must be made in order to clarify this matter. After the fall of Feng Ling Tu, the operations of Central Shansi and Suiyan troops were more guerilla than orthodox in nature. In this connection the precise character of Generalissimo Chiang's instructions to the effect that independent brigades would carry out guerilla operations should be recalled. In spite of such temporary activities, these orthodox units retained their identity and after the fall of Feng Ling Tu, they not only were able to fight along orthodox lines but often found it necessary to so do. This is an example of the fact that orthodox armies may, due to changes in the situation, temporarily function as guerillas.

Likewise, guerilla units formed from the people may gradually develop into regular units and, when operating as such, employ the tactics of orthodox mobile war. While these units function as guerillas they may be compared to innumerable gnats, which, by biting a giant both in front and in rear, ultimately exhaust him. They make themselves as unendurable as a group of cruel and hateful devils, and as they grow and attain gigantic proportions they will find that their victim is not only exhausted but practically perishing. It is for this very reason that our guerilla activities are a source of constant mental worry to Imperial Japan.

While it is improper to confuse orthodox with guerilla operations, it is equally improper to consider that there is a chasm between the two. While differences do exist, similarities appear under certain conditions, and this fact must be appreciated if we wish to establish clearly the relationship between the two. If we consider both types of warfare as a single subject, or if we confuse guerilla warfare with the mobile operations of orthodox war, we fall into this error: we exaggerate the function of guerillas and minimise that of the regular armies.

A proper conception of the relationship that exists between guerilla effort and that of the regular forces is essential. We believe it can be stated this way: 'Guerilla operations during the anti-Japanese war may for a certain time and temporarily become its paramount feature, particularly in so far as the enemy's rear is concerned. However, if we view the war as a whole, there can be no doubt that our regular forces are of primary importance, because it is they who are alone capable of producing the decision. Guerilla warfare assists them in producing this favourable decision. Orthodox forces may under certain conditions operate as guerillas, and the latter may, under certain circumstances, develop to the status of the former. However, both guerilla forces and regular forces have their own respective development and their proper combinations.

In sum, while we must promote guerilla warfare as a necessary strategical auxiliary to orthodox operations, we must neither assign it the primary position in our war strategy nor substitute it for mobile and positional warfare as conducted by orthodox forces.

GUERILLA WARFARE IN CHINA 1927 – 1936

From 1927 to 1936 the Chinese Red Army fought almost continually and employed guerilla tactics constantly. At the very beginning a positive policy was adopted. Many bases were established, and from guerilla bands the Reds were able to develop into regular armies. As these armies fought, new guerilla regimes were developed over a wide area. These regimes co-ordinated their efforts with those of the regular forces. This policy accounted for the many victories gained by guerilla troops relatively few in number, who were armed with weapons inferior to those of their opponents. The leaders of that period properly combined guerilla operations with a war of movement both strategically and tactically. They depended primarily upon alertness. They stressed the correct basis for both political affairs and military operations. They developed their guerilla bands into trained units. They then determined upon a ten-year period of resistance during which time they overcame innumerable difficulties and have only lately reached their goal of direct participation in the anti-Japanese war. There is no doubt that the internal unification of China is now a permanent and definite fact and that the experience gained during our internal struggles has proved to be both necessary and advantageous to us in the struggle against Japanese imperialism. There are many valuable lessons we can learn from the experience of those years. Principal among them is the fact that guerilla success largely depends upon powerful political leaders who work unceasingly to bring about internal unification. Such leaders must work with the people; they must have a correct conception of the policy to be adopted as regards both the people and the enemy.

After 18 September 1931 strong anti-Japanese guerilla campaigns were opened in each of the three north-east provinces. Guerilla activity persists there in spite of the cruelties and deceits practised by the Japanese at the expense of the people, and in spite of the fact that her armies have occupied the land and oppressed the people for the last seven years. The struggle can be divided into two periods. During the first, which extended from 18 September 1931 to January 1933, anti-Japanese guerilla activity exploded constantly in all three provinces. Ma Chan Shan and Ssu Ping Wei established an anti-Japanese regime in Heilungkiang. In Chi Lin the National Salvation Army and the Self-Defence Army were led by Wang Te Lin and Li Tu respectively. In Feng T'ien, Chu Lu and others commanded guerilla units. The influence of these forces was great. They harassed the Japanese unceasingly, but because there was an indefinite political goal, improper leadership, failure to co-ordinate military command and operations and to work with the people, and finally, failure to delegate proper political functions to the army, the whole organisation was feeble and its strength was not unified. As a direct result of these conditions, the campaigns failed and the troops were finally defeated by our enemy.[1]

During the second period, which has extended from January 1933 to the present time, the situation has greatly improved. This has come about because great numbers of people who have been oppressed by the enemy have decided to resist him, because of the participation of the Chinese Communists in the anti-Japanese war and because of the fine work of the volunteer units. The guerillas have finally educated the people to the meaning of guerilla warfare, and in the north-east it has again become an important and powerful influence. Already seven or eight guerilla regiments and a number of independent platoons have been formed, and their activities make it necessary for the Japanese to send troops after them month after month. These units hamper the Japanese and undermine their control in the north-east, while at the same time they inspire a Nationalist revolution in Korea. Such activities are not merely of transient and local importance but directly contribute to our ultimate victory.

However, there are still some weak points. For instance: National defence policy has not been sufficiently developed; participation of the people is not general; internal political organisation is still in its primary stages, and the force used to attack the Japanese and the puppet governments is not yet sufficient. But if present policy is continued tenaciously, all these weaknesses will be overcome. Experience proves that guerilla war will develop to even greater proportions and that, in spite of the cruelty of the Japanese and the many methods they have devised to cheat the people, they cannot extinguish guerilla activities in the three north-eastern provinces.

The guerilla experiences of China and of other countries that

[1] The operations referred to in this paragraph were conducted by the Chinese Nationalists.

have been outlined prove that in a war of revolutionary nature such hostilities are possible, natural and necessary. They prove that if the present war for the emancipation of the masses of the Chinese people is to gain ultimate victory, such hostilities must expand tremendously.

Historical experience is written in iron and blood. We must point out that the guerilla campaigns being waged in China today are a page in history that has no precedent. Their influence will not be confined solely to China in her present anti-Japanese war but will be world-wide.

CAN VICTORY BE ATTAINED BY GUERILLA OPERATIONS?

In the war the Japanese brigands must depend upon lines of communication linking the principal cities as routes for the transport of war materials. The most important considerations for her are that her rear be stable and peaceful and that her lines of communication be intact. It is not to her advantage to wage war over a vast area with disrupted lines of communication. She cannot disperse her strength and fight in a number of places, and her greatest fears are thus eruptions in her rear and disruption of her lines of communication. If she can maintain communications, she will be able at will to concentrate powerful forces speedily at strategic points to engage our organised units in decisive battle. Another important Japanese objective is to profit from the industries, finances, and manpower in captured areas and with them to augment her own insufficient strength. Certainly, it is not to her advantage to forgo these benefits, nor to be forced to dissipate her energies in a type of warfare in which the gains will not compensate for the losses. It is for these reasons that guerilla warfare conducted in each bit of conquered territory over a wide area will be a heavy blow struck at the Japanese bandits. Experience in the five northern provinces as well as in Kiangsu, Chekiang, and Anhui has absolutely established the truth of this assertion.

China is a country half colonial and half feudal; it is a country that is politically, militarily and economically backward. This is an inescapable conclusion. It is a vast country with great resources and tremendous population, a country in which the terrain is complicated and the facilities for communication are poor. All these factors favour a protracted war; they all favour the application of mobile warfare and guerilla operations. The establishment of innumerable anti-Japanese bases behind the enemy's lines will force him to fight unceasingly in many places at once, both to his front and his rear. He thus endlessly expends his resources.

We must unite the strength of the army with that of the people; we must strike the weak spots in the enemy's flanks, in his front, in his rear. We must make war everywhere and cause dispersal of his forces and dissipation of his strength. Thus the time will come when a gradual change will become evident in the relative position of ourselves and our enemy, and when that day comes, it will be the beginning of our ultimate victory over the Japanese.

Although China's population is great, it is unorganised. This is a weakness which must be taken into account. For this compelling reason, we must unite the nation without regard to parties or classes and follow our policy of resistance to the end.

Energies must be directed towards the goal of protracted war so that should the Japanese occupy much of our territory or even most of it, we shall still gain final victory. Not only must those behind our lines organise for resistance but also those who live in Japanese-occupied territory in every part of the country. The traitors who accept the Japanese as fathers are few in number, and those who have taken oath that they would prefer death to abject slavery are many. If we resist with this spirit, what enemy can we not conquer and who can say that ultimate victory will not be ours?

The progress of the war for the emancipation of the Chinese people will be in accord with these facts. The guerilla war of resistance will be in accord with these facts, and that guerilla operations correlated with those of our regular forces will produce victory is the conviction of the many patriots who devote their entire strength to guerilla hostilities.

ORGANISATION FOR GUERILLA WARFARE

How Guerilla Units are Originally Formed
The unit may originate in any one of the following ways:

(a) From the masses of the people.
(b) From regular army units temporarily detailed for the purpose.

(c) From regular army units permanently detailed.
(d) From the combination of a regular army unit and a unit recruited from the people.
(e) From the local militia.
(f) From deserters from the ranks of the enemy.
(g) From former bandits and bandit groups.

In the present hostilities, no doubt, all these sources will be employed.

The Method of Organising Guerilla Regimes[1]

As an example of such organisation, we may take a geographical area in the enemy's rear. This area may comprise many counties. It must be sub-divided to accord with the sub-divisions. To this 'military area', a military commander and political commissioners are appointed. Under these, the necessary officers, both military and political, are appointed. In the military headquarters there will be the staff, the aides, the supply officers and the medical personnel. These are controlled by the chief of staff who acts in accordance with orders from the commander. In the political headquarters there are bureaus of propaganda organisation, people's mass movements, and miscellaneous affairs. Control of these is vested in the political chairman.

The military areas are sub-divided into smaller districts in accordance with local geography, the enemy situation locally and the state of guerilla development. Each of these smaller divisions within the area is a district, each of which may consist of from two to six counties. To each district a military commander and several political commissioners are appointed. Under their direction military and political headquarters are organised. Tasks are assigned in accordance with the number of guerilla troops available. Although the names of the officers in the 'district' correspond to those in the larger 'area', the number of functionaries assigned in the former case should be reduced to the least possible. In order to unify control, to handle guerilla troops that come from different sources and to harmonise military operations and local political affairs, a committee of from seven to nine members should be organised in each area and district. This committee, the members of which are selected by the troops and the local political officers,

---

[1] On page 276 is a chart summarising the organisation given below.

should function as a forum for the discussion of both military and political matters.

All the people in an area should arm themselves and be organised into two groups. One of these groups is a combat group, the other a self-defence unit with but limited military quality. Regular combatant guerillas are organised into one of three general types of unit. The first of these is the small unit, the platoon or company; in each county three to six units may be organised. The second type is the battalion of from two to four companies; one such unit should be organised in each county. While the unit fundamentally belongs to the county in which it was organised it may operate in other counties. While in areas other than its own it must operate in conjunction with local units in order to take advantage of their manpower, the knowledge of local terrain and local customs, and their information of the enemy.

The third type is the guerilla regiment, which consists of from two to four of the above-mentioned battalion units. If sufficient manpower is available a guerilla brigade of from two to four regiments may be formed.

All the people of both sexes from the ages of sixteen to forty-five must be organised into anti-Japanese self-defence units, the basis of which is voluntary service. As a first step they must procure arms, then they must be given both military and political training. Their responsibilities are: local sentry duties, securing information about the enemy, arresting traitors and preventing the dissemination of enemy propaganda. When the enemy launches a guerilla-suppression drive, these units, armed with what weapons there are, are assigned to certain areas to deceive, hinder and harass him. Thus the defence units assist the combatant guerillas. They have other functions. They furnish stretcher-bearers to transport the wounded, carriers to take food to the troops and comfort missions to provide the troops with tea and rice.

These groups should be organised not only in the active war zones but in every province in China. 'The people must be inspired to co-operate voluntarily. We must not force them, for if we do, it will be ineffectual'.

Equipment of Guerillas

In regard to the problem of guerilla equipment, it must be understood that guerillas are lightly armed attack groups which require simple equipment. The standard of equipment is based upon the nature of duties assigned; the equipment of low-class guerilla units is not as good as that of higher-class units. For example, those who are assigned the task of destroying rail communications are better equipped than those who do not have that task. The equipment of guerillas cannot be based on what the guerillas want, or even what they need, but must be based on what is available for their use.

The question of equipment includes the collection, supply, distribution and replacement of weapons, ammunition, blankets, communication materials, transport and facilities for propaganda work. The supply of weapons and ammunition is most difficult, particularly at the time the unit is established, but this problem can always be solved eventually.

As for minimum clothing requirements, these are that each man shall have at least two summer-weight uniforms, one suit of winter clothing, two hats, a pair of wrap puttees and a blanket. Each man must have a pack or a bag for food. In the north, each man must have an overcoat. In acquiring this clothing we cannot depend on captures made from the enemy, for it is forbidden for captors to take clothing from their prisoners. In order to maintain high morale in guerilla forces all the clothing and equipment mentioned should be furnished by the representatives of the government stationed in each guerilla district.

Telephone and radio equipment is not necessary in lower groups, but all units from regiment up are equipped with both. This material can be obtained by contributions from the regular forces and by capture from the enemy.

In the guerilla army in general, and at bases in particular, there must be a high standard of medical equipment. Besides the services of the doctors, medicines must be procured.

The problem of transport is more vital in North China than in the south, for in the south all that are necessary are mules and horses. Small guerilla units need no animals, but regiments and brigades will find them necessary.

Propaganda materials are very important. Every large guerilla unit should have a printing press and a mimeograph stone. They must also have paper on which to print propaganda leaflets and notices. They must be supplied with chalk and large brushes. In guerilla areas there should be a printing press or a lead-type press.

Guerilla equipment will in the main depend on the efforts of the guerillas themselves. If they depend on higher officers too much, the psychological effect will be to weaken the guerilla spirit of resistance.

THE POLITICAL PROBLEMS OF GUERILLA WARFARE

First of all, political activities depend upon the indoctrination of both military and political leaders with the idea of anti-Japanism. Through them the idea is transmitted to the troops. One must not feel that he is anti-Japanese merely because he is a member of a guerilla unit. The anti-Japanese idea must be an ever-present conviction, and if it is forgotten we may succumb to the temptations of the enemy or be overcome with discouragements. In a war of long duration those whose conviction that the people must be emancipated is not deep-rooted are likely to become shaken in their faith or actually revolt. Without the general education that enables everyone to understand our goal of driving out Japanese imperialism and establishing a free and happy China, the soldiers fight without conviction and lose their determination.

The political goal must be clearly and precisely indicated to inhabitants of guerilla zones and their national consciousness awakened. Hence, a concrete explanation of the political systems used is important not only to guerilla troops but to all those who are concerned with the realisation of our political goal.

There are three additional matters that must be considered under the broad question of political activities. These are political activities; first, as applied to the troops; second, as applied to the people; and, third, as applied to the enemy. The fundamental problems are: first, spiritual unification of officers and men within the army; second, spiritual unification of the army and the people; and, last, destruction of the unity of the enemy.

A revolutionary army must have discipline that is established on a limited democratic basis. In all armies obedience of the subordinates to their superiors must be exacted. This is true in the case of guerilla discipline, but the basis for guerilla discipline must be the individual conscience. With guerillas a discipline of compulsion is ineffective. In any revolutionary army there is unity of purpose as far as both officers and men are concerned, and, therefore, within such an army discipline is self-imposed. Although discipline in guerilla ranks is not as severe as in the ranks of orthodox forces, the necessity for discipline exists. This must be self-imposed, because only when it is is the soldier able to understand completely why he fights and why he must obey. This type of discipline becomes a tower of strength within the army, and it is the only type that can truly harmonise the relationship that exists between officers and soldiers.

There is also a unity of spirit that should exist between troops and local inhabitants. The Eighth Route Army put into practice a code known as 'The Three Rules and the Eight Remarks', which we list here.

Rules
1. All actions are subject to command.
2. Do not steal from the people.
3. Be neither selfish nor unjust.

Remarks
1. Replace the door when you leave the house.[1]
2. Roll up the bedding on which you have slept.
3. Be courteous.
4. Be honest in your transactions.
5. Return what you borrow.
6. Replace what you break.
7. Do not bathe in the presence of women.
8. Do not without authority search those you arrest.

The Red Army adhered to this code for ten years and the Eighth Route Army and other units have since adopted it.

Many people think it impossible for guerillas to exist for long in the enemy's rear. Such a belief reveals lack of comprehension of the relationship that should exist between the people and the troops. The former may be likened to water, the latter to the fish who inhabit it. How may it be said that these two cannot exist together? It is only undisciplined troops who make the people their enemies and who, like the fish out of its native element, cannot live.

We further our mission of destroying the enemy by propagandising his troops, by treating his captured soldiers with considera-

---

[1] In summer, doors are frequently lifted off and used as beds.

tion and by caring for those of his wounded who fall into our hands. If we fail in these respects we strengthen the solidarity of our enemy.'

CHART SHOWING ORGANISATION
OF A GUERILLA REGIME

AREA HEADQUARTERS

MILITARY COMMANDER	POLITICAL COMMISSIONER
Chief of Staff	Political Chairman
Staff	Propaganda bureau
Aides	Mass Movement Organisation
Supply officers	
Medical personnel	Miscellaneous

From these a committee is formed of from 7 – 9 members.

DISTRICT HEADQUARTERS —————— DISTRICT HEADQUARTERS

DISTRICT HEADQUARTERS

MILITARY COMMANDER	POLITICAL COMMISSIONER
Military Staff	Political Staff

From these a committee is formed.

COUNTY   COUNTY   COUNTY

Guerilla Battalion (4–5 Coys)

Guerilla Platoon or Company (3–6 per county)

Self-defence Units – – – – – – – – Units

Note: If manpower is available regiments (of 2–4 battalions) and brigades (of 2–4 regiments) may be formed.

————————— Chain of Command.

– – – – – – – – – – Co-operation.

Chapter 13

Introduction to concluding chapters

'The laws of war – this is a problem that anyone directing a war must study and solve.
The laws of revolutionary war – this is a problem that anyone directing a revolutionary war must study and solve. The laws of China's revolutionary war – this is a problem that anyone directing a revolutionary war in China must study and solve.'

MAO TSE-TUNG IN 'STRATEGIC PROBLEMS OF
(CHINA'S) REVOLUTIONARY WAR' – DECEMBER 1936

The purpose of the two final chapters in this book is to summarise the lessons relevant to the conduct of guerilla warfare which arise out of the past in the hope that they may be of some value in the future. It is impossible in so small a space to cover in detail every aspect of such a complex subject, but it may be of value to set out the main essentials which leaders of both guerilla and counter-guerilla forces must attend to if they are to be successful.

The two chapters may appear to lay down a set of rules to be rigidly applied in any situation; they most emphatically do not. It is comparatively easy to lay down a set of principles for conventional warfare because we have a long history to draw from and the most thorough analyses have been made and recorded. We can, for example, assume that the strongest camp usually wins; that if both sides are equal, the most resolute will win; that if strength and resolution are equal, initiative and surprise will influence the outcome; that the principles of security and economy of force and effort have continuing value. But for guerilla warfare, particularly in a revolutionary setting, we have only a short history to draw from, most of it post-1939, and we also find that the same principles do not necessarily hold good for both sides as they do in conventional war. Furthermore, the factors affecting any given situation in revolutionary war are far more numerous and in many ways more complex than those affecting conventional war, and they vary more widely between one situation and another. It is therefore of vital importance thoroughly to assimilate the first principle of revolutionary war which is so ably presented for us by Mao Tse-tung at the head of this narrative. The same advice holds good for counter-revolutionaries as for revolutionaries.

All that we can hope to do is to draw from our experience to date some laws for revolutionary warfare, to deduce principles and to suggest suitable strategy and tactics which may serve both the revolutionary and the counter-revolutionary of the future, provided they are properly applied to the situation prevailing at the time.

These final chapters deal with guerilla warfare as a form in a war of revolutionary type. This setting is chosen because this type of warfare includes the full scope of guerilla activity, not only the military aspect. However, many of the laws and principles discussed and much of the strategy and tactics proposed, if properly applied, are relevant to guerilla warfare in total, general or limited war settings.

Chapter 14

Successful revolution

Revolutionary war is a struggle between a government party and an anti-government party, in which the latter aims to overthrow the former, generally employing all the means at its command in its attempt to do so; the government party attempts to destroy its opponents by some or all the means at its command. Occasions have occurred when revolutionary situations have given rise to spontaneous insurrection, but more often the situation has produced a group of leaders, who proceed to plan and organise the revolution. Any such group, inevitably small and with no other assets than the qualities of leadership and the inspiration of recent history, must carefully consider whether certain conditions prevail which will give them some chance of victory. Further, they must make a detailed study of each condition, leading up to a final assessment of how vulnerable the country is to revolution. What are these conditions?

A CAUSE

A *cause* is essential to a revolution since it is only by offering them something worth fighting for that the revolutionaries will divorce the population from the government to whom their loyalty is wedded and stimulate active opposition to the existing regime. It is possible for the revolutionary to acquire the support of a people by terrorist methods, but it has been clearly demonstrated, for example by the peoples of the Philippines and Kenya, that popular support given as a result of intimidation alone is passive rather than active, and lasts only for so long as the counter-revolutionary forces show any signs of weakness. The revolutionaries need active support from at least a proportion of the population, not only passive approval or timid submission. Active and lasting support

279

can be gained only by persuasion; acts of terror should be regarded only as subsidiary means of persuasion or as methods of removing people who oppose the cause.

The Communists in Greece provided an excellent example of how a revolution can fail for lack of a good *cause*. During World War II, EAM and ELAS gained thousands of adherents and won the support of the people in the cause of patriotism. After the war, when this cause no longer existed, EAM could find no substitute in a country which had only a small proletariat, where there was no severe agrarian problem and where no class divisions existed. As soon as the government forces were fully mobilised with good leadership, the Greek people withdrew their support from EAM and ELAS and the revolution withered.

The best *cause* is one that will attract the largest number of supporters for as long as is necessary while repelling the smallest number of opponents. The cause must also be one with which the revolutionary can totally identify himself. The cause of 'One Arab Nation', offered somewhat diffidently by Lawrence to the Arabs, fell upon the stony ground of tribalism; the cause of independence from colonial rule offered by the Communists to the people of Malaya was not embraced by the majority of the population, i.e., the Malays, because the membership of the Communist Party was 90% Chinese. On the other hand, the cause of independence from colonial rule offered to the peoples of Indo-China and Algeria proved to be a good one in the particular situations prevailing in those countries.

The *cause* must be carefully chosen with a view to ensuring that its appeal lasts at least for so long as it takes the revolution to get well under way. It need last no longer than that because, once the contestants are engaged in open warfare the cause is likely to be forgotten or temporarily shelved in the day-to-day excitements of the struggle. The appeal of the cause will last provided that it arises from a deep-seated problem, and so long as it is one which cannot be espoused by the counter-revolutionaries without their surrendering the power for which they intend to fight. From 1945 onwards the Hukbalahaps fought for land reform, a cause which Ramon Magsaysay was able to espouse without surrendering one iota of the power of his government; rather he enhanced it.

The *cause* may be of a political, social, economic, racial or even of a trumped-up nature. In Cuba, Fidel Castro fought for the destruction of a bad political regime; any country in which one class exploits another is vulnerable to social revolution; many of the developing countries of today are in danger of revolution for economic reasons; South Africa is exposed to revolution on racial grounds; in China the Communists artificially intensified the agrarian problem, shifting the emphasis from peasant to landlord and back as the occasion demanded.

The problem which gives rise to the *cause* need not necessarily be of immediate import. The people of the Philippines had long been accustomed to feudal living before the Huks highlighted its evils in an attempt to bring down the government.

The *cause* need not remain the same throughout the period of revolution and indeed, in certain situations, should not. Anti-colonialism will almost certainly secure the co-operation of most of the people most of the time because it includes all the necessary ingredients; in other situations, however, there may be a need to make a cat's paw of the cause. Between 1921 and 1925, the Communist Party in China presented itself as the champion of the workers; between 1925 and 1928 they embraced the cause of their enemies, the Kuomintang, for the destruction of war-lord rule, thus appealing to a wider section of the public; between 1929 and 1934 they split with the Kuomintang and advocated land reform, thus winning over the peasants; during the time of Japanese aggression they advocated a united front against the invaders while moderating their policy of land reform, thus appealing on the grounds of patriotism to the whole of the population while appeasing the landlord class; after the surrender of Japan they reverted to land reform in its more moderate form and persuaded all classes of the need to throw out the corrupt regime of the Kuomintang.

At the outset, the revolutionary is faced with the problem of presenting his *cause* to the people. Most of the post-war revolutionary organisations were built up during the war under the guise of patriotic movements. Lacking a war-time situation, the revolutionary has to alert the public to the need to fight while himself remaining concealed, or at least partially concealed, from the government's intelligence agencies. The Mau Mau uprising in Kenya received a severe initial set-back because the leaders had over-reached themselves in this respect. The police special branch knew who the leaders were; they were apprised of the methods to be adopted and had even recorded the details of the bestial initiation ceremonies to which the Mau Mau leaders subjected recruits. In Cyprus, on the other hand, Colonel Grivas was able to build up his organisation and arm his terrorists in almost complete secrecy. The cause was presented to the people of Cyprus by a crash programme of pamphlets and sermons within the island and radio broadcasts delivered from outside the island, which coincided with the outbreak of the revolution.

There is no ready solution to this problem. In most situations the revolutionary would be well-advised to seek aid from outside the country or to devise means within the country by which to disseminate his propaganda in such a way that at least a majority of his activist leaders are protected from the risk of discovery.

GEOGRAPHY

Geography plays an important role in revolutionary guerilla warfare because the guerilla, weak at first, must have some help from geography if he is to survive.

The *larger the country* which forms the battleground the better for the guerilla because it is more difficult for a government to maintain control over a large area than over a small one. If this large country is also *difficult to regionalise* and has long *borders* contiguous to nations which are sympathetic with the revolutionary's cause, then further enormous advantages accrue to the guerilla.

The Chinese Communists, after defeat at the hands of the Kuomintang in the Fukien-Kiangsi provinces in 1934, were able to retreat over an immense distance and finally to find refuge in the remote province of Shensi over which General Chiang Kai-shek's government had only the loosest control. The ELAS guerillas in the Peloponnese proved an easy prey for the Greek government's forces because they were unable to withdraw across the water on to the Greek mainland; similarly the Hukbalahap were unable to spread out of Luzon into the many islands of the Philippines. In Algeria the FLN benefited from the sanctuaries provided by the sympathetic and neighbouring states of Morocco and Tunisia; even when the French closed these borders by constructing physical barriers, the manning of these obstacles tied down thousands of the French armed forces.

Terrain is another important aspect of geography. The mountains of Greece, the swamps and forests in Russia, the Aberdare forests in Kenya, the Sierra Maestra in Cuba and the jungles of Malaya provided cover and refuge for guerillas for very long periods of time. On the other hand, open plains are obstacles to guerillas because they have to concede mastery of the air to their opponents. Before the onset of air power, Lawrence and his Arabs were able to retreat at will into the Arabian deserts, but the FLN in Algeria, opposed by a powerful French air force, were denied access to the vast reaches of the Sahara. Towns are ideal for terrorism and mass uprisings of short duration, but are quite unsuitable for lasting guerilla activity, as was clearly demonstrated in Nicosia in Cyprus and in the town of Algiers.

It is generally thought, possibly because of the experiences in Russia of the French army (in 1812) and the Wehrmacht (in 1941–1944) that a tough *climate* favours guerillas, but the reverse is true. Russia is exceptional in that much of the vast battleground offers few facilities for food and shelter to either side in the winter months, so that the logistic facilities of the anti-guerillas are inevitably strained to breaking point: in this situation the guerillas, being indigenous, are better able to withstand the rigours of climate. But in Spain and Yugoslavia the guerillas suffered untold hardships during the winter months which were not shared by their enemies, whose logistic support provided food and shelter wherever they happened to be. The monsoon rains in Asia also have a more adverse effect on guerillas than on their opponents. In extreme *climates* guerillas, who have to live continuously in the open, are faced with terrible problems of survival and with extraordinary difficulties in keeping war material in working order. A temperate *climate* is best for the guerilla.

The *size and distribution of the population* has an important bearing on the conduct of revolutionary war. It is a comparatively easy matter for a government to control a small number of people, particularly if they are concentrated into a few towns and villages, but it is another matter to control a large population widely spread over huge areas. The more numerous and the more scattered the population the better for the revolutionary. The Boer War in South Africa, the Mau Mau uprising and Communist banditry in Malaya provided examples of the benefits which accrue to guerillas from scattered populations, small as they were. In each case the government concerned was compelled to re-group the people at

283

enormous effort and expense in order to separate them from the guerillas and to re-establish control. In China, where 700,000,000 people were scattered over unbounded space, the counter-revolutionaries found no solution to this crucial problem.

The *economy* of a country needs careful study. A prosperous country is open to terrorism and mass uprisings, but if such methods are much prolonged or intensified to an unendurable degree, they will antagonise the people unless the cause is genuinely embraced by an overwhelming majority. Terrorism continued in Cyprus in varying degrees for three years, yet the Greek Cypriots never turned sour. In the more highly developed parts of Greece, however, the people turned upon ELAS, the instigators of terrorism, as soon as they felt safe to do so. If terrorism and riots are to be inflicted upon the people they must be kept within such bounds as the people can reasonably be expected to endure; the higher their standard of living, the less can be expected of the people in terms of suffering.

The under-developed country is more exposed to prolonged guerilla warfare because the administrative facilities so essential to the efficient operating of counter-guerilla forces just do not exist.

The ideal *geographical conditions* for a revolutionary are a very large country which is in itself one entity and with no coast-line, a temperate climate, a numerous and scattered rural population and an under-developed economy, with afforested mountains on the borders and swamplands in the plains.

WEAKNESSES IN GOVERNMENT

Once the revolutionary has decided that he has a *cause* which will win the active support of a section of the population and the acquiescence or passive approval of the majority of the remainder, once he has assessed the effects of *geography* on his chances of success, he must then take a close look at his opponents. What are the weaknesses in a political regime which the revolutionary should look for?

The *lasting strength* of a regime depends on the support it receives from the nation. One should not examine this aspect in generalities such as, 'People loathe a dictatorship'; or 'People support only democratically-elected governments'. The regime in

Spain has the support of the people of Spain; a similar regime under Batista lost the backing of the people in Cuba. There is no national backing for the government of East Germany; there is strength in Yugoslavia.

The *leadership* required by a governing regime in revolutionary war needs to be strong and resolute because its opponents have a good cause and because the people, ignorant of the danger, will respond reluctantly to the call to fight. The leadership should also possess a knowledge of counter-revolutionary warfare. The Greek Communists made a series of appalling mistakes between 1945 and 1948 but flourished none the less because the government was weakened by inter-party strife and by doubts about the role of the monarchy. When Field Marshal Papagos, who was not only resolute but also understood Communist guerilla warfare, was given the necessary powers the Communist movement perished.

A government controls a population by several means, four of which are of importance in a revolutionary war, namely, the *governmental system,* the *administrative service,* the *police force* and the *armed services.*

In a country where political opposition is not allowed (as in most countries behind the Iron Curtain), where every private thought and action is strictly controlled, where a father will betray his son and a sister her brother, there is virtually no hope for the revolutionary. He can exist in complete secrecy; he can indulge in individual acts of terrorism; he can retire with a small party into a deep hinterland; but in the main he will have to bide his time and wait for a change in the regime. In a country in which there is complete anarchy, on the other hand, or utter administrative inefficiency under a *system of government* which is either idle or corrupt, the revolutionary will flourish because he has every facility for subversion and recruitment. Between these two extremes are any number of governmental systems which may either open or close the door to the growth of a revolutionary movement. Countries which might attract the revolutionary today are those which have recently been released from colonial rule and, while playing with democracy, have not yet established a settled system of government, particularly if at the same time they have failed to find a wise and strong leader.

Countries are run from day to day by an *administrative service* which gives off a force of its own. In France, for example, the administration is of exceptional strength and is likely to remain strong no matter what happens to the top leadership. In South Vietnam the reverse is true because the majority of efficient civil servants and local government officials have been liquidated during twenty-three years of war. In Algeria the FLN found a particularly weak administrative apparatus and benefited accordingly. The revolutionary should try and assess the extent to which the administration will stand up to the stresses and strains of war; its junior members, i.e. those in close touch with the people, should in any case be high on his list for murder.

In a *police force* it is numerical strength which counts in a revolutionary situation and also the support which the police are likely to be given by other government departments, particularly by the judiciary. Know-how, efficiency, loyalty and equipment are other factors to be looked at, but are of secondary importance. Algeria provides an example of an understrength but efficient police force giving due warning before the terrorists showed their hand, but as fast as the police arrested suspects the judges released them. It was not until twelve months after the revolution broke out that special powers were given to the police and the judiciary, but by this time the police force had been severely mauled by the FLN and the loyalty of its Moslem members was under the greatest strain.

The revolutionary should relate the numbers in the *police force* to the situation which he hopes to bring about, and should study the way in which the judicial system will protect his supporters. The police force should in any case be his first target for destruction, starting with the members of its intelligence service.

The *armed services* available to the government demand very careful scrutiny by the revolutionary with a view to counting their *numbers* in relation to the population and with regard to their *loyalty* and *equipment*.

The *armed services* will be fighting for the support and control of the population. They will, in addition, be compelled to protect the major administrative facilities of the country, e.g., lines of communication and base installations. They must never abandon any section of the population for more than a short period of time, nor can they afford to draw far away from the essential services because the government is fighting to maintain these very services for the benefit of the people. Experience shows that counter-revolutionary armed services need a superiority of at least ten to one over their opponents, and in difficult circumstances of as much as thirty to one. The French in Indo-China never came near to achieving this superiority and consequently they were bound to be defeated, despite the excellence of their soldiers and the high quality of their equipment.

There have been a number of occasions in recent years when the armed services have sponsored revolution and have succeeded in substituting military dictatorships for existing regimes. Excluding such situations, the revolutionary should beware of taking too optimistic a view of his chances of undermining the *loyalty* of the armed services, particularly if they have a long tradition of service behind them. Examples of lack of loyalty are provided by the mutiny led by Chu Teh at Nanchang in 1929 and by certain Moslem units of the French army in Algeria which had to be withdrawn from front line service. Any opportunity for seducing members of the armed services should be seized upon by the revolutionary because it needs only a few defections to undermine the morale of the whole force.

Most countries' armies are designed to deter an aggressor from outside and are therefore well-balanced and provided with modern *equipment*; but in a revolutionary war the prime requirement is for infantry. France's *Groupements Mobiles* were of limited value in the campaigns in both Indo-China and Algeria; in Malaya artillery regiments were quickly converted to the infantry role. A navy needs boats and ships which will effectively enforce a blockade of a coastline. An air force, which is assured of mastery in the air, needs slow-flying assault aeroplanes, short take-off transport planes and helicopters. The fast-flying, heavily-armed jet aircraft is likely to repel the population because it is almost impossible for the pilots to discriminate between friend and foe when selecting targets. The French attacked many friendly places from the air in Indo-China; the Americans are experiencing similar difficulties in target selection in South Vietnam today.

The fourth factor to be considered regarding the regular *armed services* is the *time* that may elapse before they *intervene*. In conventional war there is no time interval; the armed forces are deployed as soon after the declaration of war as facilities allow. This is not so in revolutionary war. There is invariably delay and hesitancy in deploying the armed forces and the decision is a difficult one for the counter-revolutionary political leaders. At the outset the government's cry will be 'minimum force', and too many fail to see that minimum force is achieved only by deploying maximum strength. A hundred men will normally capture one man without using any force at all, but if the two sides are equal a struggle is almost certain to ensue which will involve the use of force. The activities of the revolutionaries themselves may well dictate the speed at which the armed forces are brought into the fray; the longer they are delayed the better for the revolutionary.

Given a cause and suitable geography, the revolutionary must base his decision on the right moment to strike in the light of the *strengths or weaknesses of the government* opposed to him. If the government is weak, the moment is ripe. If it is strong, the revolutionary might well have to wait until some event or crisis weakens it. No single revolution succeeded against a modern colonial power before 1938, and few were attempted. World War II, however, weakened the colonial powers to a degree which produced favourable situations for guerilla warfare in many colonies. In China, the rise and fall of the Communist Party can be directly related to the various crises and events which affected the Kuomintang between 1925 and 1945. In 1935, for example, when General Chiang Kai-shek's power was at its height, and after the Long March, the strength of the Communist Party fell to only 40,000. The Japanese invasion then seriously weakened the fighting capability of the Kuomintang and by the end of the war with Japan the Communist Party possessed a regular army 900,000 strong, a supporting militia of 2,400,000 and controlled an area of 350,000 square miles.

SUPPORT FROM OUTSIDE

Outside support need not be an essential to a revolutionary movement at any stage; it will, however, always be a help. The wise revolutionary leader will not, in any case, accept a superfluity of aid at the start, except in the moral and political fields, because his main concern will be to steel his soldiers and to make his movement self-reliant. At a later stage he may well need moral and political support and material aid, particularly at that stage when he goes over from guerilla warfare to mobile warfare involving deployment of those massed forces which are designed finally to crush his enemy. In many situations material aid may be essential at this stage.

Moral and political support differ in origin and in the means by which they should be obtained. Moral support originates with people and can best be acquired by propaganda; political support originates with governments and can best be acquired by diplomacy. Moral support was given to the EOKA movement in Cyprus without any effort on their part because their cause appealed to many people outside the island and as a result, the terrorists received much encouragement by means of radio, the press and public speeches which are the normal means of giving expression to moral support. Political support, voiced in various international forums, strengthened the FLN in Algeria while bedevilling the French government.

Material support varies from the provision of money and advisers to open military aid. The latter, provided that it is given at a time when the revolutionaries have the organisation and the numbers to absorb it, can have a decisive effect.

The turning point in the war between the Vietminh and the French in Indo-China came in 1950 when Red China started giving open military aid to the Vietminh. The French estimate that by September of that year 20,000 Vietminh soldiers had been supplied with heavy equipment from this source. Without this aid the Vietminh would have been able to inflict upon the French a protracted guerilla warfare, but could not have staged the final showdown. In Greece, the Communists flourished while receiving military aid from over the borders of Yugoslavia, but once this aid was withdrawn by Marshal Tito in 1949, at that critical period just after ELAS had re-organised into regular formations, they suffered defeat within the year. The Mau Mau in Kenya and the Hukbalahap in the Philippines received no material aid from outside and were unable to flourish.

The revolutionaries' only alternative source of sufficient supplies to enable him to develop from small-scale guerilla war to full-scale attack is his enemy. In all revolutions initiated since the end of World War II the counter-revolutionary forces have made it impossible for the guerilla to capture supplies on this scale, except only in the latter stages of the struggle in China when Mao Tse-tung's armies boasted that their supply depots were conveniently located forward in the hands of the Nationalists!

Another valuable form of outside support is '*the sanctuary*'. If the revolutionary can withdraw his armed guerillas over the border into a friendly country he can offer them a haven for rest and re-training. If he has no such sanctuary his only alternative is to establish 'liberated' areas within the country, but no matter how much effort he expends on the security of these areas they will always be liable to attack by ground troops or from the air. The sanctuary also affords a safe refuge and a secure meeting-place to the revolutionary leaders. There are many examples of the value of sanctuaries.

With the East-West conflict as it is today, it should not be impossible for a revolutionary to obtain *support from outside*. The Communists can be relied upon to support, at least with political and material aid, any revolution which might further their long-term aims, whether or not they are in sympathy with the cause, because they hope that it will produce that state of anarchy so beloved by Communist infiltrators. Such aid, however, is unlikely to be given without strings attached. If the revolutionary fails with the Communists or finds the strings too unpalatable, he should turn elsewhere. The United Arab Republic mobilised moral, political and material support for the FLN; Greece for EOKA.

But while looking for outside support, the wise revolutionary will bear in mind that at least in the initial stages of the long and hard struggle which lies ahead he should rely in the main upon his own forces.

It can be seen that there is a wide variety of factors to be taken into account by the revolutionary leader before he resorts to open rebellion. He would do well to summarise them with a view to deciding on his best course of action and assessing his chances of success. A simple method of summarising is to list the factors in tabular form, allotting himself 'marks' (out of ten, say) against each factor, giving the balance of the total marks available to his opponents. As an example I offer a tabular summary which Chen Ping, the Chairman of the Malayan Communist Party would have done well to have made (but clearly did not make) in 1947 when he was urging open insurrection upon his colleagues. We must assume that his aim was to wage a protracted guerilla war with a view to overthrowing the existing regime in Malaya and substituting for it a Soviet Republic.

Serial	Factor	Marks to:		Notes
		Revolutionaries (Malayan Communist Party)	Counter Revolutionaries (Malayan Government)	
1	Own leadership	5	5	Organised and enthusiastic, but inexperienced and in disarray due defection Lai Teck.
2	Own forces	7	3	An army 6,000–10,000 strong, either in service or awaiting call-up (in the event only 50% answered call-up). Weapons available.
3	Cause	4	6	Cause of independence a good one, but Malays (one half population) unlikely actively embrace due 90% membership of Communist Party being Chinese.
4	Location of Malaya	2	8	Isolated by sea, except on northern border.
5	Size	2	8	Small.
6	Formation	9	1	One entity; impossible to regionalise.
7	Borders	2	8	One short border with unsympathetic country beyond.
8	Terrain	9	1	Nine parts jungle.
9	Climate	6	4	Sub-tropical.
10	Population	2	8	Small and only partially scattered.
11	Economy	2	8	Highly developed.
12	Solidity of regime	2	8	Although a colonial government a prosperous people in the main behind it, expecting independence by constitutional means.

table (*cont.*)

Serial	Factor	Marks to:		Notes
		Revolutionaries (Malayan Communist Party)	Counter Revolutionaries (Malayan Government)	
13	Government's leadership	0	10	Resolute and likely to remain so. Also experienced in counter-guerilla warfare.
14	Government's administrative machine	3	7	Solidly based, if inexperienced in decision-making
15	Political structure	6	4	An alert democracy.
16	Police	5	5	Intelligence good, loyalty sound, but weak in numbers.
17	Enemy's armed forces	0	10	Numerous in relation to population, skilled, loyal and with almost unlimited resources.
18	Outside support	1	9	None guaranteed; moral and political from Communist countries hoped for.
	Totals	67	113	

This table does not, of course, present a completely accurate picture. It does, for example, allot the same number of total marks to each factor, whereas some factors are more important than others. It does, however, provide a useful summary, and from it Chen Ping could have deduced that he had only a remote chance of achieving his aim in the conditions prevailing at the time.

The table also shows clearly that his opponents' *changeable* assets were the strong economy of the country, the solidity of the regime, its leadership, administrative machine and armed forces, while the revolutionaries' major changeable weakness was lack of outside support. Faced by these facts Chen Ping might well have concluded that, rather than resort at once to guerilla war, it would have been better to undermine the economy by instigating industrial unrest, and to penetrate the administrative service while awaiting some event such as independence (which any intelligent man could have foreseen for Malaya) in the hope that it would weaken the solidity of the regime and its leadership and lead to the withdrawal of the strong British armed forces. While waiting he might well have solicited support for his movement from the Chinese Communists who in 1947 were on the path to victory.

In fairness to Chen Ping we must admit to the advantage of hindsight, but he himself had some advantage in this respect in that the Communist Party of Malaya had staged a dress rehearsal for guerilla warfare during the time of Japanese occupation. The leaders could, for example, have foreseen that the Malays would not embrace their cause (Serial 3 of table) because they had refused co-operation with the guerillas during the war: rather the guerillas were compelled to avoid Malay kampongs for fear of betrayal.

HOW TO CONDUCT A REVOLUTION

Let us assume that the revolutionary has assessed his chances of success as being reasonably favourable. He must now decide how he is to conduct his affairs, stage by stage and right up to the time when he has achieved his aim. Drawing from history he has one of two methods to follow – the Communist method as exemplified in China, the Philippines and Malaya, or the Nationalist method as exemplified in Cyprus and Algeria.

THE COMMUNIST METHOD

For details of the Communist method he has only to study the writings and sayings of various Communist leaders from Karl Marx to Mao Tse-tung. These writers are unanimous in claiming that their methods are applicable to countries other than their own and the Chinese Communists are adamant that their methods – Mao's way to victory – apply to all colonial and semi-colonial countries; by their definition this includes all of Asia except the Communist states and all of Latin America and Africa.

The *first stage* in the Communist method is the creation of a party, which is the basis for the whole struggle. The party should be of the proletariat, but must include the peasants and must find its leaders from among the intellectuals and students. It must be strong and pure and possessed of an iron discipline. Strength is ensured by frequent testing; purity is maintained by dismissal or conversion of all deviators; discipline is imposed by ruthless but 'democratic' centralised control. The party may operate openly at first, but must retain an underground element in case the party is outlawed, or, when the time comes, to work secretly in support of open insurrection. The creation of a party is a long process, however, even in countries in which political opposition is permitted. The Chinese Communist Party spent five years in raising its first thousand members: it was ten years from its inception before the Malayan Communist Party became an organisation to be reckoned with, despite a fairly strong membership.

The *second stage* is to win allies for the party. Any form of deception, trickery or political manoeuvre is justified to this end, short of open rebellion. The aim should be to win over to the party's side the maximum numbers among the people, particularly in the rural areas where the battle is to be fought. The seduction of politicians is only a means to this end. The party must be careful to retain its identity during this time, and to avoid being overwhelmed by its allies.

The *third stage* is guerilla warfare. The Chinese Communists claim that this stage is indispensable and that even if opportunity offers, the revolutionaries should not seize power by political compromise. There is something to be said for this viewpoint, because theoretically a party that has emerged successfully from the hardships of a protracted struggle must be strong and well-tested. Events in China today may, however, give rise to some practical questions on this subject. History has not yet provided us with a certain answer but it may well prove that the party remains strong only for so long as it retains those leaders who have been through the fire. Whether adopted as a resort or for reasons of convenience, guerilla warfare itself is conducted in three steps:

Step 1
The guerilla's first concern is survival, his second the securing of the active assistance of the population. He achieves the latter by means of political cells living among the people, supported by force in the shape of guerilla bands. Commissars ensure the political reliability and proper behaviour of the guerilla soldiers. This stage is best conducted in areas remote from the centres of govern-

ment control and which are difficult of access to the government's security forces.

Step 2
The establishment of guerilla bases ('liberated areas') where the revolutionaries' political organisation controls the population and where the armed guerillas can recruit, train and equip.

Step 3
Expansion outwards from these bases.

Throughout the period of guerilla warfare the revolutionary must make sure of maintaining a central direction of effort, although the actual operations may be widely dispersed. He does this by ensuring that a common doctrine is accepted and worked to by all his people. The revolutionary must also take steps to ensure that his allies do not desert him during this period.

The *fourth stage* is the transfer from guerilla warfare to mobile warfare preceded by the conversion of guerilla units to regular troops. The selection of the timing for this transfer is of the utmost importance, and certain prior conditions must prevail if the revolutionary is to avoid losing much of what he has gained during the period of guerilla activity.

He must be sure that his *regular bases* are firmly established, governed and administered in every way by his political organisation and defended by the people rather than by his regular troops. The population within these bases needs to be fully organised, by villages and districts, to conduct full-scale war on the side of the revolutionaries. If military aid is being provided from abroad, some of these regular bases should be near the border. The revolutionary also needs additional *guerilla bases*, again under his own political control. Sufficient properly trained *political cadres* must be available to take control of areas which are to be 'liberated' by his regular forces, and to organise the population for war in these areas. His *regular forces* must be sufficiently well-armed and equipped to give them a good chance of success in battle against government troops. Many of the initial operations mounted by the regular troops, making full use of their advantage of extensive mobility, may have to be launched for one purpose only – to capture large amounts of weapons and equipment.

We have a number of examples of revolutionary movements moving into the mobile warfare stage too early; the best is provided by General Nguyen Vo Giap, when he launched his Vietminh in massed attacks against the French forces in the Red River Delta in 1951, and was severely beaten.

The *fifth stage* is the final annihilation of the enemy regime. Before moving into this last offensive, the revolutionary must be sure of his political and psychological strength vis à vis the people and the strength of his military and subversive forces vis à vis his enemy.

THE 'NATIONALIST'[1] METHOD

This method varies from the Communist's only in regard to the first and second stages, the remaining being the same. The 'Nationalist' rejects the long and sometimes agonising process of creating a party and winning allies. Instead, he recruits a small group of terrorists (in Cyprus the group numbered less than a hundred; in Algeria no more than five hundred) and suddenly and without warning inflicts a wave of terrorism upon his country.

In the *first stage* the terrorist need select no particular targets, because the aim is to draw the attention of the people, and of the world, to the revolutionaries, to make a noise and to show that they are a party to be reckoned with. The initial bombings and arson instigated by EOKA on 1 April 1955 did no military or administrative damage whatsoever, but within days the Greek Cypriots respected the movement while the hotels of Cyprus were taken over by the international press.

The *second stage* in terrorism needs to be more selective, the aim being to divorce the people from their government. This is best done by killing a number of junior government officials who are in touch with the people, such as policemen, village chiefs and teachers, and by attacking administrative installations, a process which should be continued until the government's authority is thoroughly undermined.

Once terrorism has had a fair measure of success, the 'Nationalist' revolutionary passes to the third stage, guerilla warfare.

There are two inherent dangers in terrorism. If it is developed to

[1] For the purpose of this chapter I use this word to describe all types of revolution other than those inspired by Communism.

an intensity which the people can no longer endure it will back-fire. If it proves successful, the revolutionaries may find themselves suddenly projected into a position of power for which they are un-prepared, and will then be unable to maintain their position during the long struggle to follow. They may even disintegrate, partic-ularly in the face of the bitterness which terrorism will almost certainly have created.

Before adopting this 'Nationalist' method the revolutionary needs to be sure of the strength, skill, determination and dedica-tion of his leadership, unless, of course, he is opposed by a weak regime or possesses a cause which is bound to succeed with the people.

Chapter 15

Successful counter-revolution

From the counter-revolutionary's standpoint, there are two phases in a revolutionary war – the covert or 'cold' war phase and the overt or 'hot' war phase.

COLD WAR

During this phase the revolutionary restricts himself to lawful and moderate activities while building up his organisation and strength and, so far as he is able, publicising himself and his aims. The hot war period is that which follows the onset of unlawful and violent actions. In relation to the various stages outlined in the previous chapter, the hot war starts with stage 3 of the Communist method of revolution and applies, theoretically, to the whole course of the Nationalist method. However, the transition from cold to hot war is a gradual process and one which is far from clear-cut, and in practice the moment of change from one to the other is not always easy to recognise. Even in the Nationalist method there is a period of preparation before the revolutionaries initiate acts of terrorism.

To illustrate this change from cold to hot war with examples from the past; we find that in China the cold war period lasted from 1921 until 1927, during which time the revolutionary Communist Party was allied to its opponents, the Nationalists, in order to eliminate the evils of war-lord rule; the hot war could be said to have been started by the counter-revolutionaries when Generalissimo Chiang Kai-shek broke with the Communists in 1927 and killed a number of the Party's leaders. In Kenya, Algeria and Cyprus the revolutionaries started the hot war with a bang, but in all these countries the ruling regimes were aware that something was afoot some time before the rebels came out into the open. In the Philippines the government countered the Huks' initial outbursts of terrorism by police action only; it was not until four years later that the armed forces of the Philippines were committed to the war.

For the purposes of discussion, however, we will assume that the moment of commencement of the hot war is that moment when the counter-revolutionary commits his armed forces to the struggle, a point of time which may often, but will not necessarily, follow shortly upon the adoption by the revolutionary of unlawful and violent activity.

During the period of the cold war the counter-revolutionary is faced with a situation in which his enemy is conducting his affairs within the law, except in regard to certain subversive activities which may be on the fringe of illegality or even downright criminal, e.g. Ben Bella's raid on the central post office at Oran in 1949. In any case, unless the revolutionary leaders over-reach themselves, no one but a few members of the police and government is aware of what is threatening. But even if there is some awareness of the reality of the threat, the people can hardly be expected to accept as proof of danger the few facts which the government may be able to put before them, and they will be most unlikely to condone severe or unseemly measures which will affect their day-to-day life.

In such a situation the counter-revolutionary has four courses open to him:

1. Direct Action

The most direct course is to arrest the leaders, restrict their movements and ban their organisation; by these means the revolution may be effectively laid low. This is the obvious and easiest course for a totalitarian regime, but it is hardly practicable in a democracy unless the government has taken the precaution of equipping itself with special powers to deal with revolution; even then the government will have to take care to make the arrests and hold the rebel leaders under restriction without giving undue publicity to the facts, because it is at this stage that the rebels most need publicity.

Without special powers the counter-revolutionary government is placed in a serious dilemma in that it has to justify to the people every action taken against the enemy and any restriction that it may have to impose on everyday life. The revolutionaries will claim the right of political opposition; they will exploit every form of protection offered by the law; they will use the law-courts as publicity agencies; and if their organisation is outlawed they will re-appear under another name. Under pressure, the government may be tempted themselves to act beyond the law; if they do they may well create a public outcry and so play into the hands of the revolutionaries.

Prompt and drastic action can therefore be safely taken by a democratic government against revolutionary leaders during the cold war period only if that government has special powers and can prevent the revolutionary gaining publicity from the implementation of those powers, unless, of course, the rebels are no more than a gang of hot-heads without a popular cause. This is not to say that in certain situations democratic governments would not be right to lay the revolution low by placing the leaders under restriction, but the risks of taking this course must first be carefully weighed.

2. Infiltration

Should the direct course prove an unacceptable risk then every attempt should be made to infiltrate the revolutionary movement. As was clearly demonstrated by the Malayan Communist Party and the Algerian FLN, the leaders of embryo revolutionary movements are inexperienced and are often divided in opinion. In this state they are vulnerable to penetration by agents who should be insinuated into the movement, both to bring about its disintegration by playing upon the weaknesses of its members and to inform on it.

Although agents may bring quick results, their infiltration should be planned as a long-term investment. They must be given time to establish themselves in positions of trust in the revolutionary movement, and their security should not be jeopardised by insistence on early and frequent reporting to their sponsors.

3. Attack the revolutionaries' assets

A more indirect approach is to attack those assets which even at this early stage may have accrued to the revolutionaries. Such assets are most likely to be their cause (there is explanation in the previous chapter of how essential a good cause is to the revolutionary) and the promise or reality of outside support. Geography may be an asset but one which cannot be much altered in peacetime.

Dispossessing the revolutionary of a well-chosen cause may prove to be impossible since it will involve the government either in ridding the country of all its problems or in an open espousal of the cause with a consequent unacceptable surrender of power. There are no clear-cut examples from the past of governments espousing or seriously undermining a revolutionary cause during the cold war period, although there are a number of cases where this has been done during the hot war, e.g. in the Philippines and Malaya.

It should be possible to foretell where the revolutionaries will look for outside support, and diplomatic activity should be directed at depriving them of such support, particularly if it is likely to be offered by a neighbouring country.

4. Strengthen the regime

Bearing in mind the difficulties which will be encountered in undermining the revolutionary's cause or in depriving him of outside support, the best indirect approach would appear to be a strengthening of the governing regime by an increase in the powers and numbers of the bureaucracy, police, armed services and judiciary, with the dual purpose of showing the revolutionaries that the government is determined to fight, and of strengthening the machinery by which to fight. Even more important is a strong political machinery; the government needs to look at every means by which control is exercised over the population with a view to eradicating corruption and ensuring both sufficiency and efficiency at all levels.

Whatever may be the course which the counter-revolutionaries may feel able to adopt during this cold war period, one thing is certain. As Field Marshal Papagos concluded after the campaign against the Communists in Greece: 'When a nation reaches a point where it is forced to engage in military operations against the guerillas, the Communists have already won the first round. Thereafter the process will be painful'.[1] Every example offered by history shows that once the first shot has been fired, a revolution can be exterminated only after enormous expenditure of blood and money and goodwill. Counter-revolutionary regimes should bear this in mind when they are assessing the risks involved in early direct and ruthless suppression.

[1] From an article in *Foreign Affairs*, January 1952.

HOT WAR

The Situation

The circumstances under which the armed forces are first committed to the struggle are likely to be as follows:

1 With the revolutionaries. They have a political organisation in being. They have a cause around which a belligerent movement has sprung up. Part of this movement may be revealed, part will certainly be concealed. They have an army of terrorists or guerillas or regular troops, or all three, although the latter will be a rarity unless part of the country's armed forces have joined the revolt. They control the population in certain areas (black); they have partial control over the population in other areas (grey); they have infiltrated and threaten the remaining areas (white). They have the psychological initiative.

2 With the counter-revolutionaries. They have a political organisation which possesses the means for controlling the population, but the means are not strong enough in terms of numbers to deal with an emergency situation. The loyalty of every citizen is in question. The population, except in the black areas, is unaware of the danger which threatens. Confusion exists as to where priorities lie – the economy sags while expenses rise; the guarding of administrative installations and essential services is a necessity, yet it is important to hunt down the armed enemy.

Conventional Military reaction?

In such a situation, the counter-revolutionary may be tempted to take military action as prescribed by the experiences of conventional warfare. The objectives of conventional warfare, however, are the enemy's territory, his armed forces and his material means of making war. But in revolutionary warfare the enemy holds no territory, nor is he prepared to fight for it; his armed forces, part civilian, part uniformed, are either too well-concealed or too small and mobile for immediate destruction; while his material requirements are infinitesimally small compared with those of conventional forces and can mostly be acquired from local resources. Only if the counter-revolutionary regime has the means to saturate the country with its armed forces and maintain widespread operations for months on end will conventional military operations eliminate revolution. History provides no single example of a counter-revolutionary regime's ability to maintain such operations, although the British came near to this position during the Boer War.

Guerilla-type Military reaction?

In the absence of an ability to mount suppressive operations by conventional means, the counter-revolutionary might consider opposing guerillas with guerillas. In the situation prevailing at the outbreak of the hot war, such a method would be most unlikely to succeed because the revolutionary has the support of the population in the black areas, and in part in the grey areas; without such support he would not have opened guerilla warfare. Furthermore, experience shows that there is insufficient room in one territory for two or more guerilla forces to co-exist – e.g., Tito's partisans and Mihailovic's Cetnics in Yugoslavia, ELAS and other guerilla organisations in Greece, the Communist and Nationalist guerillas in North China. Those guerillas who have the support of the majority of the population will either destroy or absorb the others. Guerilla forces may serve the counter-revolutionary well in a subsidiary role, as the Scout Ranger teams served Ramon Magsaysay in the Philippines, but not as a main form. The strength of the counter-revolutionary lies in his open assets; he should not sacrifice them in exchange for subversion.

STRATEGY

Since neither conventional nor guerilla warfare will work, one must conclude that the counter-revolutionary should develop a form of warfare suitable to revolutionary war. What are the principles upon which he should base his strategy and tactics?

The support of the population

This is as essential to the counter-revolutionary as it is to his enemy. But how is he to gain it in the face of the fact that at least in the black areas, and partially in the grey and white areas, the revolutionaries have already established their political organisation among the people and have organised them to conduct the struggle on their side? The previous chapter explained how the revolutionary, before adopting open rebellion, must be sure of the active support of a minority and at least the neutrality of the majority of the people. There will, however, always be a third element, a minority who support the government. In areas where the revolutionary has gained control this third element will have disappeared, afraid to show themselves.

The government's first step, therefore, is to find this element, to place its members in positions of authority and provide them with security which will enable them to win over to the government's side the neutral majority. Every operation, whether civilian or military, should be designed for this purpose. Furthermore, the physical security which will alone enable the government's political organisation to work among the people should be maintained for so long as is necessary to establish or re-establish locally the political regime, and allow time for the mobilisation of the people in defence against a possible come-back by the revolutionaries.

This may prove to be a long process, but experience shows that victory is not won until the revolutionaries are isolated from the people and the people have the determination, organisation and facilities permanently to maintain that isolation.

Concentration

The resources of manpower, material and effort required permanently to isolate the revolutionaries from the population are enormous, while the operations involved are of an intensive nature and of long duration. The resources cannot, therefore, be spread all over the country; they must be concentrated area by area.

The Strategic Concept

These are the two vital principles relevant to revolutionary warfare and they alone dictate the strategy of the counter-revolutionary regime, which should be based on the following programme:

1 Deploy into a selected area sufficient military and police forces, and political teams, to break the hold over the population of the enemy's armed guerilas.
2 Hold the area secure while making contact with and re-establishing control over the population. Security must be maintained to enable all three services to go to work among the population unmolested.

3 Hold the area secure while eliminating the revolutionaries' political cells.

4 Hold the area secure while carrying out political, social, economic and other reforms. The reforms will not take effect if the guerillas are allowed to return at this stage – for example, land reform in Algeria in 1957 was rendered ineffective by the slaughter of a number of Moslems who had accepted land from the government.

5 Hold the area secure while elections are held to appoint local leaders, while organising the people into self-defence units and indoctrinating them until their determination to keep the revolutionaries out is no longer in doubt. Sufficient volunteers will not appear for armed service if the guerillas are still active in the area – for example, in South Indo-China, at the time of the battle of Dien Bien Phu, a call-up of 100,000 citizens produced only 9,000 volunteers.

6 Organise the new leaders into a political party.

7 Transfer the major effort to another area while continuing a policy of public education and hunting down any guerilla remnants which may remain in the selected area.

This programme was successfully adopted, in degrees of thoroughness which varied according to prevailing conditions, by General Papagos in Greece in 1949, by General Briggs and Sir Gerald Templer in Malaya, by the war cabinet in Kenya against the Mau Mau and by the French in Algeria in 1959–60.[1]

Certain aspects of this strategy merit further detailed attention:

1 The initiative. Because the counter-revolutionary exerts his efforts on the population and not against the armed guerillas alone, the system gives him the initiative. The French discovered in Indo-China that an attack in one direction against the Vietminh failed to relieve pressure elsewhere. For example, the operation of *Groupement Mobile* 100 on the Plateaux Montagnards and the simultaneous landing of a large force on the adjacent coastline of Central Annam (*Opération Atlante*) although intended to do so had no effect on the battle of Dien Bien Phu. If the guerilla does not wish to fight in any given place he simply disappears, but if the government's political and military forces

---

[1] A detailed description of the methods adopted by the French is given under the title 'Operation Pilote' in Narrative 11, pp. 247–9.

attempt to capture and hold the population in any given area, the guerilla is compelled either to fight or to admit defeat in that area, because the population is his source of strength.

2 Economy of force. The system also allows of the maximum economy of force, an essential aspect of counter-revolutionary war, because operations into selected areas can be spread over a period of time and can be mounted anywhere the counter-revolutionary chooses. While concentrating his main forces on the chosen area, the counter-revolutionary need deploy only sufficient forces to other areas to ensure that the guerilla does not establish safe bases there. The raids by land or air necessary to deprive the guerilla of security in his bases need be comparatively small and of short duration, and, although they may have to be frequent, will not tie down large forces. In Kenya the security of the Mau Mau's bases in the forests was constantly disturbed by the RAF and a number of small patrols operating round the perimeter of the selected area.

3 Best use of assets. The system also makes best use of the counter-revolutionary's assets – his economic and administrative resources, his public information facilities and, in areas where reasonable or better communications exist, the heavy equipment of his armed forces. All these assets are of limited value when deployed against armed guerillas, but are of inestimable value when applied to the population.

4 Simplicity. The system is simple, in a situation which calls for simplicity above all else. Confusion inevitably reigns during the initial stages of a hot revolutionary war. The counter-revolutionaries' intelligence services seldom know who or where the guerillas are, or where they will strike next; objectives are difficult to define because the enemy is everywhere yet nowhere, and the real objective is in any case millions of people spread all over the country, many of whom are unaware of the danger. The outbreak of hostilities clarifies the problems for both protagonists in conventional war, but there is no such clarification during the gradual transition from cold to hot in revolutionary war. A simple strategy is essential to the counter-revolutionary.

5 Continuity and control. The system is continuous and also allows the counter-revolutionary to evaluate results at each stage, thus leaving him at all times in control of the situation. Furthermore, the revolutionary cannot reverse the process or

even prohibit progress, because each area in turn is eventually permanently denied to him by the very people upon whom he depends for strength, i.e., the local population.

Command

The strategical concept outlined in the preceding paragraphs presents the counter-revolutionary with the problem of how best to ensure that there is proper co-ordination of the political, police and military tasks involved in the operations. The problem is complicated by the fact that the tasks of the three services overlap in time and in function. When the initial intensive effort is made in the selected area all the government's services will be working side by side with the same object in view, i.e., permanently to isolate the revolutionaries from the population. The initial tasks of expelling the guerillas from the area and preventing their return are military; the arrest and rehabilitation of the revolutionary political cells are tasks for the police and judiciary; while establishing contact with the people, controlling them and carrying out reforms are political tasks. But the military is the only service with the numbers and resources available to carry out effectively all the tasks required. It is inevitable, therefore, that soldiers, sailors and airmen will become involved not only in fighting armed bands, but also in police functions such as crowd control, enforcement of curfew, manning of road blocks and house-to-house searches, and in activities solely designed to control and win the support of the people, such as census-taking, road construction, food and water distribution, provision of transport and communications and training of self-defence units.

With the military in such predominance, it is tempting to hand over control of the whole operation to a military man. However, it is the political regime which is threatened by the revolutionaries and it is the politicians' business to defend it, although the armed services have been called in to help. Furthermore, the goal of every individual, no matter to which service he belongs, is a political one, and the military, even though they may be wearing the uniform of their service, are likely to be engaged rather more in civil tasks than in fighting. The responsibility at every level, therefore, should remain with the civil power. If military men have to be appointed to command for lack of good civilian officers they should serve in a civilian capacity.

Field Marshal Papagos, although given responsibility in 1949 for the expulsion of the Communist guerillas from Greece, was responsible to a civilian head of government. General Sir Gerald Templer was appointed as High Commissioner and Commander-in-Chief in Malaya for two vital years during the emergency, his primary function as head of state, his secondary as head of the armed forces. The French in Algeria, on the other hand, vested power wholly in the military for a short period during 1959, and in certain areas for longer periods, with resultant handicaps.

Assuming that command at all levels is vested in the civil power, there remains the problem of providing the civilian commander with the wherewithal to co-ordinate the activities of the three services. This is no simple problem because of the inter-relation of the three services' activities and the contrariety of their demands. Police intelligence is directly related to military action; the military thirst for intelligence is urgent and insatiable, yet the police must exercise caution to protect agents. Civil action can neither begin nor continue without the military first removing the threat posed by armed guerillas and then maintaining security by fighting for it; yet military action is destructive while civil action is constructive. How can the civilian commander co-ordinate the efforts of all three services and decide on the many conflicting priorities?

There are two possible systems – the integrated civil-military staff, in which the military is subordinated to the civilian, or the committee system as illustrated in Narrative 8 and applied in Malaya, Kenya and Cyprus. The integrated staff is speedy but rigid; the committee system is slower but flexible, and allows for decision by committee in planning but gives responsibility for execution to the service concerned. There seems to be room for both in a counter-revolutionary war, the committee system at the higher echelons where time is of less importance, the integrated staff at lower echelons where fleeting opportunities have to be acted upon at a moment's notice.

But whatever system is adopted, its success or failure depends upon the individual members. The author has twice served on a committee system during the early stages of a hot revolutionary war. In spite of the fact that the three committee members were strangers to each other and were weighed down with their own particular burdens and anxieties in very unpleasant situations, the committee worked admirably on both occasions because all three members had been given a clear-cut doctrine to work to which was well-understood, and they also served a head of government whom they knew would unhesitatingly remove them from office if they failed to make the system work for the common aim. A clear-cut and well-understood doctrine, and a ruthless determination to see it through, are essential parts of any counter-revolutionary's armoury.

At various stages during the war the counter-revolutionary will be faced with the problem of territorial command. Government forces, the military certainly but possibly also police reserve units and political cadres, will be divided into two categories:

1 The mobile units whose task it will be to move from sector to sector dealing with armed guerillas, the enemy's political cells and emergency civil works, and

2 Static units whose task it will be to remain in a sector, living among the people, in order to maintain security and carry out the civil actions required.

Since the commander of the static units will know both the situation and the people in his sector, it is logical that, once the static organisation has been established, any mobile units moving into the area should be placed under his command even though the officer-in-charge of the mobile units might be his senior in rank.

The business of command does not end with the setting-up of the command structure. There is also a need to prepare the government's forces for counter-revolutionary warfare in regard both to their organisation and equipment and to their mental attitude.

So far as organisation and equipment are concerned:

1 The army will normally consist of balanced formations designed for conventional warfare, yet in counter-revolutionary warfare the primary and continuing need is for infantry, mobile in every type of terrain likely to be encountered, and lightly armed. The conversion of as many specialist units as possible to the infantry role will be a first requirement. Engineer and signals units should not, however, be converted because there will be many calls on their resources and expertise.

2 Military units allocated to the static role will become involved in a multitude of civil tasks because only they will have the material and numerical resources required. Their primary tasks

will include such activities as control of civilian movement, implementation of social and economic reforms, census-taking, intelligence gathering and propaganda work. They should be organised and equipped accordingly.

3 The police and administrative services need numbers far above any required in peace-time; recruiting and training programmes should be put in hand at the earliest opportunity.

As regards mental adaptation:

1 Military forces designed for conventional war are trained to kill; their power stems from the sword and from the sword alone. This is not so in revolutionary war when it is seldom right, and often disastrous to bring to bear the full weight of the armed forces' potential for destruction and killing. 'Firmness with courtesy'[1] is more likely to be the right approach for soldiers, particularly among those in contact with the population. Their minds need to be conditioned accordingly. Their tasks will also take them into the political field and the soldier's ingrained habit of 'no politics' has to be cast out.

2 The police and administrative services find themselves in unfamiliar situations while depending upon a third service, the military, to carry out tasks which they would normally consider their own. At the same time they cannot maintain the neutral attitude which in normal times they would adopt towards the population; instead, they have to support those citizens who co-operate and take firm action against those who do not. This requires a new mental approach which should be inculcated as soon as possible.

The search for civilian leaders who understand counter-revolutionary warfare will exercise the government for a considerable time. Because the requirement is immediate, the government will not have time fully to train and indoctrinate leaders; instead, it will be compelled to resort to a system of trial and error, the selected leaders learning while at their work. Those who prove themselves should be promoted; those who fail removed. This problem is not so acute in the military services because those who cannot reconcile themselves to working with the population can be posted to mobile units. Any man whose political reliability is in

---

[1] This motto was given to his security forces by Field Marshal Sir John Harding, Governor of Cyprus, during the campaign against the EOKA terrorists.

doubt should not be allowed a position of responsibility which brings him into contact with the people.

Political precautions

Before launching an intensive drive into a selected area the counter-revolutionary should take certain political steps aimed at undermining, so far as possible, his opponent's cause. If the cause is badly chosen the government has only to espouse it, or make a promise in general terms to solve the somewhat ephemeral problem on which it is based. If it is well-chosen, deep-seated and dynamic, and if its espousal will lead to an unacceptable surrender of power, the government can counter only by promoting secondary issues which may appeal to the population. It is true to say that people will in the main accept something small today rather than a promise of something large tomorrow, particularly if the smaller gift is offered by a regime on whom they normally depend for an orderly life, i.e., their government. Ramon Magsaysay proved this point in the Philippines; the land reforms which he offered his people were not as sweeping as those promised by his Communist opponents, but the people gladly accepted them and the Communists lost their cause. In any case a government should find out what the people really want and determine to meet those demands which can safely be met.

Just as a revolutionary faces the problem of how to sell his cause to the people, so does the counter-revolutionary. It is no use promising reforms which cannot be carried out, as was proven in Algeria, between 1954 and 1957, where attempts at reform were successfully sabotaged, either by the non-Moslems or the FLN, and thus had no effect on the sympathies of the people. It will not be practicable fully to implement reforms, except possibly in certain white areas, until the guerilla bands and their supporters have been removed from the area concerned.

Political precautions should therefore take the form of an announcement of a political programme in general terms only, followed by announcements of specific reforms as the situation allows of their implementation.

Selecting an area

We have seen many different examples of how counter-revolutionary leaders have gone about selecting an area for intensive effort.

In Greece, the National Army, during 1947 and 1948, attacked unsuccessfully the Communist's strongest positions in the mountains of Thessaly; in 1949, however, Field Marshal Papagos made his first intensive attack upon their weakest area, in the Peloponnese, and then successfully worked northwards. In Kenya, the war cabinet selected the Kikuyus' strongest sector in the heart of their own land unit, and successfully established there a people's defence system based on the Home Guard. In Algeria, the French army operated with limited success over the whole country until 1959 when they worked from west to east, starting in the province of Oran, and meeting with immediate and resounding success.

Although the decision as to which area to select will be influenced by a large number of factors relevant to the situation prevailing in the country at the time, there are two factors which should be considered by any counter-revolutionary leader faced with this problem:

1 The counter-revolutionary forces need an early success.
2 The counter-revolutionary forces need to gain experience in this type of warfare.

These two factors indicate that it would pay the counter-revolutionary best to start in an easy area in order to gain a certain tactical victory while taking strategic risks elsewhere, and then proceed to the more difficult areas. This argument does not of course apply if the counter-revolutionary feels that he is strong enough to reverse the process.

Important tactical factors bearing on the selection of the area for intensive effort are:

1 Terrain, economic development and climate.
2 Can the area be physically cut off from the remainder of the country, bearing in mind that the only natural obstacles to guerillas are water and plains, and that artificial obstacles, although expensive, are effective (e.g. the block-house system of the Boer War; the Tunisian border in Algeria)?
3 The population – their size and spread, and their political attitude.

The easiest type of area to deal with tactically is one which is small and flat, is cut off from the remainder of the country by natural obstacles, and has a population concentrated in towns and villages among which a reasonable proportion can be relied upon to favour the counter-revolutionary regime.

It is impossible to lay down a yard-stick for the size of the selected area. It must be small enough to allow of thorough saturation by the forces at the government's disposal. It should, if possible, be large enough to compel any revolutionary forces despatched to it to travel, on foot, for more than one night before making a deep penetration; this precaution will give the counter-revolutionary forces an opportunity of intercepting them in daylight.

TACTICS

We will now consider the strategic concept, step by step, and make suggestions for the tactics which should be employed in the implementation of the strategic plan. Tactical dogma is dangerous, because the situations at field level will vary greatly even within the same country, but certain principles can be safely admitted.

There is one basic theme underlying the recommendations which follow, i.e. that cruel or harsh behaviour towards the population may yield short-term results, as it did for Generalissimo Chiang Kai-shek in China in 1933 and has since in other revolutionary wars, but it is unlikely to be forgotten by the people in the long term. Massacres, mass arrests and holding people in detention for long terms, are not therefore recommended as good tactics, while collective punishments and restrictions, although they may prove necessary, should be imposed on the population only after careful thought and with a full explanation of the need for them.

We will assume that the selected area is a black area in which the counter-revolutionary has to implement every step of the strategic plan; in the white and grey areas it may be possible to omit or telescope some of the steps.

Deployment to break the hold over the population of the enemy's armed guerillas

The aims of the counter-revolutionary forces at this stage are:

1 To destroy all guerillas in the area, or
2 To drive all guerillas from the area, or
3 To disperse the guerillas into very small groups within the area and force them into hiding.

Bearing in mind that this stage is only a preliminary to the permanent deployment of security forces in the area, the successful completion of either of the two latter aims will prove satisfactory, although it is obviously desirable to destroy the guerillas and so prevent them from transferring to another area where they will have to be dealt with. Tactics to be employed at this stage are as follows:

1 Suddenly deploy round the perimeter of the selected area all the mobile units required, and also those static military, police and political units which are ear-marked for the area.

2 All units then drive inwards in the 'fiery wall' pattern as adopted by Chiang Kai-shek against the Chinese Communists in 1933, and by Field Marshal Papagos in the Peloponnese and Thessaly in 1949. Troops should operate in depth round the perimeter; a 'thin red line' is quite inadequate because the guerillas will find it easy to break out of the encirclement. Chiang Kai-shek's 'fiery wall' was established in considerable depth, but the Chinese Communists were none the less able to break out, albeit at considerable loss to themselves. The need for depth is particularly applicable to night-time, when the counter-guerilla forces' main means of keeping the enemy in the net will be by night patrols and ambushes, both extremely difficult operations even for the best troops. If the guerilla succeeds in avoiding one patrol or ambush under cover of darkness, there must be many more for him to pass through before he can escape the encirclement.

3 The inward drive continues until the troops meet in the centre of the area. Unless intelligence is good – an unlikely contingency in a black area because intelligence originates with the population – the counter-guerilla may have difficulty in finding the guerillas. When under pressure guerillas can be expected to decline battle and to go into hiding, but although they may refuse to fight, they must eat. Searches should therefore be based on sources of food which are normally easy to find, apart from secret caches which cannot last for long. The supply lines running out from the sources of food will lead the hunters to the guerillas' hiding places. This principle applies to all stages of fighting against armed guerillas when other forms of intelligence are scarce.

4 When the inward drive is completed the counter-guerilla forces turn about and sweep outwards, towards the perimeter, with a view to driving the guerillas out of the area.

5 The area is then divided into sectors. The static units are allotted to sectors and the mobile units drawn into a central reserve. All units then hunt down the remaining guerillas, the mobile reserve operating in sectors as required.

Throughout this initial period of intensive operations, patrolling should be stepped up by troops stationed in areas adjacent to the selected area, in order to intercept guerillas who may be trying to make their way out.

Police and other government officials who were originally in the area will give the incoming forces all the help they can, particularly in the provision of intelligence, but apart from this, there is little scope for civil action during this stage except in the field of propaganda. All units must be thoroughly briefed as to what propaganda is to be disseminated and must carry sufficient equipment, e.g. loud hailers in vehicles and aircraft, pamphlets, duplicating machines, etc. to enable them to spread the word. Propaganda should be directed as follows:

1 At the armed guerillas. It must be made clear to them that the government and its forces are in the area to stay, the aim being to induce the guerillas to accept the challenge and stand to fight.

2 At the counter-guerilla forces. They must be told, and frequently reminded, to restrict damage to a minimum and to pay promptly for any incurred, to alleviate hardship and to be kind to the people. They must be so well-indoctrinated in this policy that they will adhere to it in the face of extreme provocation. That they will meet with provocation is certain; fighting for and among an unco-operative population is infuriating enough, but in addition the guerillas will go to any lengths to set the population against them, e.g. Stalin in Russia during World War II.

3 At the population. They must be told that if they continue to support the guerillas there will be more fighting and more damage, bloodshed, restrictions and hardship, whereas if they remain neutral, peace will return. It would be premature at this stage to court the active support of the people because successful counter-action by the guerillas, such as murder of informers

and officials, or sabotage of a constructive reform, will inflict on the government a psychological defeat.

Hold the area secure while making contact with and re-establishing control over the population

However successful the initial drive against the armed guerillas may have been, remnants will still remain in the area. They may be in hiding in difficult terrain, or in disguise among the population, and their support organisation and political cells are still in being. Successful disposal of these remnants will depend on the counter-guerilla's ability to win the support of the population. In order to win this support a re-deployment of resources is necessary at this stage, so designed that the counter-guerilla can best:

1 Direct his main effort at the population;
2 Give the people an increasing sense of security.

The area should now be sub-divided into sectors, which may not necessarily coincide with those selected for the previous stage, and again into sub-sectors. Static units of all three services should be deployed into the sectors and sub-sectors while a mobile reserve is retained in the area.

The following principles should be observed in this re-deployment:

1 The mobile reserve units.

(a) Their primary function is to maintain security throughout the whole area by constantly harassing the armed guerillas: the majority will, therefore, be military units, although police reserve units and political teams may be included. Units may be allocated to sectors from time to time, but control must be exercised direct by the area commander in order to make best use of their mobility and to retain the ability at the highest level to direct them to where they are most needed.

(b) When not engaged on military operations, the mobile reserve should help with the work among the people.

2 Static units.

(a) Their primary function is constructive work among the population, provision of security being only a secondary function. Their deployment must therefore be directly related to the numbers and distribution of the population, and can follow no set pattern. It may, for example, be possible to control the population of a small town with one company of soldiers, one centralised police unit and one political team, yet an area of scattered villages may require a battalion of soldiers, numerous small police detachments and several political teams, even though the number of people in the rural area is smaller than that in the town. If the population is too scattered to be controlled by the forces available, it will be necessary to concentrate the people into 'new villages', as in Kenya and Malaya, but there is danger in this procedure in that the people will not immediately realise the benefits which will accrue to them; they will more likely resent being forcibly removed from their homes. A mass movement of the population should be undertaken only after careful thought and thorough preparation, and in the full realisation that the necessity for it arises from weaknesses in the counter-revolutionary forces.

(b) The boundaries of sectors and sub-sectors should conform with the peace-time administrative boundaries, even although such divisions make no military sense, because the civil aspects of the role of the static units take priority over the military.

(c) Soldiers should not be deployed on ground or in places of purely military value, such as mountain passes or hilltops, because they have no value in a revolutionary war. Power stations or water reservoirs, on the other hand, have value because they serve the people, and will therefore need to be guarded.

(d) The counter-guerilla forces should live among the population and under the same conditions as those in which the people live. The well-worn military principle that, when living among the people, soldiers should remain largely out of sight with only a few 'in the shop window' is not applicable to revolutionary warfare. Furthermore, if the people live in *cainhas*, so should the soldiers; if they live in town houses, so should the soldiers. The building of barracks and police compounds is expensive, the requisitioning of the best buildings is unpopular, and both will tempt the counter-revolutionary forces to remain in their comfortable quarters rather than go out to meet and live among the people in less amenable surroundings.

The following chart (see p. 319) shows a suitable deployment and command system for counter-revolutionary forces at the beginning of the battle for the control of the population.

With the re-deployment completed, the battle for the control of the population begins, and in this the counter-revolutionary has three aims in view:

1 Physical isolation of the population from the guerillas.
2 Re-establishing control over the population.
3 The gaining of the intelligence required to eliminate the remaining armed guerillas and their support organisation and political cells.

The tactics to be employed in achieving these aims are as follows:

1 By mobile reserve units.

(a) Their main task is to eliminate the remaining armed guerillas either by killing or capture. The latter should by this time have been broken up into small groups and driven into hiding in difficult terrain. The tactics to be employed against them approximate to guerilla tactics, i.e., small patrols by day and night, day and night ambushes, raids and encircling operations. The soldiers must be prepared to go into the difficult terrain and out-stay the guerillas there, while ruthlessly pursuing them by day and night. They should make maximum use of helicopters, particularly for encircling operations, and should be given maximum air support in the form of slow-flying ground attack and transport aircraft. Units should reduce administration to the minimum necessary for the task and should look for all available administrative means, e.g., pack animals, porters, local trackers, etc., to enable them to stay in the difficult terrain and there locate and destroy the enemy. Where intelligence is scarce, searches for the guerillas should start at their sources of food supply.

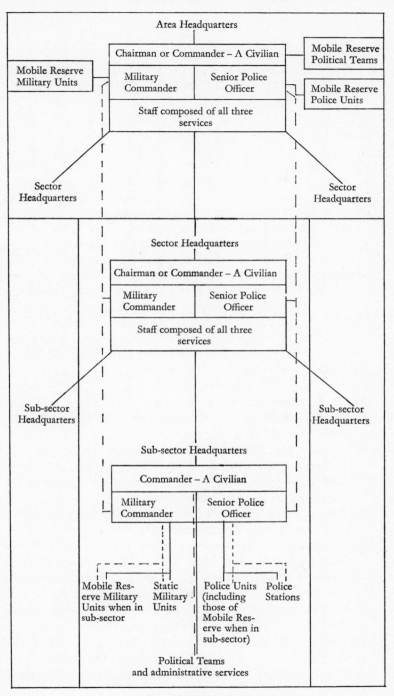

Area Headquarters

Chairman or Commander – A Civilian

Mobile Reserve
Political Teams

Mobile Reserve
Military Units

| Military Commander | Senior Police Officer |

Mobile Reserve
Police Units

Staff composed of all three services

Sector Headquarters

Sector Headquarters

Sector Headquarters

Chairman or Commander – A Civilian

| Military Commander | Senior Police Officer |

Staff composed of all three services

Sub-sector Headquarters

Sub-sector Headquarters

Sub-sector Headquarters

Commander – A Civilian

| Military Commander | Senior Police Officer |

Mobile Reserve Military Units when in sub-sector

Static Military Units

Police Units (including those of Mobile Reserve when in sub-sector)

Police Stations

Political Teams
and administrative services

——————— Chain of Command for planning operations.

– – – – – – – – Chain of responsibility for executing operations.

Note: Variation may be made in this organisation to suit prevailing conditions,
e.g., a capital town would normally be treated as an autonomous area; a 'prohibited'
area would normally need no static units.

(b) When not engaged in operations against armed guerillas, mobile reserve units should assist in the task of winning over the population wherever they may be needed.

2 By military, police and political static units.

(a) The first problem is to break down the barrier which is bound to exist between the counter-revolutionary forces and the people. Even if the population is sympathetic towards the government, the revolutionaries, certainly in the black areas, will deliberately have erected such a barrier, and while guerillas are in the area the people will be afraid to come forward and show where their sympathies lie. The population should, therefore, be given simple tasks to do, such as opening the shops, repairing buildings or improving the streets. These initial administrative tasks should lead to further tasks of military value, such as constructing village defences and carrying military supplies. The people should at first be asked to perform these government-sponsored tasks, and only if they do not comply with requests should compulsion be brought to bear. The people should, however, be given orders with which they can reasonably be expected to comply, and they should then be firmly but courteously made to obey; a too diffident approach will achieve little, too arrogant an attitude will antagonise. Any work done should be paid for. By way of this persuasion or compulsion to work for the government the people are gradually committed to the government.

(b) Control is best established over the population by taking a census and issuing identity cards. The taking of a census will tell the counter-revolutionary forces all they want to know about the population, while the compulsory issue of identity cards will place the people firmly under their control. The institution of an identity card system in Malaya delivered a stunning blow to the Communist guerillas there, and all their efforts to sabotage the system by forcing citizens to destroy their cards came to nought because the citizen without an identity card could obtain nothing from his government, no work, no pay, no food, no luxuries – nothing.

(c) A further method of control is the curfew, because it provides a check on movement. It has a useful side effect in that it gives the citizens an excuse for not helping the guerillas.

(d) Control of material goods is difficult and costly to enforce. However, in certain situations, as in Malaya, control over the distribution of items useful to guerillas might well be justified.

(e) Throughout this period of breaking the ice and establishing control the people must be protected against intimidation. Static units should therefore engage in small patrols and ambushes by day and night, and should in particular take care to avoid the situation which was allowed to develop in Indo-China where at night 'the land belonged to the Vietminh'. If static units are likely to become embroiled in military activities to such an extent that they are unable to devote their attention to the population, then mobile reserve units should be called in to help.

(f) Gathering intelligence is the task of every individual engaged in counter-guerilla operations, but a proper intelligence organisation should be established in each town and village, based on the police, or intelligence will not flow in. If it is slow in coming, pressure must be brought to bear, not as a rule directly on the whole community but indirectly on individuals. It is easy for a government official to make life difficult for a non-cooperative citizen. He may, for example, call in a citizen's identity card for 'checking' and prolong the 'check' for as long as is needed to get the information which he is sure the citizen possesses. But the best way to stimulate the flow of information is to make opportunities for the military, the police and political cadres to meet the citizens as frequently as possible, for example, when paying workers or arranging holiday festivities, or through welfare and medical services.

(g) During this period also, the first steps should be taken to win the active support of the population. It is too early yet to appoint leaders from the co-operative minority because the revolutionaries' political cells and support organisation are still able to take counter-action. But reforms of a social and economic nature should be set in train, preferably by the people themselves with the government's forces as help-mates.

3 By psychological warfare teams.

The mobile and static units, and the local headquarters will be too busy to concern themselves with the planning of psychological warfare, although every man will have his part to play in its implementation. Psychological warfare teams and personnel should therefore be allocated to take care of this aspect of operations, and direction should come from the higher echelons of command. Propaganda should be directed –

(a) At the guerillas. They should be further induced to stand and fight on the same lines as advocated for the previous stage. Propaganda should also aim at creating divisions in their ranks, rather than cementing their organisation by treating them all as one common enemy.

(b) At the counter-revolutionary forces. The government's security forces are turning from familiar to unfamiliar tasks, particularly the military. At the same time they are widely scattered among the population whom they will meet initially as strangers and with whom they will finally become friends. Propaganda, disseminated by their officers, should at first be slanted towards explaining to soldiers and policemen what their new role is and what tasks are involved, and later towards instructing them in how to remain on their guard while showing friendship to the people, in conditions in which the war-like atmosphere of the initial operations has dispersed. Discussion between officers and men about their tasks and occupations should become a daily routine.

(c) At the population. Full explanation should be given to the people, as individuals rather than en masse, as to the reasons for the various actions taken by the counter-revolutionary forces. In addition, it must be made clear to them that the government's forces are in the area to stay – a few long-term contracts for food and housing is one way of doing this. But the most difficult aspects of propaganda work at this stage are laying the groundwork for the separation of the population from the revolutionaries, and making preparations for the future of the active minority sympathetic to the government. Local commanders cannot be expected to carry out this work; they should be given psychological warfare personnel to help them, and the policy should be decided and direction given by the higher echelons of command.

Elimination of the revolutionaries' political cells

Although stress is laid on political cells at this stage, because they are the basis for the revolutionaries' activity among the people, the operations should also be directed against armed guerillas who have reverted to civilian life, and the guerillas' support organisation. The main problem is to assess the correct timing for rounding up the political cells. There are two main factors to consider:

1 Intelligence. There is no need to wait for precise information on all the revolutionary leaders and their chief sympathisers. It is sufficient to have listed a number of suspects who, under interrogation, will normally produce the information required to catch the leaders.

2 Follow-up. Before any action is taken, the counter-revolutionaries must be in a position in which they can be sure of placing security forces in the town or village in which arrests have been made. If this is not done, new cells will be created by the revolutionaries, as they were in Cochin by the Vietminh in 1952–3.

Responsibility for the decision to act against the political cells rests with the local commander, although the action itself is a matter for the police, supplemented, when necessary, by the military. A number of suspects should first be arrested and interrogated by professionals – interrogation by amateurs is at best futile, at worst disastrous. The innocent should then be released, the guilty detained, and any further arrests indicated by the information arising from interrogations promptly made. The whole operation should be conducted in the shortest possible time. It is bound to create some bitterness, because those arrested are of the people and, technically, have committed no crime; indeed, the people may look on them as men and women guided by the highest motives. If the operation is allowed to drag on, bitterness will increase.

Intelligence will often indicate who should be arrested, but will seldom tell where they are in hiding. One method of overcoming this difficulty is by the 'cordon and search' operation in which a village or part of a town is surrounded, the people assembled and screened by agents, and every single building searched from roof to basement. This type of operation should, however, be avoided whenever possible. It seldom achieves any results because the area of search is so wide, while the targets for search are easily hidden.[1] It never achieves results to compensate for the ill-will created by an operation which leaves every housewife distraught, with her house turned upside down and every corner of her privacy invaded. The 'cordon and screening' is justifiable and can be conducted without leaving bitterness, but searches should be restricted to a few buildings which are indicated as suspect by the intelligence available. If the intelligence is not precise enough, it is better not to search at all.

When the arrests have been made and interrogations completed, there remains the problem of how best to deal with those detained. A number of different techniques have been adopted in the past. The Greek government set up rehabilitation camps, returning to units or civilian life those who forswore Communism. The British in Malaya and Kenya drafted into the local police force many who recanted, and they subsequently became excellent intelligence agents. President Magsaysay settled reformed Huks on land of their own and provided them with the wherewithal to start farming. The best policy appears to be to treat leniently those who genuinely disavow their previously-held beliefs, while punishing those who do not on the grounds of conspiracy against the government.

Psychological warfare at this stage should be aimed at convincing the people of the necessity to make the arrests while stressing the policy of leniency.

Carrying out reforms while organising the people for their own defence
These two steps are shown separately in the proposed strategic

---

[1] One hide, uncovered by policemen working with the author in Cyprus and concealing eight terrorists, was constructed underneath the living room of a cottage. The only entrance was covered by the concrete slab of the fireplace. When the police entered, a fire was burning, granny was rocking to and fro in a chair by the fire, the housewife was engaged in sewing and two babies swung in cloth cradles suspended from the ceiling. A thorough examination revealed no clue that the concrete slab was movable or concealed an entrance. The hide was pointed out by a terrorist who had recently surrendered to the security forces.

programme, but in practice they will run concurrently. The initiation of reforms should come first in order to win sufficient co-operation from the people to enable the counter-revolutionary to start organising them, but the reforms should continue throughout the period of re-organisation.

One of two situations will prevail at this stage. Either the population, relieved of the presence of the revolutionaries, will come forward readily to help the government, or they will still hold back because they genuinely espouse the revolutionaries' cause. The latter situation is by no means hopeless, but will involve the counter-revolutionary forces in a more protracted campaign with emphasis on severity and compulsion rather than on leniency and inducement. In either case the counter-revolutionary should set about organising the population as follows:

1 Arrange for free elections to be held to appoint local leaders; the elections should be free and should be seen to be free. The risk that the people may elect the wrong leaders can readily be taken while counter-revolutionary forces are in strength in the area.
2 Test the local leaders by giving them definite tasks. The tasks should be of two kinds; those of direct benefit to the people, such as running local government concerns and organising public works; and those related to the future defence of the area, such as recruiting self-defence units and organising village defence systems. Help should be provided by the government's forces whenever needed, but the responsibility for carrying out each task should be allowed to rest firmly on the shoulders of the local leaders. The population can then be relied upon to dispose of leaders who fail them and replace them with better ones.
3 Organise local leaders into a national political party. Not until this has been done will the counter-revolutionary have firmly re-established his regime in the selected area.

At some time during this process the counter-revolutionary should achieve the break-through he is looking for, i.e. the active support of the population, but the break-through will not occur over the whole of the selected area at the same time. It will appear, and will be easily recognisable by an improvement in the general atmosphere and an increasing flow of intelligence, in a village here or a small township there. Propaganda should be brought into play, preferably disseminated by the people themselves, to promote the forward places and encourage the citizens of the more backward places to emulate them.

Throughout this period of reform and re-organisation the security of the area, and particularly of the local leaders, will be the primary responsibility of mobile reserve units and a secondary responsibility for static units.

Suppression of the last guerilla remnants

With the population organised for their own defence and with his regime re-established at the grass roots, the counter-revolutionary is within sight of victory, but he still cannot afford to leave unmolested in the area a last hard-core of guerillas. However, the demands made by large military forces on the population are exacting, and the people can hardly be expected to accept the need for them when the enemy is no longer on his door-step. Furthermore, the counter-revolutionary leaders will wish to switch their major effort to another area, or, if there is no other area, they will wish to concentrate and re-train their military forces for their normal role of external defence.

This problem was solved by President Magsaysay in the Philippines by withdrawing his regular military combat teams from the revolutionary war while leaving his Scout Ranger groups available to deal with the Huk remnants. The Malayan government, on the other hand, brought the campaign against the Communist bandits to a formal end in 1960, leaving a handful of guerillas to rot in the jungles, while establishing military watch on the border with Thailand beyond which a larger body of guerillas had sought refuge.

The best solution must depend on the situation prevailing at the time. The counter-revolutionaries can either conduct a final massive drive on the same lines as the initial operation into the area, but this time with the population on their side, or they can leave the matter to the population, helping them out with small and mobile forces. In either case an amnesty should now be offered to the guerillas, or, if previously offered, renewed.

CONCLUSION

At the start of the hot war, the revolutionary has the psychological initiative and he has on his side an active minority of the population with the remainder observing a fearful neutrality. The task of the counter-revolutionary is to wrest the psychological initiative from his enemy, to win the population over to his side and divorce them permanently from the revolutionaries. Every strategic plan and tactical operation should be geared to this end.

Acts of terrorism and intimidation will yield short-term dividends to the revolutionaries, but in the long-term may recoil against them. Brutal or disorderly behaviour, however, will never help the counter-revolutionaries, because they are defending a regime which is based on law and order. Ruthless suppression of the incurably guilty, and firm but courteous treatment of the innocent should be their guidelines, from the moment the first shot is fired until the time when victory is won.

Glossary of Foreign Words

aman	Pardon
ataman	Head of civil and military administration in the Ukraine: leader of popular uprisings
atap	A bush with fronds which are plaited to make roofing
Bande Noire	Lit: Black Band—French intelligence organisation
bashas	Huts built of wood or bamboo and roofed with *atap*
Batistianos	Followers of Batista
beetle	Tool with heavy head and handle used for crushing or ramming
blitzkrieg	Violent campaign aimed at speedy victory
boule	Bread
boun-youls	Natives
boukaks	Natives
burgomeister	Mayor of town or district
burnous	Arab hooded cloak
cainhas	Native grass-roofed huts
caudillo	Chief or Captain
canaille	Rabble
Colon	Farmer, settler; familiarly-colonial
Comintern	Communist International
congaies	Native concubines
cuartels	Fortified barracks in towns or villages
dai-doi du Kich	Militia units
dinh	Village community house
douar	Arab village
douk-douk	Arab knife
Einsitzgruppen	Special service squads of the SS
fellaghas	Peasants: name given in Algeria to armed Moslems
Fidelistas	Followers of Fidel Castro
Fritzes	Germans
Groupement Mobile	Motorized forces of the French Army operating in Indo-China
hika	Quick move without warning

junta	Administrative council
jus	Coffee
kampong	Malay village
Katiba	A company of rebels, normally about 100 strong
kopje	Small hill
kraal	Native village, enclosed by fence
lianas	Climbing and twining tropical-forest plants which can be used as ropes
mechta	Arab house or hut
Mau Mau	Name given to the terrorist movement in Kenya
miqueletes	Armed peasants
Morane	French reconnaissance aeroplane
Mouchard	French reconnaissance aeroplane
NKVD	State police
nullah	Stream, watercourse
otrjad	Roughly equivalent to a section/squad or platoon of soldiers
oued	Watercourse
padi	Rice
padis	Rice-fields
pakret	Quick move without warning
partidas	Partisan bands
polk	Roughly equivalent to a battalion of soldiers
pousse-pousses	Motor-driven trishaws
puppet troops	The name given by Communists to indigenous troops in the pay of their enemies
ratissage	A 'mop-up' operation
rebeldes	Rebels
rooineks	Red-necks, an uncomplimentary term applied to British soldiers
sampan	Small boat of Chinese pattern
sangar	Stone breast-work
scènes de carnage	Scenes of slaughter
spruit	Small watercourse
'Stoi!'	A challenge
Tabors	North African troops serving under French officers
Tiên-lên! Tiên-lên!	Forward! Forward!
untermenschen	Gangsters, thugs
Ustasas	Yugoslavian collaborators who aided the Germans in occupied Yugoslavia
veld	Open country, neither cultivated nor true forest
wadi	Rocky watercourse, dry except after rain
wilaya	Zone or district

Bibliography

(in alphabetical order by geographic areas)

AFRICA

The Boer War, 1899–1902

BOOKS

Doyle, C. *The Great Boer War*. London: Smith-Elber. New York: McClure & Phillips, 1902.

Kruger, R. C. *Goodbye Dolly Gray: The Story of the Boer War*. London: Cassell. Philadelphia: Lippincott, 1960.

Reitz, D. *Commando: A Boer Journal of the Boer War*. London: Faber & Faber. New York: Charles Boni Paper Books, 1930.

Wilson, H. W. *After Pretoria: The Guerilla War*. 2 vols. London: Amalgamated, 1902.

ARTICLES

Guerilla Warfare: A Historical Parallel. Blackwood's Edinburgh Magazine, 171: 102–8, 1902.

ALGERIA

1954 to 1961

BOOKS

Behr, E. *The Algerian Problem*. London: Hodder & Stoughton, 1961.

Clark, M. K. *Algeria in Turmoil: A History of the Rebellion*. London: Thames & Hudson. New York: Praeger, 1959.

OTHER BOOKS

Gillespie, J. *Algeria, Rebellion and Revolution*. New York: Praeger, 1961.

Roy, J. *The War in Algeria*. Tr. by R. Howard, New York: Grove, 1961.

ARABIA

World War I

BOOKS

Hart, L. *Lawrence in Arabia and After*. London: Cape, 1936.

Lawrence, T. E. *Revolt in the Desert*. London: Golden Cockerel, 1939. New York: Doran, 1927.

Lawrence, T. E. *Seven Pillars of Wisdom*. London: Cape. New York: Doubleday, 1935.

ARTICLES

Lawrence, T. E. *Guerilla Warfare*. Encyclopaedia Britannica. Vol. 10, 1948.

BURMA

World War II

BOOKS

Burchett, W. G. *Wingate's Phantom Army*. Bombay: Thacker, 1944.

Fergusson, B. E. *Beyond the Chindwin: Being an Account of the Adventures of Number Five Column of the Wingate Expedition into Burma, 1943*. London: Collins, 1945.

Fergusson, B. E. *The Wild Green Earth*. London: Collins, 1946.

OTHER BOOKS

McKelvie, R. *The War in Burma*. London: Methuen, 1948.

Ogburn, C. *The Marauders*. New York: Fawcett Crest Books, 1960.

Sykes, C. *Orde Wingate: A Biography*. Cleveland: World Publishing, 1959.

CHINA

Post World War I

BOOKS

De Jaegher. *The Enemy Within*. Bombay: St. Paul Publications, 1952.

Fitzgerald, C. P. *Revolution in China*. London: Cresset, 1952.

Lui, F. F. *A Military History of Modern China, 1924–49*. London: Geoffrey Cumberlege, Oxford University Press. N.J: Princeton University, 1956.

Mao Tse-tung on Guerilla Warfare. Tr. by S. B. Griffith. London: Cassell. New York: Praeger, 1961.

BIBLIOGRAPHY

ARTICLES

Dinegar, Captain W. W. *The 'Long March' as Extended Guerilla Warfare.* From US Naval Institute *Proceedings*, 1952.

Hanrahan, G. Z. *The Chinese Red Army and Guerilla Warfare.* From *Combat Forces Journal*, February 1951.

Jacobs, W. D. *Mao Tse-tung as a Guerilla – A Second Look.* From *Military Review*, February 1958.

Katzenback, E. L. Jnr., and G. Z. Hanrahan. *The Revolutionary Strategy of Mao Tse-tung.* From *Political Science Quarterly*, September 1955.

OTHER BOOKS

Band, C. and William. *Dragon Fangs.* London: Allen & Unwin, 1947. (*Two Years with the Chinese Communists.* New Haven: Yale University, 1948).

Bertran, J. M. *North China Front.* Macmillan, 1939. (*Unconquered: Journal of a Year's Adventure among the Fighting Peasants of North China.* New York: John Day. 1939).

Wint, T. H. and A. Jacoby. *Thunder out of China.* New York: Sloane, 1946.

CUBA

BOOKS

Guevara, E. *Guerilla Warfare.* Tr. by P. J. Murray. London: Cassell, 1962. New York: Praeger, 1961.

Weyl, N. *Red Star over Cuba.* New York: Hillman Books, 1961.

ARTICLES

Chapelle, D. *How Castro Won. Marine Corps Gazette*, February 1960.

CYPRUS

BOOKS

Foley, C. *Island in Revolt.* London: Longmans, 1962.

Foot, S. *Emergency Exit.* London: Chatto & Windus, 1960.

Grivas, G. *Guerilla Warfare and EOKA's Struggle.* Tr. by A. A. Pallis. London: Longmans, 1964.

OTHER BOOKS

Alastos, D. *Cyprus Guerillas: Grivas, Makarios and the British Doros Alastos.* London: Heinemann, 1960.

Barker, D. *Grivas: Portrait of a Terrorist*, New York: Harcourt, 1960.

Tremayne, P. *Below the Tide*. London: Hutchinson, 1958.

GREECE

World War II and After

BOOKS

Leeper, R. *When Greek Meets Greek*. London: Chatto & Windus, 1950.

McNeil, W. H. *Greek Dilemma: War and Aftermath*. London: Gollanz. Philadelphia: Lippincott, 1947.

Moss, S. *Ill Met by Moonlight*. London: Harrap, 1950. New York: Macmillan

Myers, E. C. W. *Greek Entanglement*. London: Hart-Davis, 1955.

Psychoundakis, G. *The Cretan Runner: His Story of German Occupation*. Tr. by P. L. Fermor. London: Murray, 1955.

Woodhouse, C. M. *Apple of Discord*. London: Hutchinson, 1947.

ARTICLES

Balcos, A. A. *Geurilla Warfare. Military Review,* March 1958.

Papagos, A. *Guerilla Warfare. Foreign Affairs,* January 1952.

Papthanasiades, T. *The Bandit's Last Stand in Greece. Military Review,* February, 1951.

INDO-CHINA

Post-World War II

BOOKS

Ainley, H. *In Order to Die*. London: Burke, 1955.

Fall, B. B. *Street Without Joy: Indo-China at War, 1946–1954*. London: Pall Mall, 1964. Harrisburg, Pa: Stackpole, 1961.

Larteguy, Jean. *The Centurions*. London: Hutchinson, 1961. New York: Dutton, 1962.

Nguyen Huy Tuong. *The Frontier Campaign*. Foreign Languages Publishing House, Hanoi, 1962.

Paret, P. and J. W. Shy. *Guerillas in the 1960's*. London: Pall Mall, 1962. New York: Praeger, 1962.

Riesen, R. *Jungle Mission*. Tr. by James Oliver. London: Hutchinson. New York: Crowell, 1957.

BIBLIOGRAPHY

Tanham, G. K. *Communist Revolutionary Warfare: The Vietminh in Indo-China*. London: Methuen. New York: Praeger, 1961.

Truong, Chinh. *Primer for Revolt: The Communist Takeover in Vietnam*. New York: Praeger, 1963.

Vo Nguyen Giap (Gen.) *Dien Bien Phu*. Hanoi: Foreign Languages Publishing House, 1959.

Vo Nguyen Giap (Gen.) *People's War, People's Army*. New York: Praeger, 1962.

OTHER BOOKS

Fall, B. B. *The Two Vietnams: A Political and Military History* (Revised edition). New York: Praeger, 1964.

Graham, A. (Lt. Col.) *Interval in Indo-China*. London: St. Martin's Press, 1956.

Lancaster, D. *The Emancipation of Indo-China*. New York: Oxford University Press, 1961.

Trinquier, R. (Col.). *Modern Warfare: A French View of Counter-insurgency*. New York: Praeger, 1964.

KENYA

BOOKS

Corfield, F. D. *Historical Survey of the Origin and Growth of Mau Mau*. London: H.M. Stationery Office, 1960. New York: British Information Service, 1960.

Henderson, J. and P. Goodhart. *Hunt for Kimathi*. London: Hamish Hamilton, 1958. (*Manhunt in Kenya*. New York: Doubleday, 1958).

ARTICLES

Erskine, G. *Kenya – Mau Mau. Royal United Service Institute Journal*, February 1956.

MALAYA

World War II and After

BOOKS

Campbell, A. *Jungle Green*. London: Allen & Unwin, 1953. Boston: Little, Brown, 1954.

Chapman, J. S. *The Jungle is Neutral*. London: Chatto & Windus, 1949. New York: Norton, 1949.

BIBLIOGRAPHY

Clutterbuck, R. L. *The Long, Long War*. New York: Praeger, 1966.
Henniker, M. C. A. *Red Shadow over Malaya*. London: Blackwood, 1955.
Miers, R. *Shoot to Kill*. London: Faber, 1959.
O'Ballance, E. *The Communist Insurgent War, 1948–1960*. London: Faber and Faber, 1966.

ARTICLES
Henniker, M. C. A. *Jungle War in Malaya. Military Engineer,* January-February, 1953.
Henniker, M. C. A. *Jungle Hunting Malaya Bandits*. ibid.
    „   „   *The Jungle War in Malaya*. ibid. November-December 1953.

OTHER BOOKS
Bartlett, V. *Report from Malaya*. New York: Criterion 1955.
Communist Banditry in Malaya. Singapore: HM Stationery Office, 1951.
Crockett, A. *Green Beret, Red Star: Describing the Jungle Operations of 42 Royal Marine Commando*. London: Eyre & Spottiswoode, 1954.
Pye, L. W. *Guerilla Communism in Malaya: Its Social and Political Meaning*. Princeton, N.J.: Princeton University, 1956.

NORTH AMERICA
Civil War

BOOKS
Henderson, G. F. R. *Stonewall Jackson and the American Civil War*. London: Longmans, 1898.
Mosby, U. S. *Mosby's War Reminiscences and Stuart's Cavalry Campaigns*. New York: Pageant, 1960.

PHILIPPINES
World War II and after

BOOKS
Baclagon, V. S. *Philippine Campaigns*. Manila: Graphic House, 1952.
Wolfert, I. *American Guerilla in the Philippines*. (London: *Guerilla* Transworld, 1958). New York: Simon & Schuster, 1945.

BIBLIOGRAPHY

ARTICLES

Bashore, B. T. (Major). *Dual Strategy for Limited War*. *Military Review*, 1960.

Hammer, K. M. (Major). *Huks in the Philippines*. *Military Review*, April 1956.

Tiron, T. C. (Lt. Col.). *The Philippine Anti-Communist Campaign*. *Air University Quarterly Review*, Summer, 1954.

Villa-Real, L. A. *Huk Hunting*. *Combat Forces Journal*, November 1954.

RUSSIA

1812

BOOKS

Caulaincourt, A. de. *With Napoleon in Russia: Memoirs*. London: Cassell. New York: Grosset.

De Segue, P. *Napoleon's Russian Campaign*. London: Michael Joseph.

Roeder, H. *The Ordeal of Captain Roeder*. London: Methuen.

Tolstoy, L. *War and Peace*. London: J. M. Dent & Sons Ltd. New York: E. P. Dutton & Sons Ltd.

RUSSIA

World War II

BOOKS

Dixon, A. and O. Heilbrunn. *Communist Guerilla Warfare*. London: Allen & Unwin, 1954. New York: Praeger, 1954.

Ponomarenko. Lt. Gen. *Behind the Front Lines*. Tr. by A. Gritsuk. London: Hutchinson, 1945.

ARTICLES

Dohnányi, E. von. *Combating Soviet Guerillas*. *Marine Corps Gazette*, February 1955.

Jacobs, W. D. *Irregular Warfare and the Soviets*. *Military Review*, May 1958.

Lenin, V. I. *Partisan Warfare*. *Orbis*, Summer 1958.

McClure, Brooks. *Russia's Hidden Army*. *Infantry Journal*, July and August 1949.

OTHER BOOKS

Agapov, B. *After the Battle and Notes of a Guerilla Fighter*. London: Hutchinson, 1943.

Dallin, A. *German Rule in Russia, 1941-45; A Study of Occupation Policies*. London: Macmillan, 1957. New York: St. Martin's, 1957.

Heinman, L. *I was a Soviet Guerilla*. London: Brown, Watson, 1959.

Kovpak, S. A. *Our Partisan Course*. Tr. by E. and M. Lesser. London: Hutchinson, 1945.

SPAIN

Peninsular War 1808-1814

BOOKS

Forester, C. S. *Rifleman Dodd and the Gun*. London: Lane, 1942. New York: Readers Club, 1942.

Forestier, M. *The Fort of San Lorenzo*. London: Hodder & Stoughton, 1960.

Napier, W. F. P. *History of the War in the Peninsular*. 6 vols. London: Frederick Warne & Co. Ltd. Philadelphia: Carey & Hart, 1842.

Oman, C. *History of the Peninsular War*. London: Clarendon Press.

Rocca, M. de. *Memoirs of the War of the French in Spain*. London: Murray, 1935.

ARTICLES

Guerilla Warfare – A Historical Parallel. Blackwood's Edinburgh Magazine. 171:102-108, 1902.

The Guerrillero. ibid. 163:540-551, 1898.

SPAIN

Civil War, 1936-1938

BOOKS

Borkeraw, F. *The Spanish Cockpit: An Eyewitness Account of the Political and Social Conflicts of the Spanish Civil War*. London: Faber, 1937.

Hemingway, E. *For Whom the Bell Tolls*. New York: Scribner, 1940.

Thomas, H. *The Spanish Civil War: The First Comprehensive History*. London: Eyre & Spottiswoode, 1961. New York: Harper, 1961.

YUGOSLAVIA

BOOKS

Dedijer, V. *With Tito through the War*. London: Alexander Hamilton, 1951.

Jones, W. *Twelve Months with Tito's Partisans*. Bedford, England: Bedford Books, 1946.

Maclean, F. *Eastern Approaches*. London: Pan Books, 1949. (*Escape to Adventure*. Boston: Little, Brown, 1950).

Maclean F. *Disputed Barricade*. London: Jonathan Cape. (*The Heretic: The Life and Times of Josip Broz Tito*. New York: Harper, 1957).

OTHER BOOKS

Armstrong, H. F. *Tito and Goliath*. London: Gollancz, 1951. New York: Macmillan, 1951.

Brown, A. *Mihailovic and Yugoslav Resistance*. London: Lane, 1943.

Martin, D. *Ally Betrayed: The uncensored Story of Tito and Mihailovic*. New York: Prentice-Hall, 1946.

Rootham, J. *Miss Fire: The Chronicle of a British Mission to Mihailovic, 1943–1944*. London: Chatto & Windus, 1946.

Thayer, C. *Hands across the Caviar*. London: Joseph, 1953.

GENERAL

BOOKS

Galula, D. *Counterinsurgency Warfare, Theory and Practice*. London: Pall Mall, 1964. New York: Praeger.

Levy, B. *Guerilla Warfare*. Washington DC: Infantry Journal – Penguin Special.

O'Sanka, F. M. *Modern Guerilla Warfare*. USA: Free Press of Glencoe, 1962.

Paret, P. and J. W. Shy. *Guerillas in the 1960's*. New York: Praeger, 1962.

Seth, R. *The Undaunted: The Story of Resistance in Western Europe*. London: Muller, 1956.

OTHER BOOKS

Callwell, C. E. *Small Wars: Their Principles and Practice*. London: HM Stationery Office, 1906.

Chroley, K. *Armies and the Art of Revolution*. London: Faber, 1943.

Dyer, M. *The Weapon on the Wall: Rethinking Psychological Warfare.*
Baltimore, Md: Johns Hopkins University, 1958.

Hunter, R. *Revolution: Why, How, Where?* New York: Harper, 1940.

Idriess, I. L. *Guerilla Tactics.* Sydney: Angus & Robertson, 1942.

Kerr, A. *The Art of Guerilla Fighting and Patrol.* London: Jarolds,
1940.

Linebarger, P. M. A. *Psychological Warfare*, 2nd ed. New York:
Duell, Sloane and Pearce, 1960.

Ney, V. *Notes on Guerilla War.* Washington, DC: Command Publications, 1961.

Tickell, J. *Moon Squadron.* London: Wingate, 1956. New York:
Doubleday, 1956.

Note: This Bibliography is not comprehensive; it gives only a list
of books and articles recommended to those readers whose
interest may have been stimulated by the contents of this
book.

Index

NOTE: This index includes only references to the portions of the book described as chapters, not to the intervening narratives, because the factual history and analysis is recorded in the chapters. Readers will, however, find the subjects listed in the index illustrated in many of the narratives.